LAURA ALDRIDGE

THINGS THAT SOAK YOU

Mousse Publishing

TABLE OF CONTENTS

5
FOREWORD
TINA FISKE

9
BRONZE AND MARBLE HAVE NO PLACE WHEN HAIR NETS, WOODEN SPOONS, AND PLANT DYES ARE TO HAND
LINSEY YOUNG

17
NO MATH METHOD

43
INSIDE ALL MY ACTIVITIES

65
JOE SCOTLAND IN CONVERSATION WITH LAURA ALDRIDGE

81
sumVIGOUR

113
THINGS THAT SOAK YOU

135
THE OUTSIDE IS INSIDE EVERYTHING WE MAKE

161
AND THIS BECOMES MATERIAL
LOUISE SHELLEY

FOREWORD

TINA FISKE

Tina Fiske is Director of CAMPLE LINE, an arts organisation and gallery based in rural Dumfries and Galloway.

I first encountered Laura Aldridge's work more than ten years ago now when I visited her exhibition *Cats are not important* at Transmission in Glasgow. At that time, the secondary eruption of the Icelandic volcano Eyjafjallajökull had thrown glass-rich volcanic ash nine kilometres into the sky, resulting in the closure of airspace across Europe. I vividly remember stepping into the gallery to the sight of *Hand Extended (I–III)* (2010)—a group of three monochrome screen prints of disembodied arms cradling cats—floating in seemingly free-form fashion across the gallery walls alongside a host of colourful plaster-filled fabric knots. In what seemed like the most immaterial of material circumstances (stratospheric ash we could not see), it was an immense relief to feel the sensation of touch so physically and visually evoked as it was in that group of work. Incorporating wall-based elements, so-called *Stones*, hangings, and elements assembled on a low, wide plinth, it seemed to promise a new spectrum of visual-tactile association that felt radical, humane, open.

The experience of being in that exhibition at that time inspired a genuine affection in me, which endures to this day. I have sought out Laura's work as often as I have been able since then, and now readily recognise those aspects of tactility, vibrancy, openness, and playfulness as fundamental aspects of her practice. There are so many more encounters I could draw on, from Studio Voltaire, Tramway, Pig Rock Bothy, Kate MacGarry, or most recently the Curfew Gallery in Edinburgh, but curiously it was *Cats are not important* that came to mind most often over the time we worked with Laura toward her exhibition *sumVIGOUR* at CAMPLE LINE. The first images that Laura sent from the studio as she was making her new ceramic works *NINE* and *Comparing my insides to other people's outsides (that's your freedom)*, both 2021, immediately recalled the real lemons and the melon she placed in water as part of her work *Holders* (2010), which appears in that exhibition. More than that, however, it has struck me that *sumVIGOUR* and likewise *The Outside is Inside Everything We Make* (with Leanne Ross and Judith Scott, Kendall Koppe) came into being in circumstances that were not so much about the confounding of touch (the Icelandic eruptions) as they were defined by its inhibition (the global pandemic).

Now especially, the range of material combinations and transitions, the richness of texture, saturation, detail, and surface quality in Laura's most recent works are like a lightning rod to the senses, their emotional affect heightened given the constraints of distance and noncontact we have collectively observed and navigated throughout the last year. As Laura installed her new ceramic work at CAMPLE LINE, I couldn't help but notice the way she lifted and held each work as she placed it, and I thought of the times she must have done that in the making, in the transporting to and from the kiln, around the studio, on and off plinth arrangements. Eleven years on, the out-stretched arms of *Hand Extended (I–III)* here become Laura's own, her process marked by a deep-seated and ever-accumulating tacit knowledge, her most recent work finding a register of the tactile, the sensory, and the seen that is as compelling as it is encompassing.

BRONZE AND MARBLE HAVE NO PLACE WHEN HAIR NETS, WOODEN SPOONS, AND PLANT DYES ARE TO HAND

LINSEY YOUNG

Linsey Young is Curator of Contemporary British Art at Tate Britain, London. Her research focuses on feminism and the work of women artists in the UK.

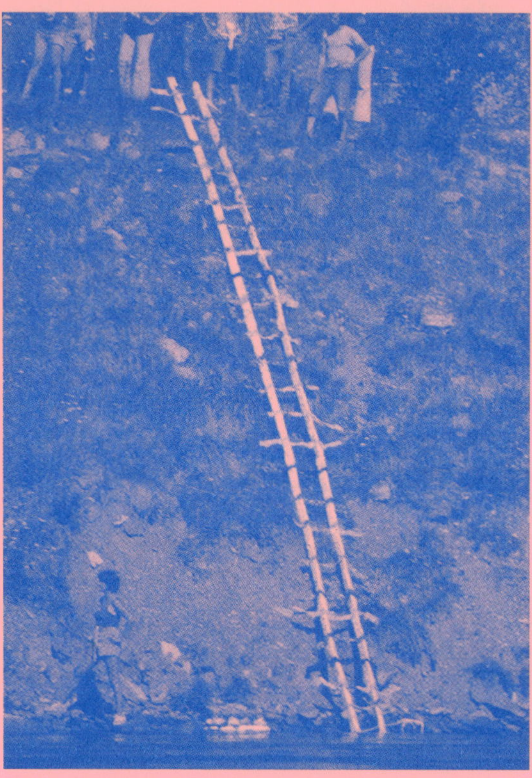

Ree Morton, *The Maid of the Mist*, 1976, Artpark, Lewiston, New York

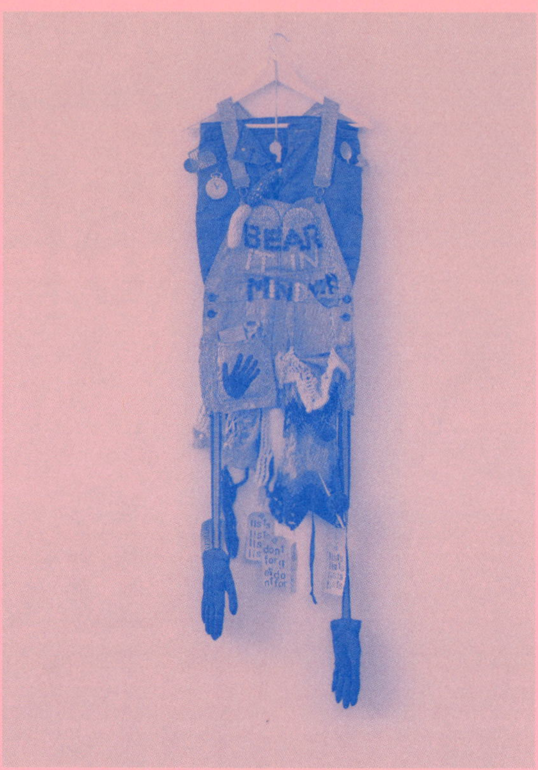

Su Richardson, *Bear it in Mind*, 1976, mixed media: fabric (cotton, silk, wool), paper, plastic, metal, 160 × 40 × 10 cm

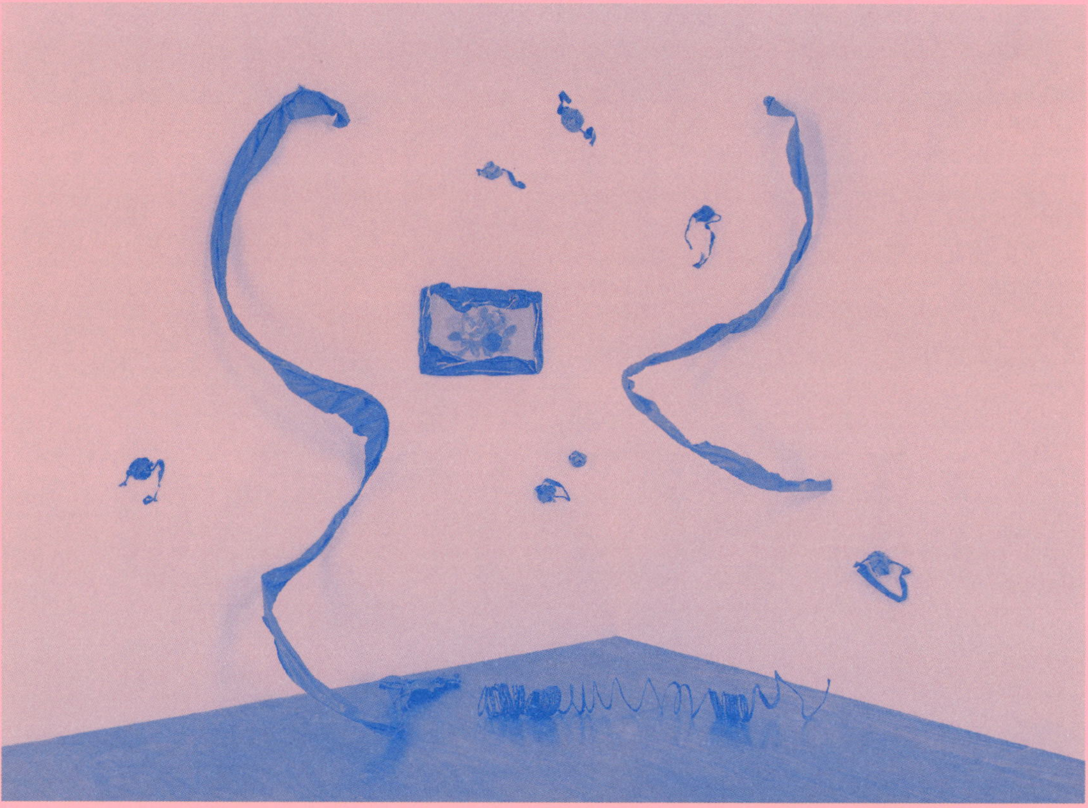

Ree Morton, *For Kate*, 1976, oil on wood and wire and enamel on plastic, dimensions variable

One of the first things we discover is that personal problems are political problems. There are no personal solutions at this time. There is only collective action for a collective solution.[1]

In essays about an artist's practice, you're supposed to maintain a distance, measure against the history of art, critical theory, cool analysis that continues a lineage of press releases and *Artforum* articles, a flattening out of people to the objects that they make. I understand the reason we do this: it's about judging a piece of work on its own out in the world, how it can stand up for itself against all the others, it's about a level of hard-to-get-ness for the artist, creating a persona you'll never really access that keeps you in your place (and the work in its place within the market), holding back questions that you might not think smart enough to ask, and ensuring the writer seems knowledgeable enough to justify them having the job in the first place.

But really, is that how anyone understands art or its relationship to them? Now particularly, when all our actions and even physical gestures are curtailed, are we going to continue to insist that art work and artists have a dispassionate relationship to the gorgeous and heartbreaking messiness of life?

In an industry (because that is what it has become) where value is placed on exclusivity, wealth, and status, Laura Aldridge's practice looks to historic artistic, political, and social models to find a place in which to settle. Her practice is informed, shaped, and grows from her relationships with people, the practical skills learned and shared, the love that holds a life together and the lessons learned from proximity to those whose lived experiences are different from your own, and for all of this, it is at its core a political practice. Political in the manner that all women's lives are political.

Aldridge entered Wimbledon College of Arts in 1997 at the exuberant dawn of the New Labour era (one of the first shows she visited as a student was *Sensation* at the Royal Academy), graduating in 2001, a year after Tate Modern opened and it became clear that bigger was better. The opportunities for young artists in London, especially those outside the commercial gallery system, were dwindling in the wake of increasingly vertiginous domestic and studio costs alongside ultracompetitive exhibiting opportunities.

Aldridge has spoken of her discomfort with the prevailing attitude of the time, one with a severe crush on object-based Conceptualism where the only perceived route to success was via gallery representation (a visiting tutor once going so far as to say that any part-time work necessitated by needing to pay the bills constituted a failure). This atmosphere of market-driven competition was and remains deeply at odds with an artist engaged with questioning what constitutes an artwork and who that work is for. Aldridge's approach to art-making was one from a different era; as she has stated, "I didn't understand why you had to be destroyed to make work."[2]

For Aldridge, as for many artists and art historians of her generation, teaching centred around the canon, around men, Conceptualism, and the YBA movement, with no mention of the history of women's art in the United Kingdom or further afield or participatory, radical practices. As Aldridge has described it, "there was no room for people."[3]

Seeking a community that welcomed and supported artists and had affordable space to play and grow, Aldridge enrolled in the MFA programme at the Glasgow School of Art and moved to that city in 2004. GSA's highly regarded course, plentiful, affordable living and working spaces in the city, and a notoriously collegial group of artists would offer Aldridge the foundations to begin to test her ideas. As well as a two-year course and small class sizes, a particular draw was the art school's exchange programme with CalArts in Valencia, California. Aldridge undertook the exchange in 2005. A key influence from this time was the presence at CalArts of feminist writer Leslie Dick. In particular, Aldridge had referred often to "Fashion Tragedies," a 2004 text by Dick that the writer insisted on reading to students when they forgot to take their work to a crit.

"Fashion Tragedies" explores Dick's relationship to garments, those lost, or not purchased and regretted, or destroyed in the throes of passion; for Aldridge, the text generated new ways of thinking about space and material.

It's always the space between things that interests me—so the space between my work and her essay, and the grey area between 3D and 2D—I think fabric has always held such appeal to me because it is at once both something flat, a surface to absorb colour and pattern, and something three-dimensional—it holds forms, houses our bodies, it has a front and a back. I made a fabric work called Double Interest*—the title seems important now in relation to this thinking.*[4]

Dick talks of garments as "materializing memory,"[5] of holding traces of the person we were or wanted to be at the time when we wore them. This notion of who we might want to be is present in Aldridge's ambitious first solo exhibition, held at Glasgow Sculpture Studios in 2006, *The Workshop Has Survived Because We Love Each Other*.

Aldridge presented three large-scale carved polystyrene sculptures, covered in foam coat to give them the appearance of ceramic. Living plants were inserted in cut-out sections as though they had naturally grown on the organic forms. Borrowing methods from prop making (which she had done as an odd job while studying) allowed her to make work to the scale that she needed to make oversize bodily forms and get close to the sensation of a large outdoor space within the gallery. Referencing Barbara Hepworth and her sculpture garden in St. Ives, the work is sensuous, bulging, and fertile. We might also relate it to a particularly seductive section of Dick's "Fashion Tragedies" that talks about the power of a Comme des Garçons dress to blow apart our understanding of the body.

I was so much in love at that time that I had sex on the floor while wearing the dress, and it tore along the pleated seams in various places. It was never quite the same, in part because the luxury dry cleaner where I took it for repair was completely perplexed by the dress. On some level, it wasn't a dress at all, it was a conceptual art work, it rested against the body in arbitrary ways, bunching up over the bottom, wrinkling around the belly, and it was precisely the disconnect between the female body inside and the rigorous logic of the garment's structure that opened up a mental space for the imagination.[6]

This desire for sensation, particularly the sensation of desire (to know and to touch), relates to a wider concern in Aldridge's practice. Where is the work? Is it in the void of a Hepworth sculpture, in the plants that grow around them, or in the collar of a dress you sewed while thinking of a friend?

Other major influences surfaced during Aldridge's time in California, in particular an introduction to the work of Ree Morton, the American sculptor who, having formed a nuclear American Dream family at a young age, rejected its confines and enrolled in art school as a mature student, exhibiting widely before her untimely death in 1977 at age forty. Although she was chronologically in step with American feminist artists of the time, there is a sense of removal with Morton; her work is often fragmentary and sometimes dreamy. She looks to nature, plants and found pieces of wood, ribbons, light bulbs, materials that are available and democratic.

Although she works with similar materials, the major draw for Aldridge seems to be Morton's ability to communicate emotional experience and to trust in the long-term development of relationships and conversations, to sit happily in spaces that are hard to define, be they a performative kiln firing, the solo production of a banner, designing a bothy, or exploring plant dye. As with Morton, a lightness of humour and visual generosity belie a sophisticated and engaged understanding of theoretical discussions.

Perhaps the most direct visual reference to Morton's work in Aldridge's practice is in her coloured knots of 2011–14, which formed the basis of her solo show at Studio Voltaire in 2011. The presentation, exploding over the gallery walls, combined vital texture and colour with the flatness of print and that particular quality of hand-set plaster that is so still but holds every gesture that went into its making. Something happens in the space between these curls and knots. The cats, so very fluffy, are held and caressed by frozen hands, the softness of their fur and heat of their bodies stilled by the transformation to monochrome Perspex. Next to the cats, the knots form a kind of cartography for language—or movement? The two together capture a particular sensory experience, a place of warmth and comfort but also of that infuriating movement of a creature you just want to stay still. There is a dynamism and a decoding of sensation into a still image—life in shorthand.

A series of works made for *Underside, backside, inside, even* at the Centre for Contemporary Arts Glasgow, in 2012, continued Aldridge's observation and elevation of the everyday. For the show, she made a series of wildly oversized pockets. You've experienced a pocket, you understand a pocket, but what happens when its ability to hold or contain is highlighted? This exploration of the domestic object through everyday materials can be seen as relating to British feminist art history of the 1970s and '80s. A little taught or even acknowledged period of art history, it is formed of a wide range of practitioners making work where the intersections between art and politics collapsed, where humble materials ruled, where the galleries and the market (that didn't care about the work of women and certainly not working-class, politicised women) were superseded by postal events, exhibitions in libraries, and embracing the base at Greenham.

Central to this activity in the early to mid-1970s were a group of women, Su Richardson, Monica Ross, and Kate Walker, who had individual practices that they managed around child-rearing, earning a living, and keeping a home. They came together through feminist conferences and consciousness-raising groups and began a series of projects and exhibitions to allow them to communicate and share their lived experiences. Richardson, in particular, worked closely with domestic textiles, creating works such as *Bear it in Mind* (1976), a crocheted pair of dungarees with pockets stuffed with all the essentials that a single mother must bear in mind to keep her daily life together as cook (sausages), plumber (spanners), and a whistle (referee), all covered in the shiny black handprints of the ever needy child.

Aldridge's pocket works (and later her banners and textile wall pieces with ceramic elements) have a relationship with this history, in the desire to explore the everyday, in respect for domestic materials, and in the very practical approach to material and the selection of those materials that allow for transportation and scaling up of size without the need for expensive equipment, shipping, or a huge studio. Aldridge has spoken often of working with expanded collage, and "expanded" in her world doesn't mean expanded to the size of a large piece of paper or extending beyond the frame; rather, it refers to an expansion into a room, onto the side of a building, into an atmosphere and the rhythms of daily life, something that is possible because of how she refuses to engage with a hierarchy of materials. Bronze and marble have no place when hair nets, wooden spoons, and plant dyes are to hand.

In 2015 Aldridge was invited to make a solo presentation at Tramway, Glasgow, one of the largest contemporary art spaces in the United Kingdom. In a show titled *California WOW!* she was able to push her play with scale to an extreme, working from a finger-sized blob of clay as part of an assemblage to full-size glazed brick walls, hugely oversized air fresheners, sculptural reclining chairs, and a Perspex house. Everything was to the max: the number of objects, the use of colour, and the wide variety of materials set on top of and in relation to one another. Of course, you were not allowed to touch, so these seductive objects teased, offering and at the same time denying a riot of sensation.

Shortly after the Tramway exhibition, on a visit to her studio, we talked about a series of boxes that Aldridge had been grappling with privately. In stark contrast to the vitality and fullness of *California WOW!*, this series was small and fragile. The original work was a simple painted box turned upside down, its contents evacuated from a great height. This box was reworked in plaster and fabric, with different placement for the folding edges and multiple orientations on the walls, but it was the original that she kept coming back to, a sad, slightly sagging cardboard box, painted fleshy pink, flipped upside down and placed on the wall, the space within hollow. The language of that original form said all she needed to about the gulf between object and desire and the impossibility of gaining and holding. This work is extremely pared back for a Laura Aldridge; composed of two materials, in a single corporeal colour way, it speaks of a person consumed with one thought.

This period and perhaps this work mark a turning point for Aldridge, a moment of extreme self-reflection that allowed her to process and acknowledge the deeply woven connections between her individual practice and her work with others. What it means to work alone versus what it means to work with others truly. What it means to be able to choose the people you will spend your life with. It is through acknowledgement of the reciprocal nature of friendships and collaborative working relationships that she has stretched, flexed, and refined her voice and opened up new spaces for making and loving.

One of the central components in this shift is the organisation Artlink, which Aldridge has worked with for more than a decade. Artlink was formed in 1984 to promote the involvement of disabled people in the arts; the studio workshop initiated by Artlink has evolved into what is now known as KMAdotcom (or "Kiss My Artist" dotcom), a studio as a place of "originality, collaboration, and imagination" where neurodiverse artists work in a non-hierarchical way with neurotypical artists. It is a space where duration has a different meaning, where it might take months or even years to come to an understanding of what a fellow artist, who is, say, nonverbal, might desire to make them feel comfortable enough to make work or of what material they like best. This patience and care for people and a process of fore-grounding collaboration and creativity that reflects lived experience (similar to that of female artists in the 1970s and '80s) still feels like a wildly radical notion.

Although she has worked with Artlink for a long time, it is only in recent years that Aldridge has begun to accept the profound and ongoing effect that it has had on how she makes and understands her own work. Perhaps it is born from the experience of moving through personal trauma, something that she has spoken about privately, but a door has opened that has allowed her to recognise and articulate how utterly essential a non-hierarchical approach to material/collaborator/audience is in resolving the work, to a realisation that this ongoing movement through textures, colours, and communication that we call artistic practice is successful, is important, only if it is truly for everyone.

In June 2021, Aldridge opened two concurrent exhibitions, *The Outside is Inside Everything We Make*, in collaboration with KMA studio member Leanne Ross, featuring work by Judith Scott, and a solo exhibition, *sumVIGOUR*, at CAMPLE LINE in Dumfries. Both feel like major shifts in energy and process. This is in part due to the enforced pandemic isolation, which allowed Aldridge the time to refine her understanding of production processes, but also due to the intensive work she and her Artlink colleagues did during lockdown, working online to ensure there were moments of productivity and joy among the terror (which is what it is if you—or a family member—are supported by a care system that is overwhelmed even before a pandemic). The proximity of death and enforced separation, the straight-up weirdness of a world turned on its head, seem to have generated a new intensity in Aldridge's work.

Works in both exhibitions, particularly the ceramics, were imagined as gifts for people she could not get close to. Made while thinking about the subject, her musings inform the finished object. A memorial urn is decorated with rough bows and ribbons made from clay offcuts because the pot's subject "cared deeply about people who went unnoticed by others," sideways thoughts that gently celebrate the essence of a life. The vessels are then placed on "texture totems," assemblages of glass jars filled with pickling liquids, scraps of netting, plaster, and wood. Surfaces that force our reading of the vessels to shift and develop their own identities, stretching their character out in different directions, providing potential. Framed textile, ceramic, and paper collages have metal bars jutting out from their brightly painted frames, from which wind chimes made of leftover clay and discarded spoons sing out through the gallery.

This new forced shift in priorities from action to reflection, from full throttle to slow and steady, reflects much of what happens as we age, as we lose people and our bodies become less reliable. They prompt questions that Aldridge has long mused over: Where is the work? How do you create a space where people feel safe and nurtured, able to engage with the creative process in whatever way they see fit? There isn't a right or a wrong answer; there isn't a good or bad material, a high or low art. There is only a limited amount of time on the planet, the task of finding a way to communicate with the people we share it with.

1
Carol Hanisch, "The Personal Is Political," http://www.carolhanisch.org/CHwritings/PIP.html

2
The artist in conversation with Linsey Young, October 2020.

3
The artist in conversation with Linsey Young, February 2021.

4
Correspondence between Laura Aldridge and Jamie Kenyon, November 2011, lauraaldridge.co.uk

5
Leslie Dick, "Fashion Tragedies," 2004.

6
Ibid.

NO MATH METHOD

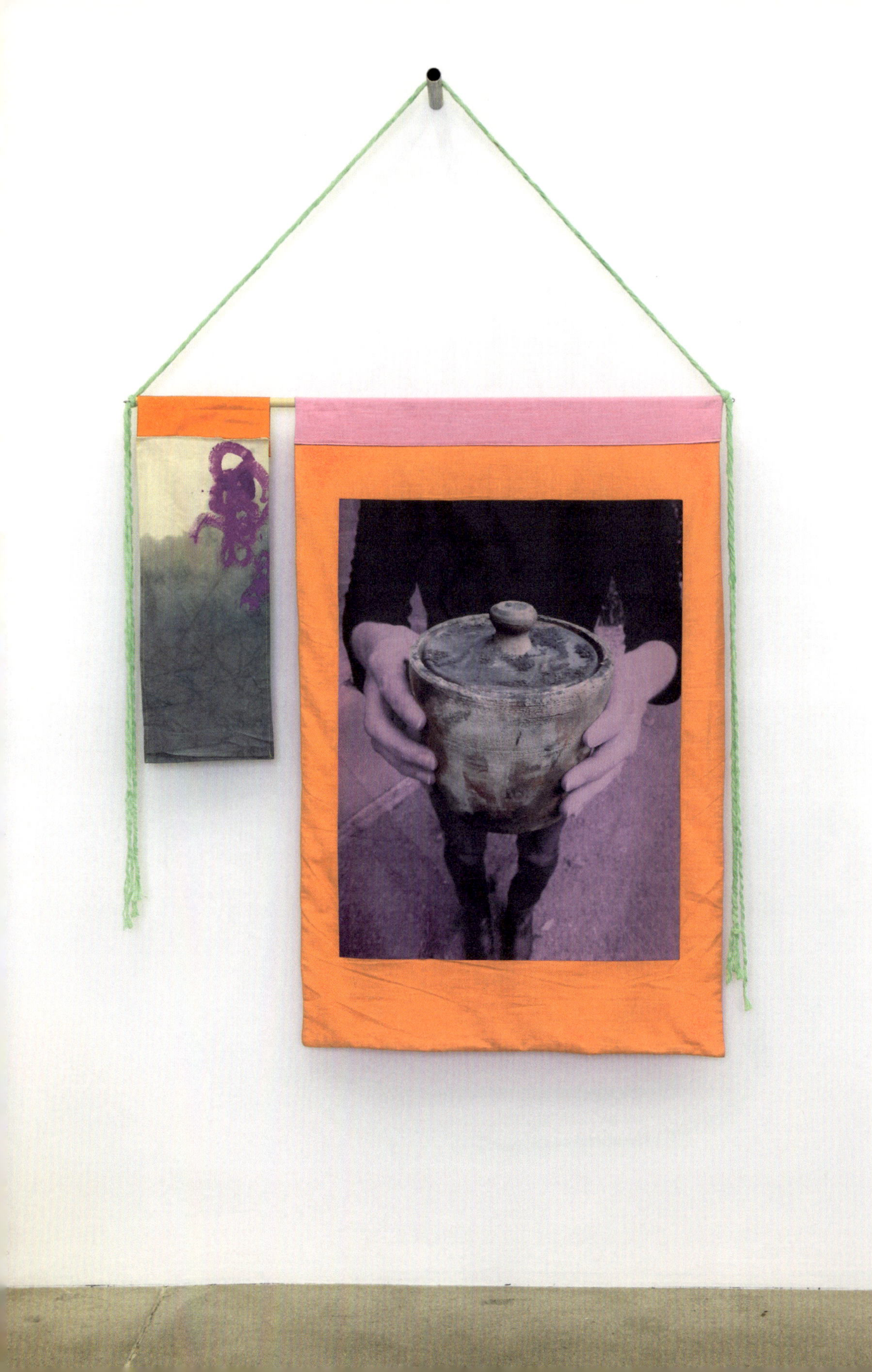

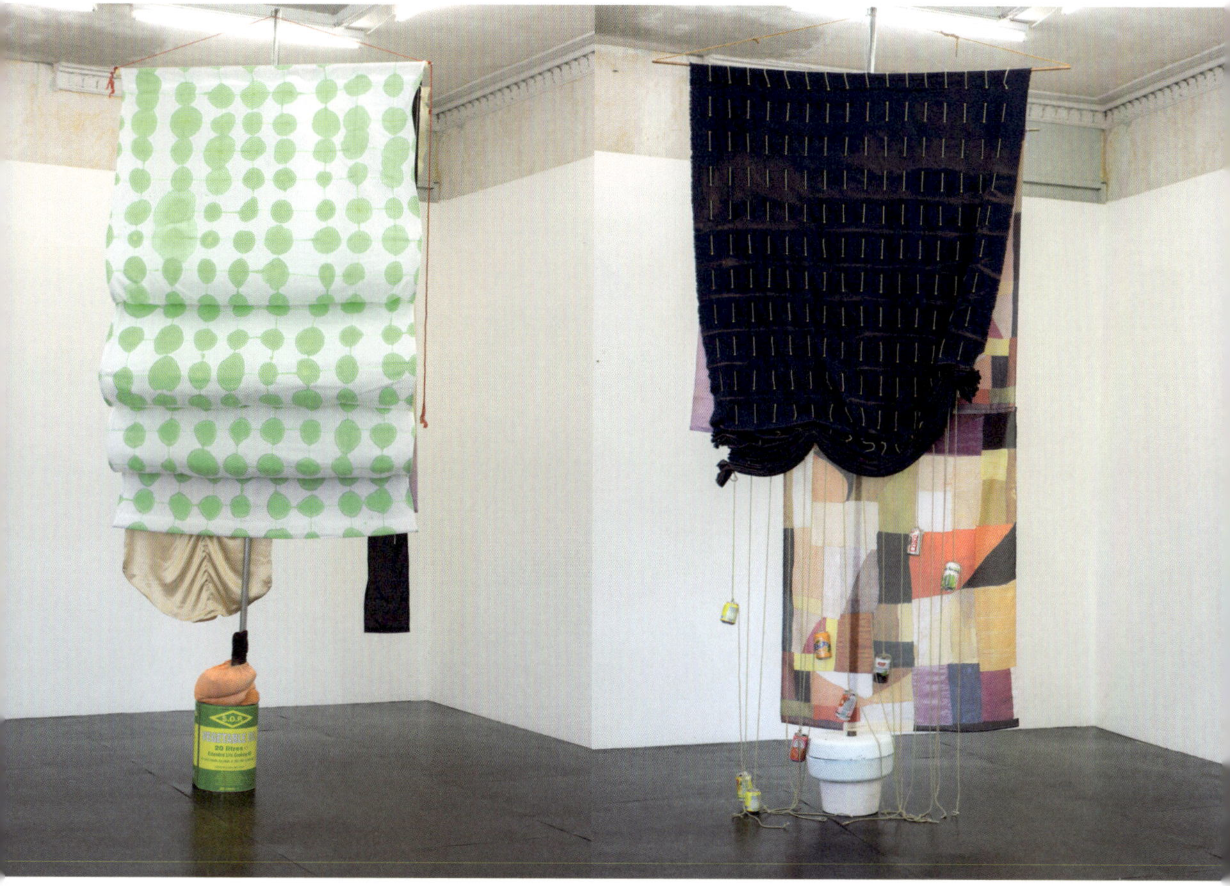

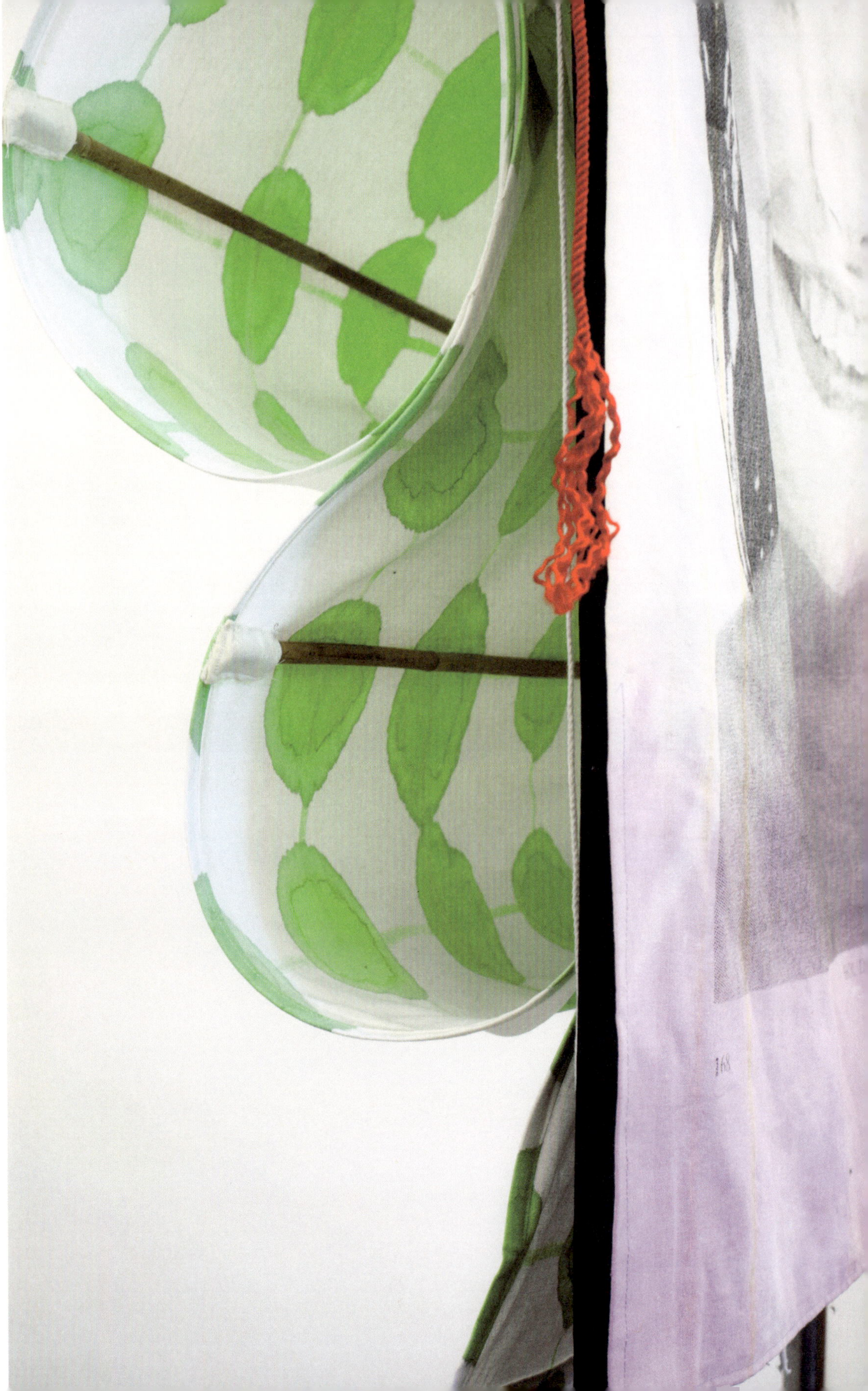

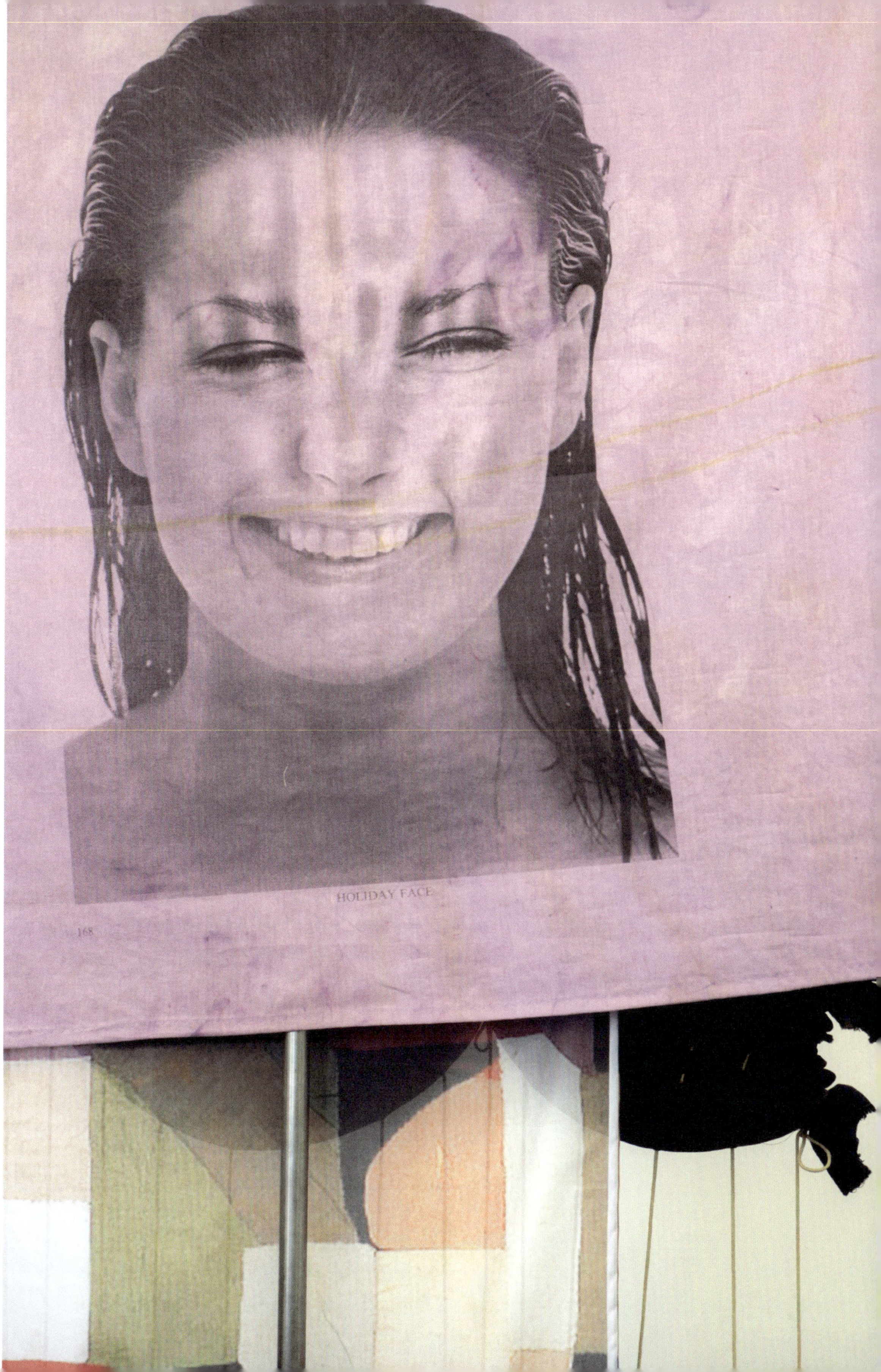
HOLIDAY FACE
168

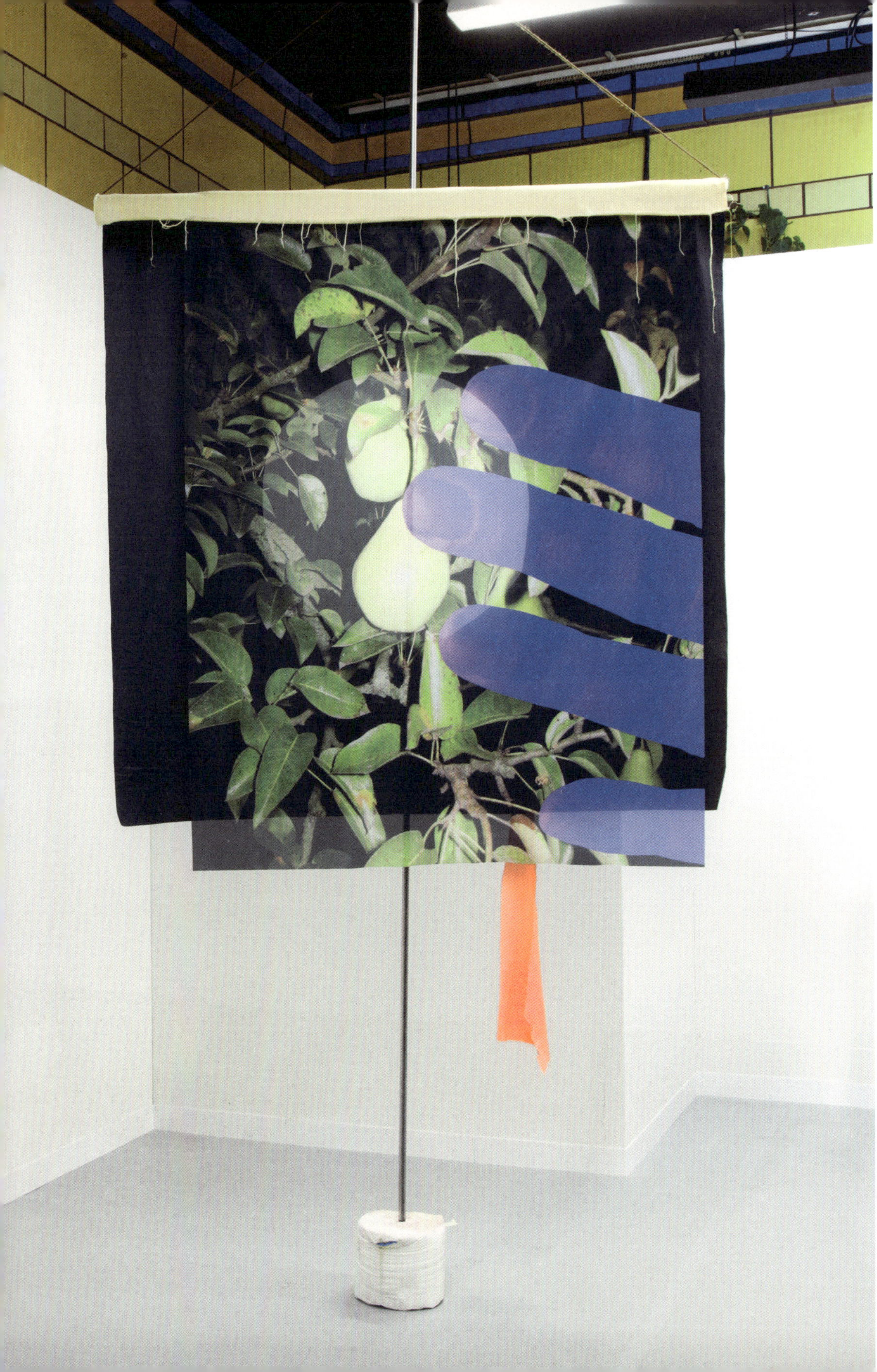

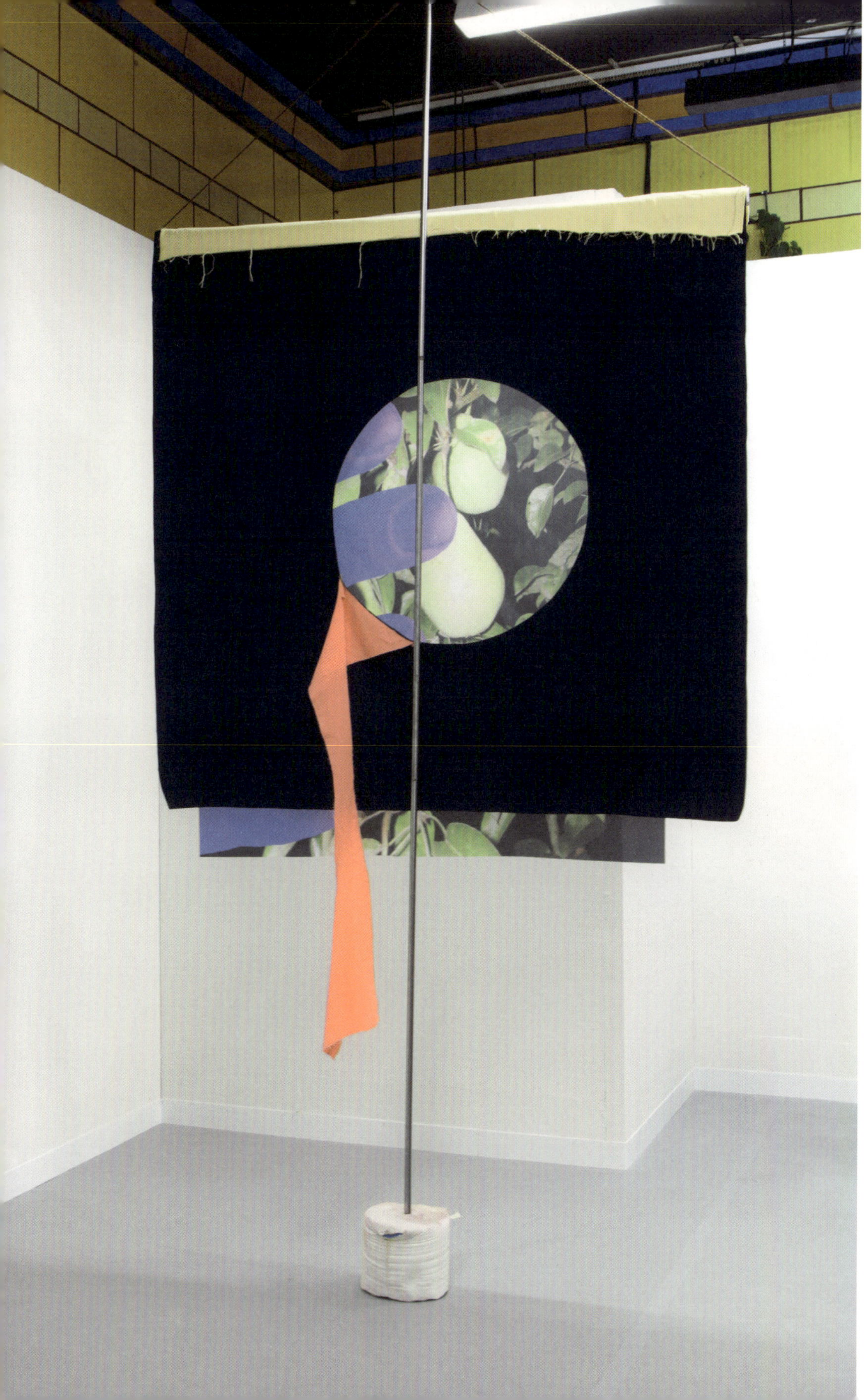

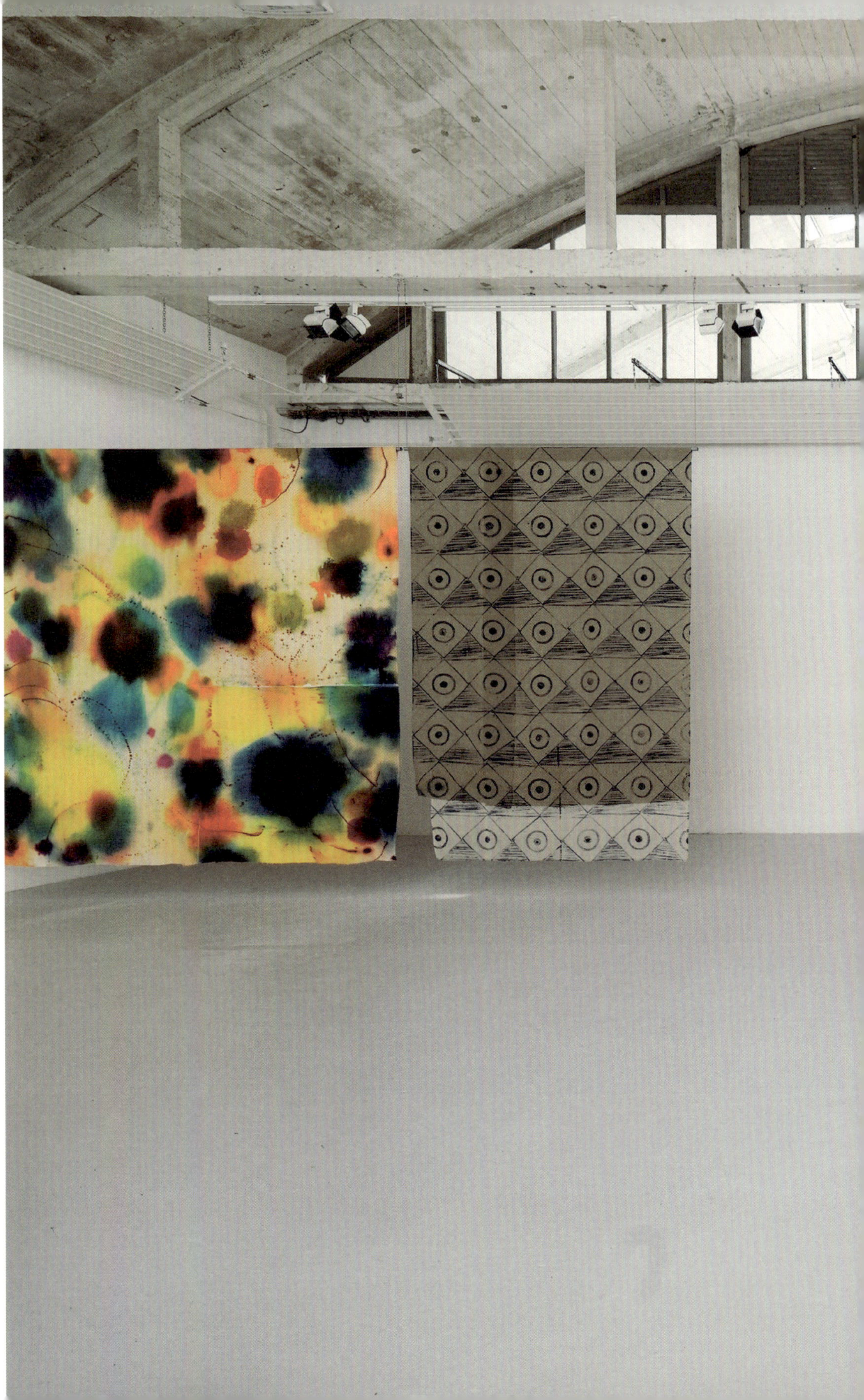

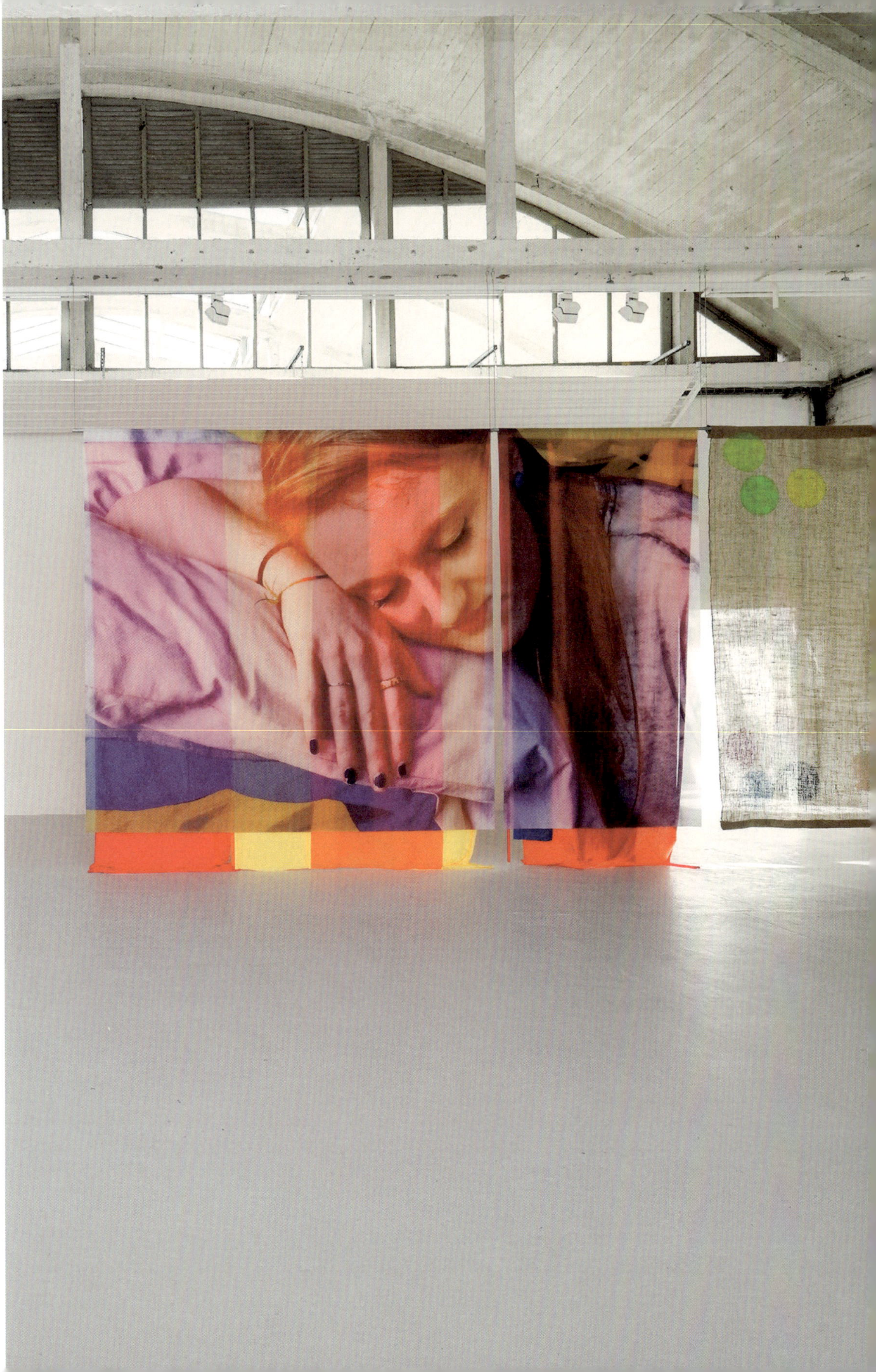

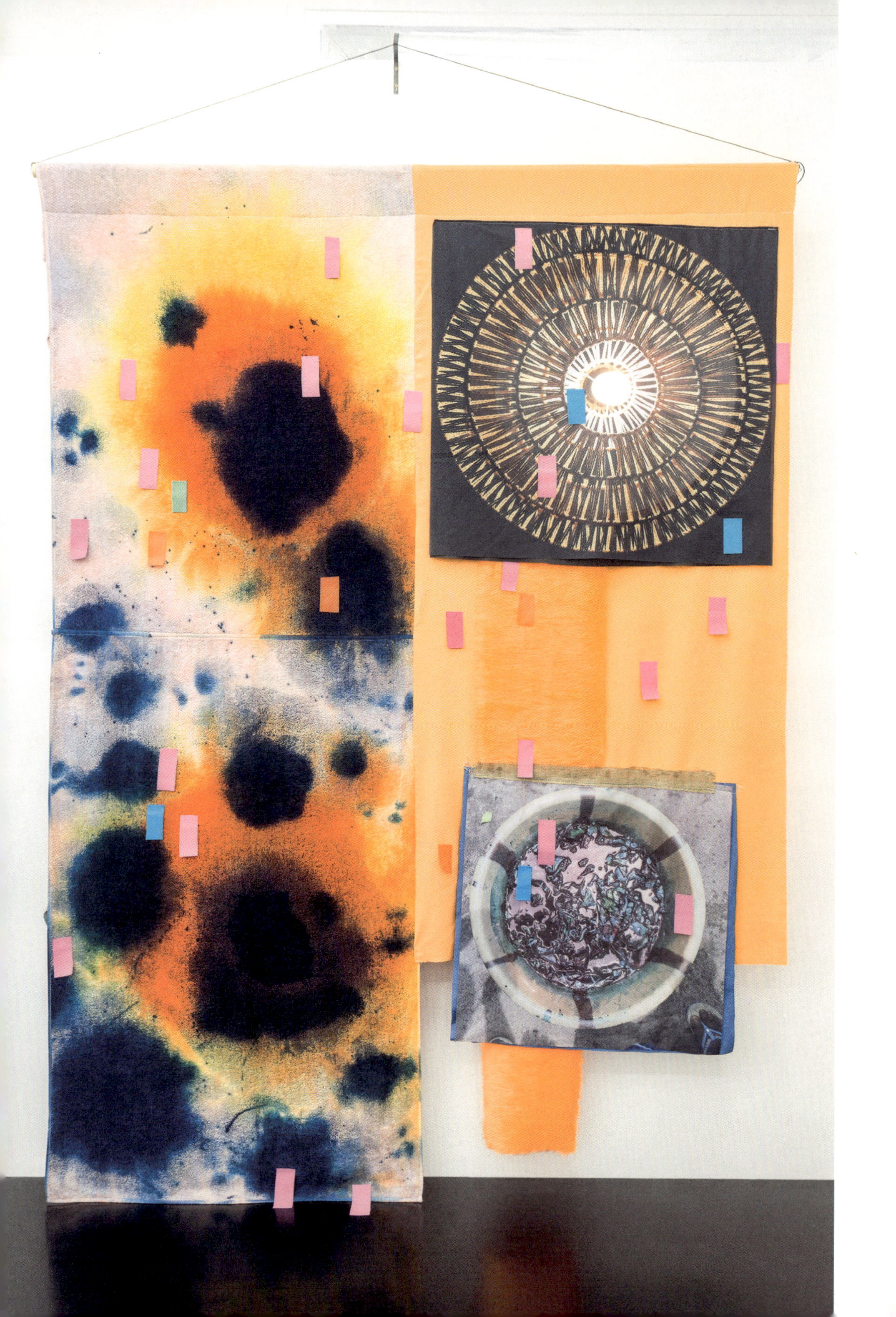

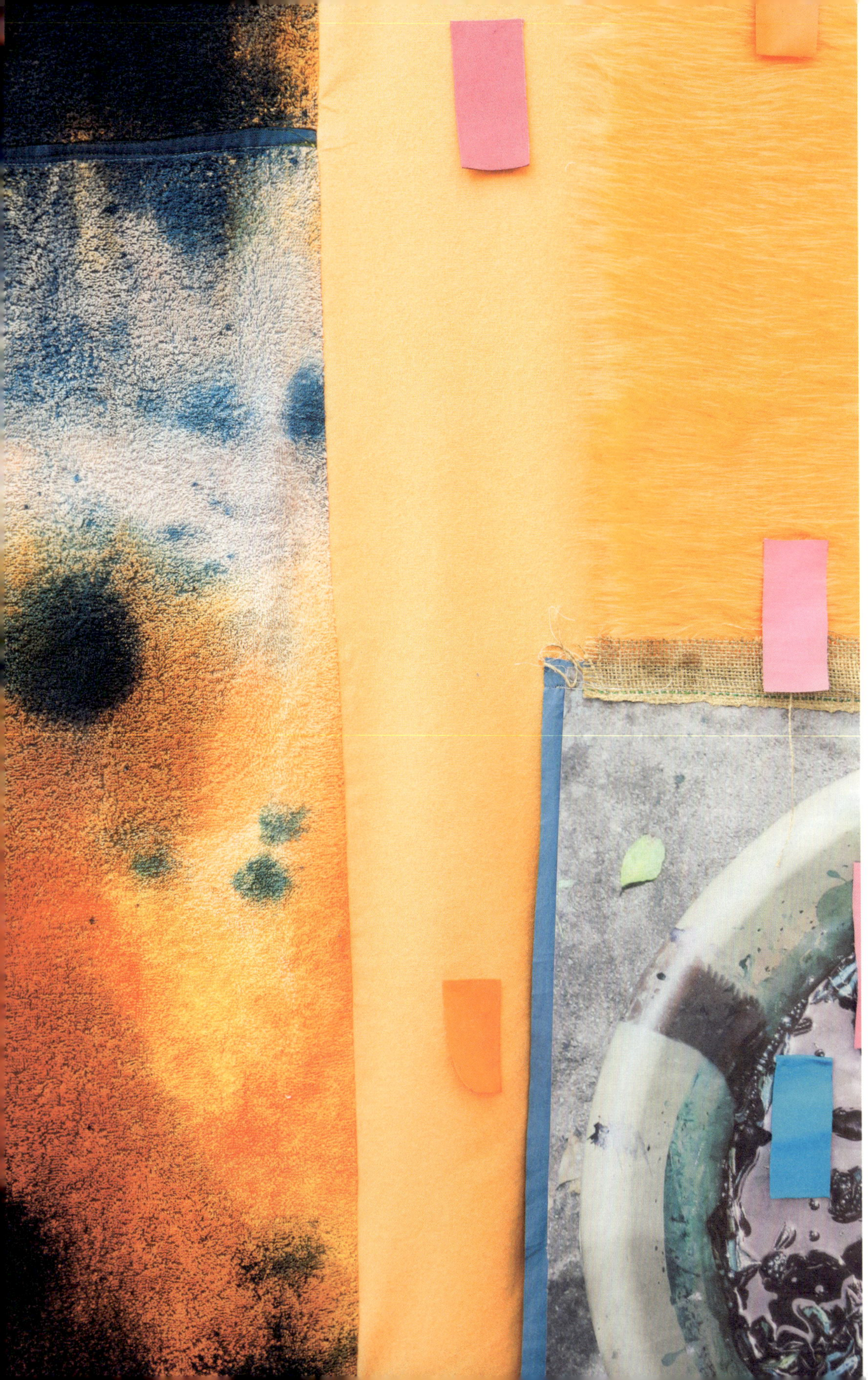

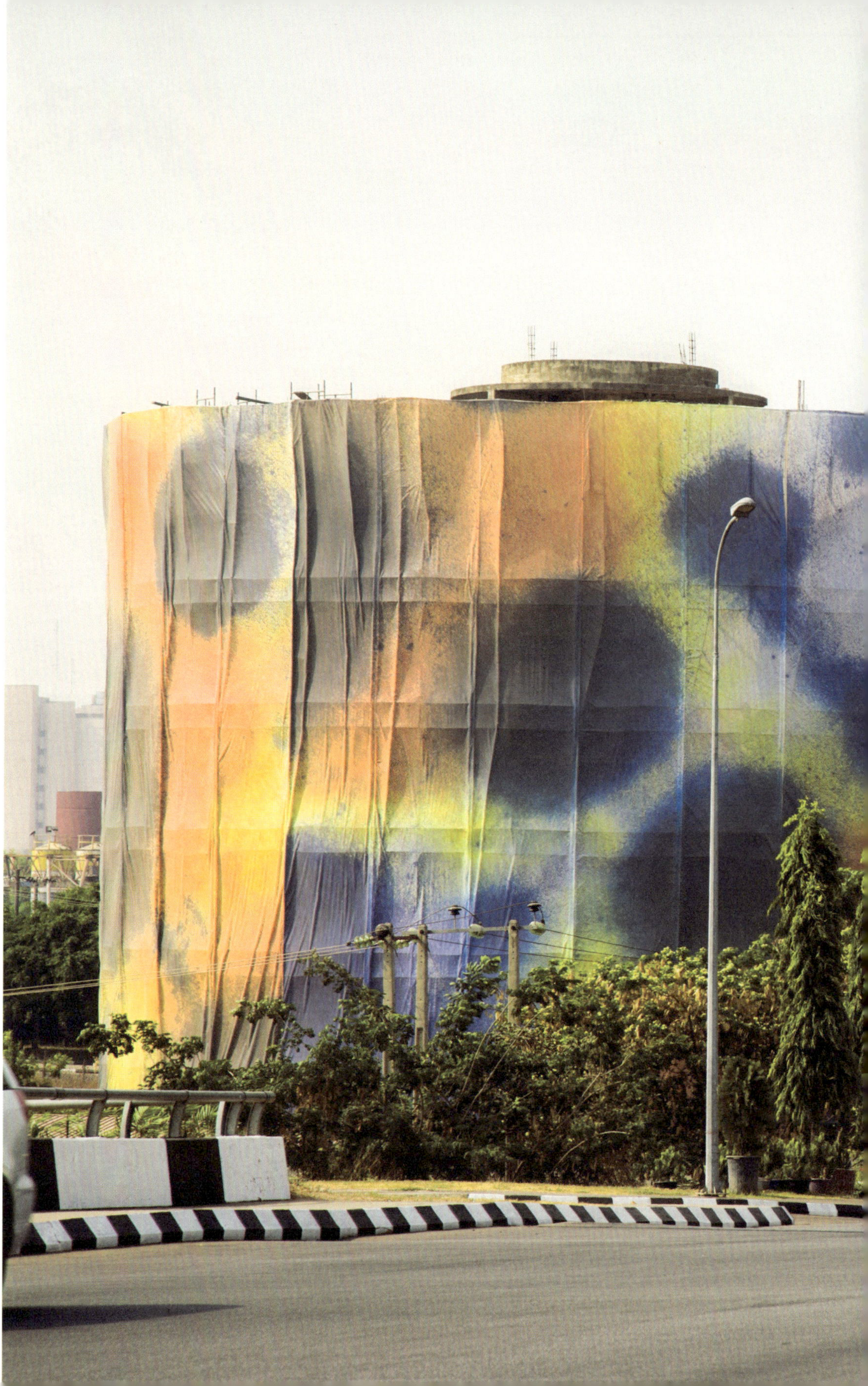

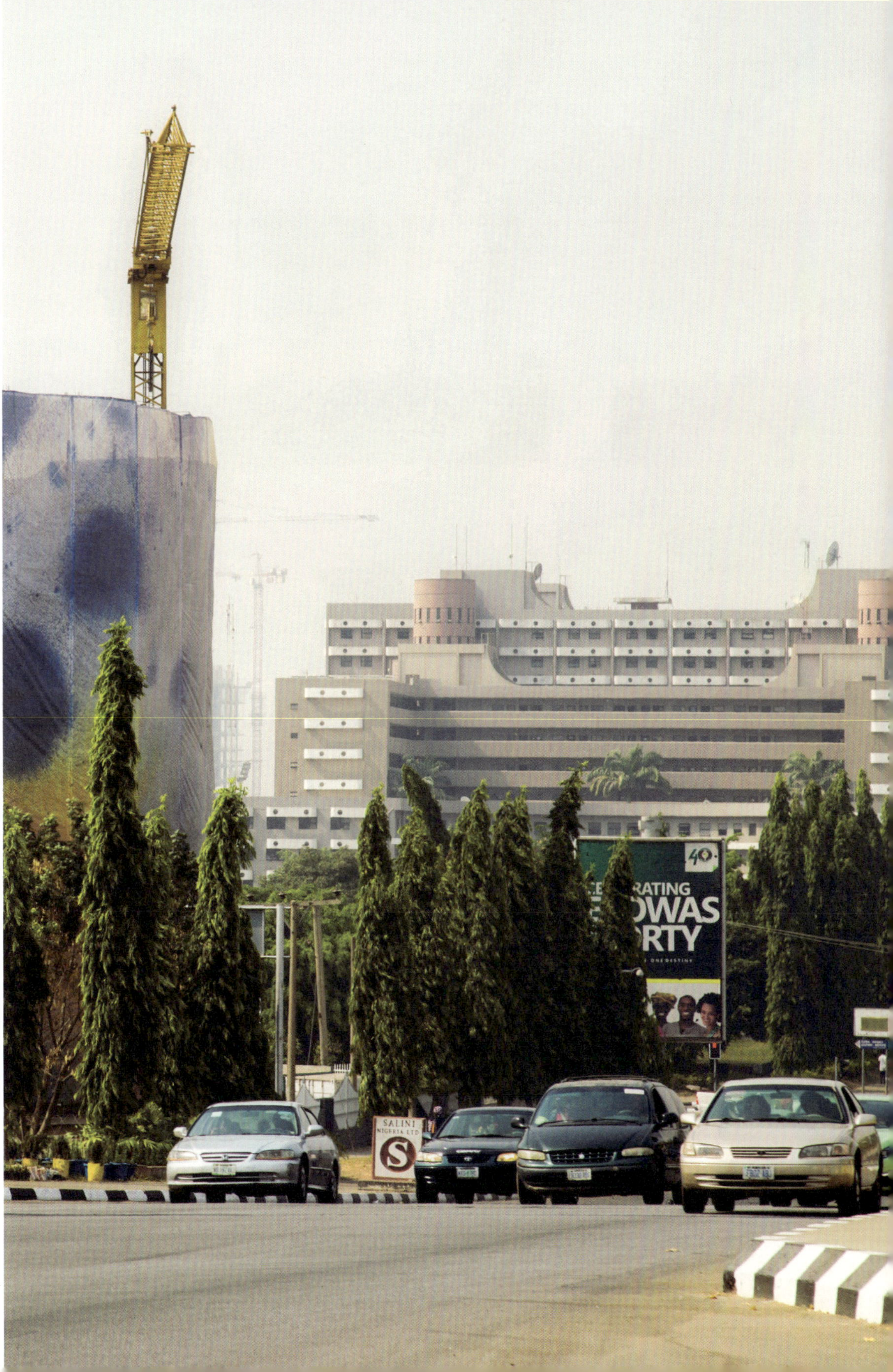
SALINI
NIGERIA LTD

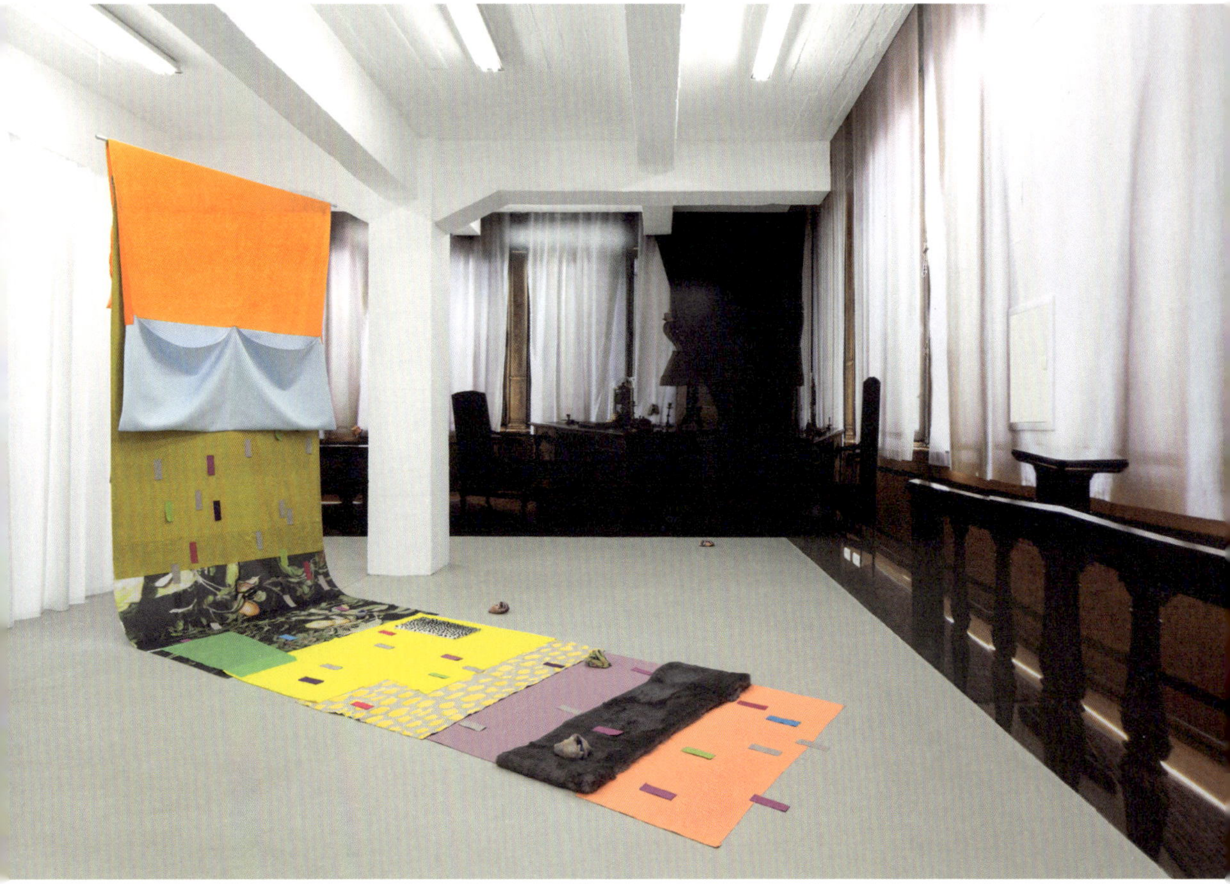

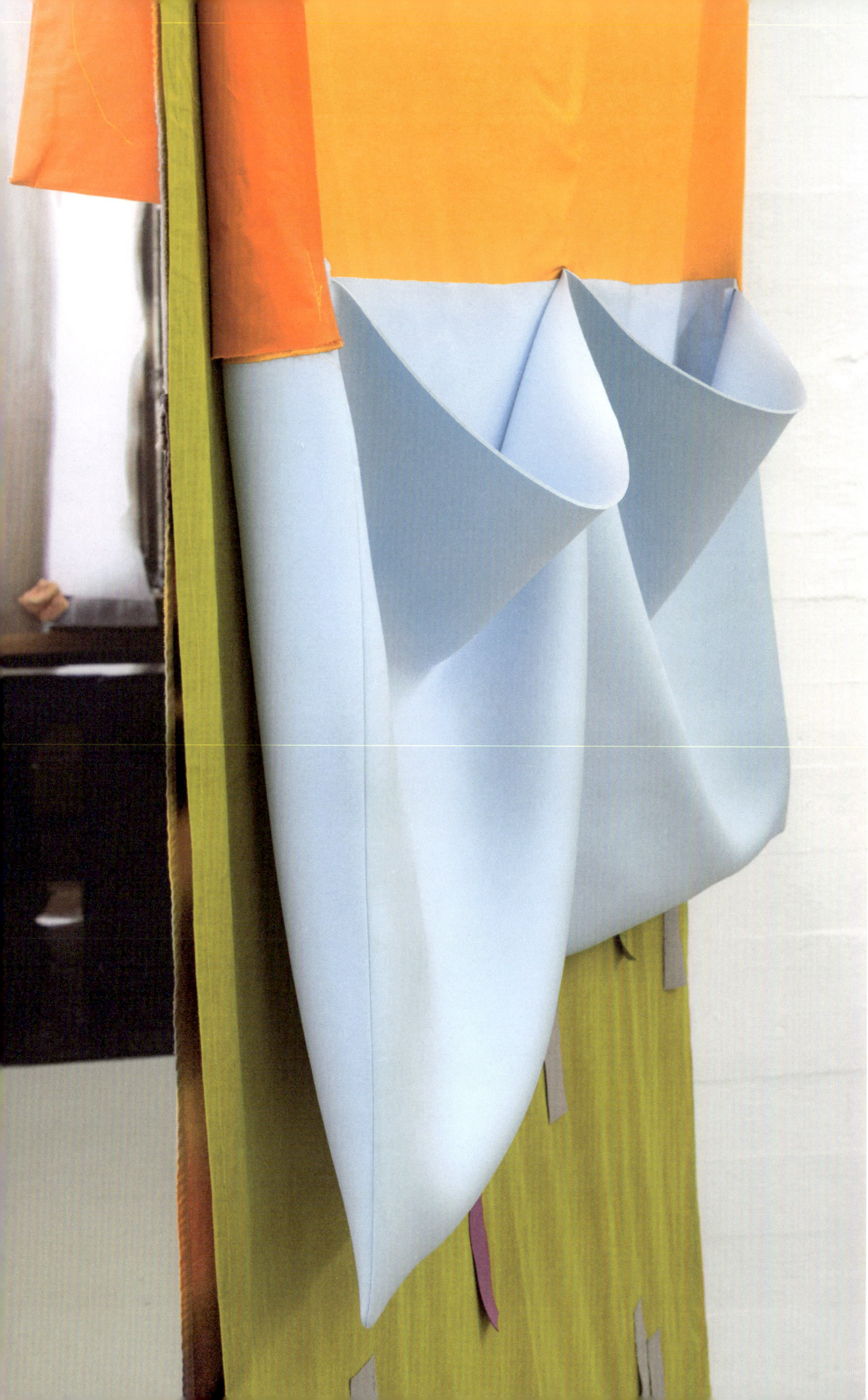

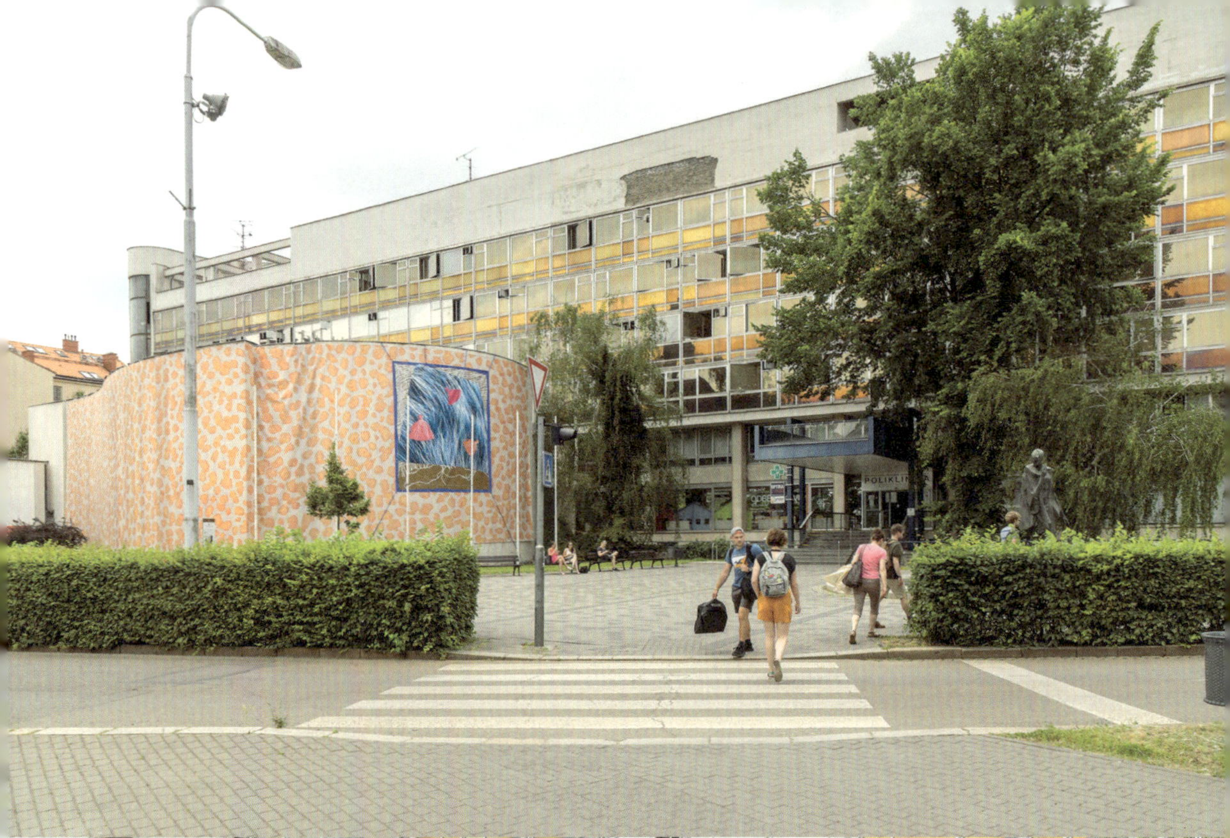

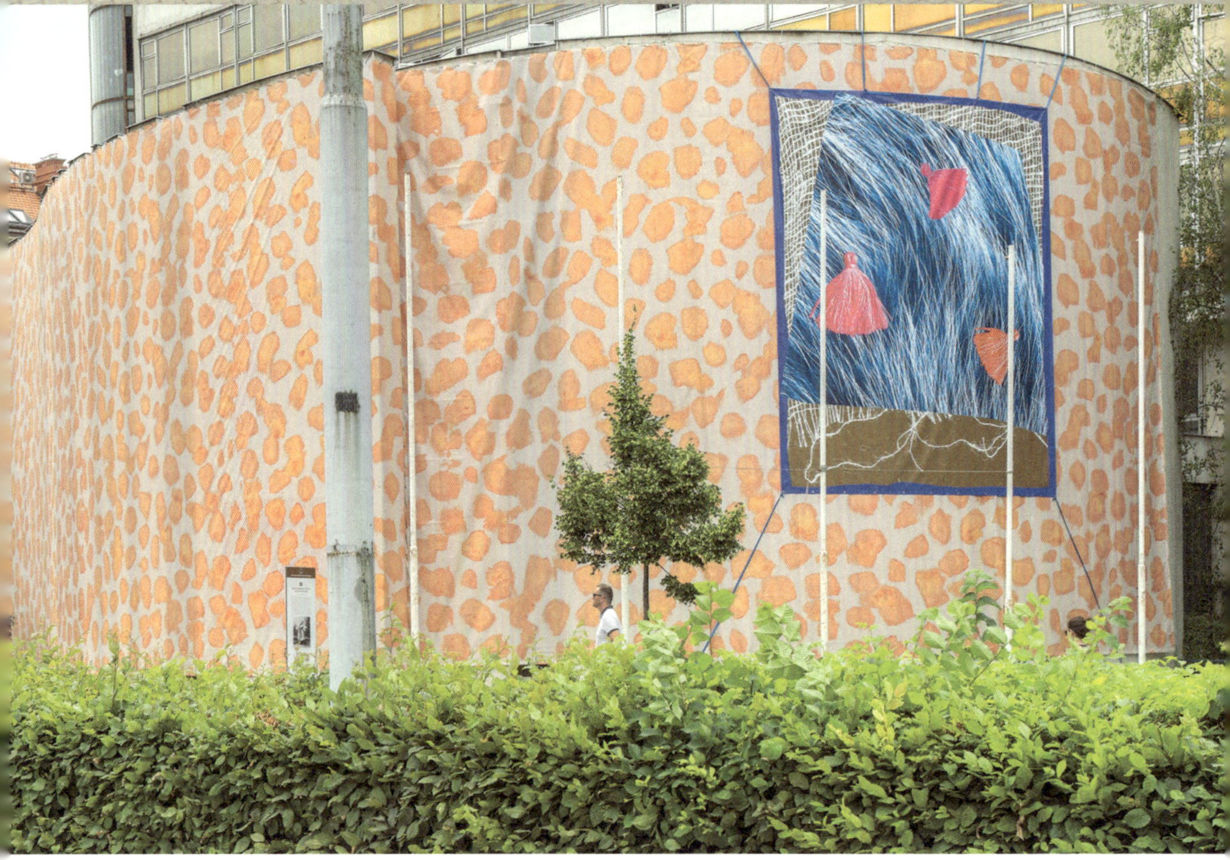

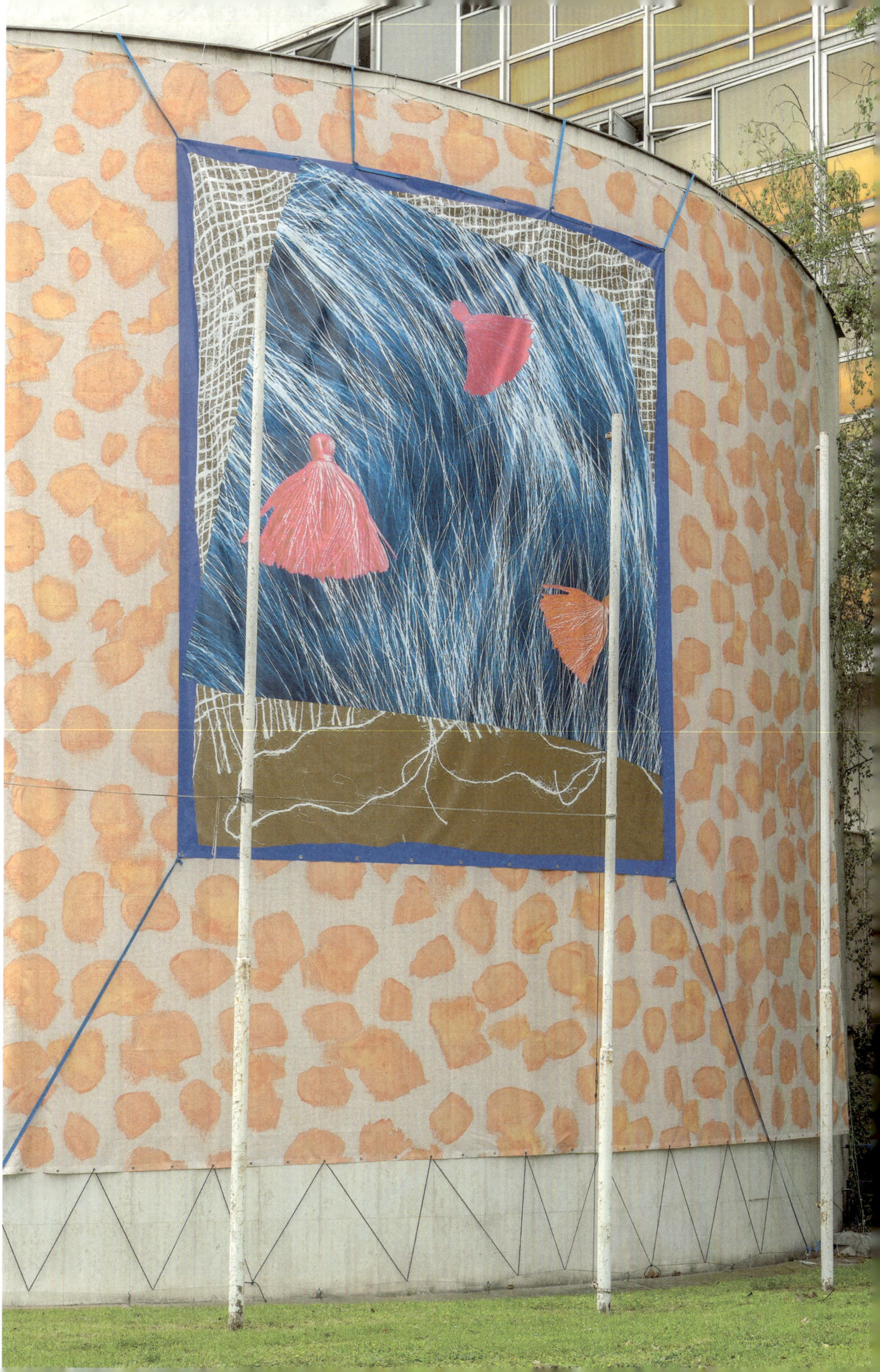

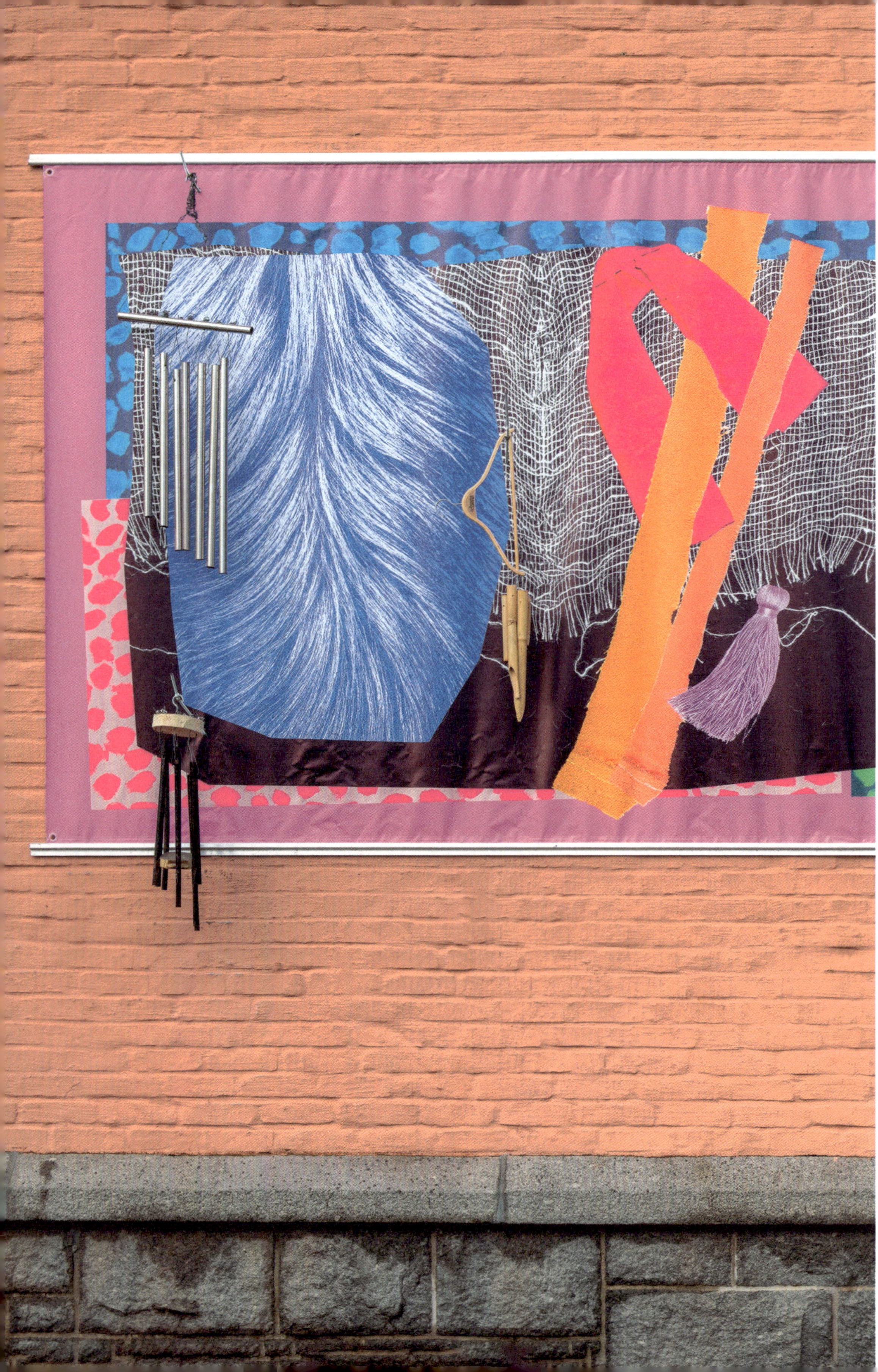

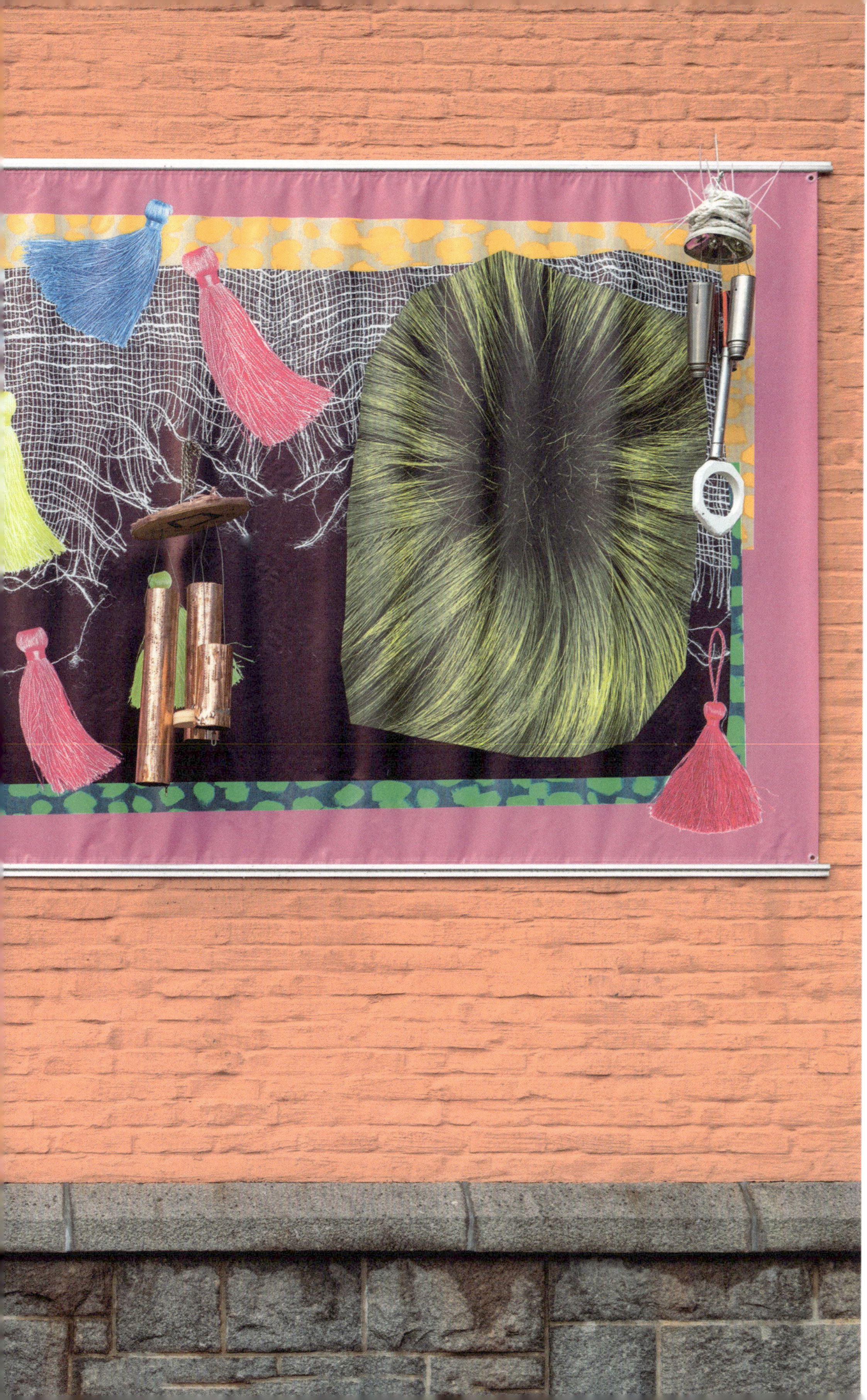

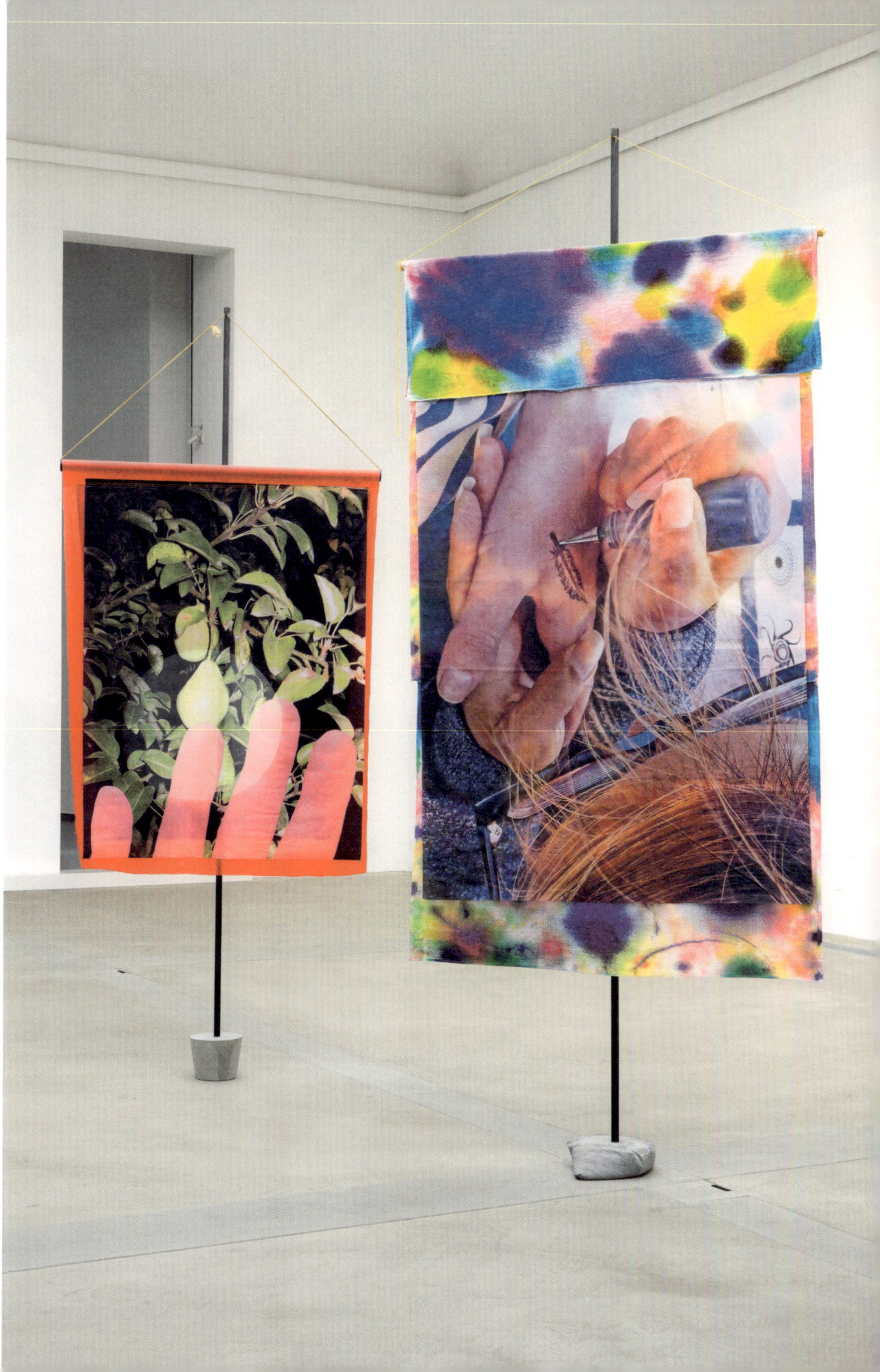

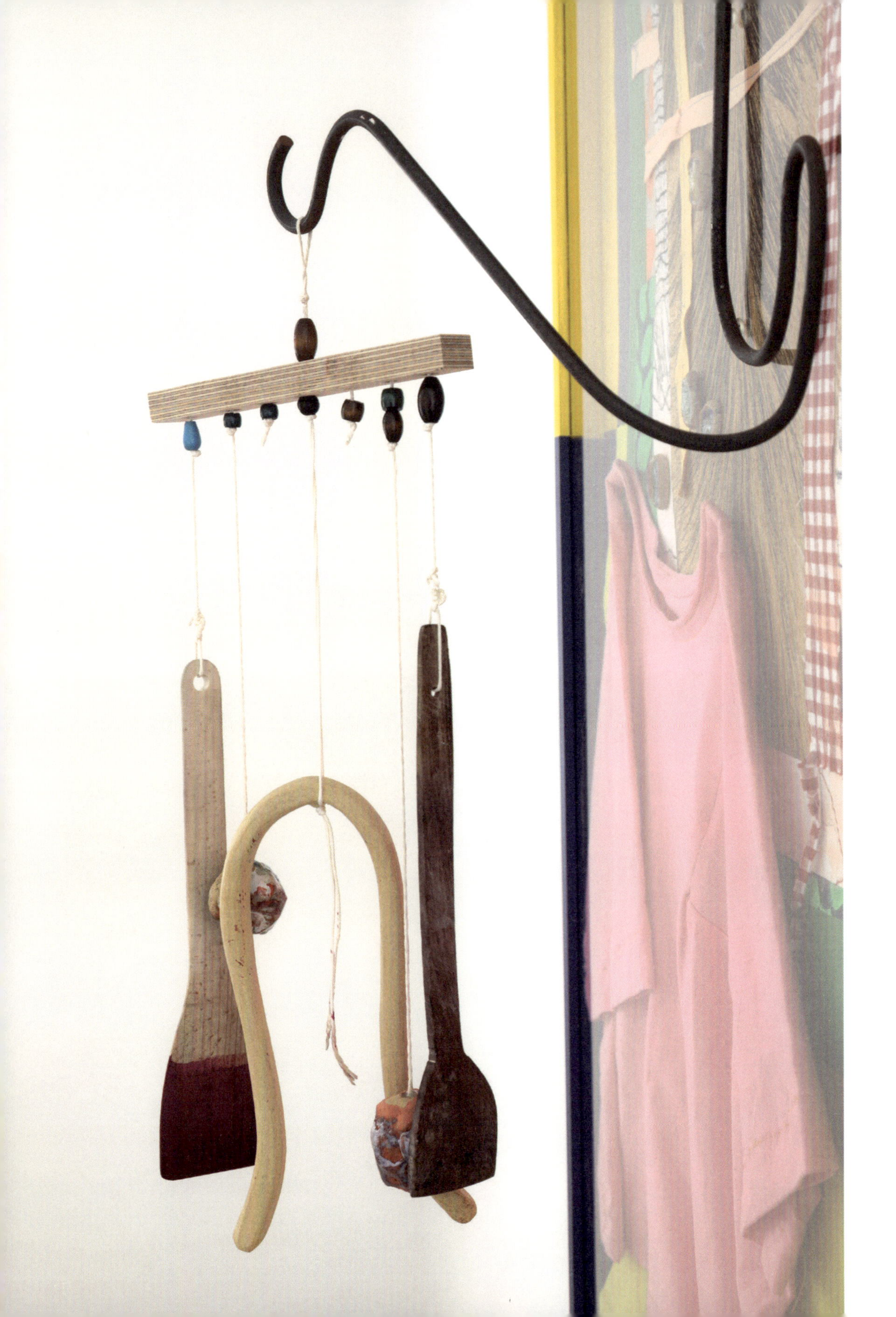

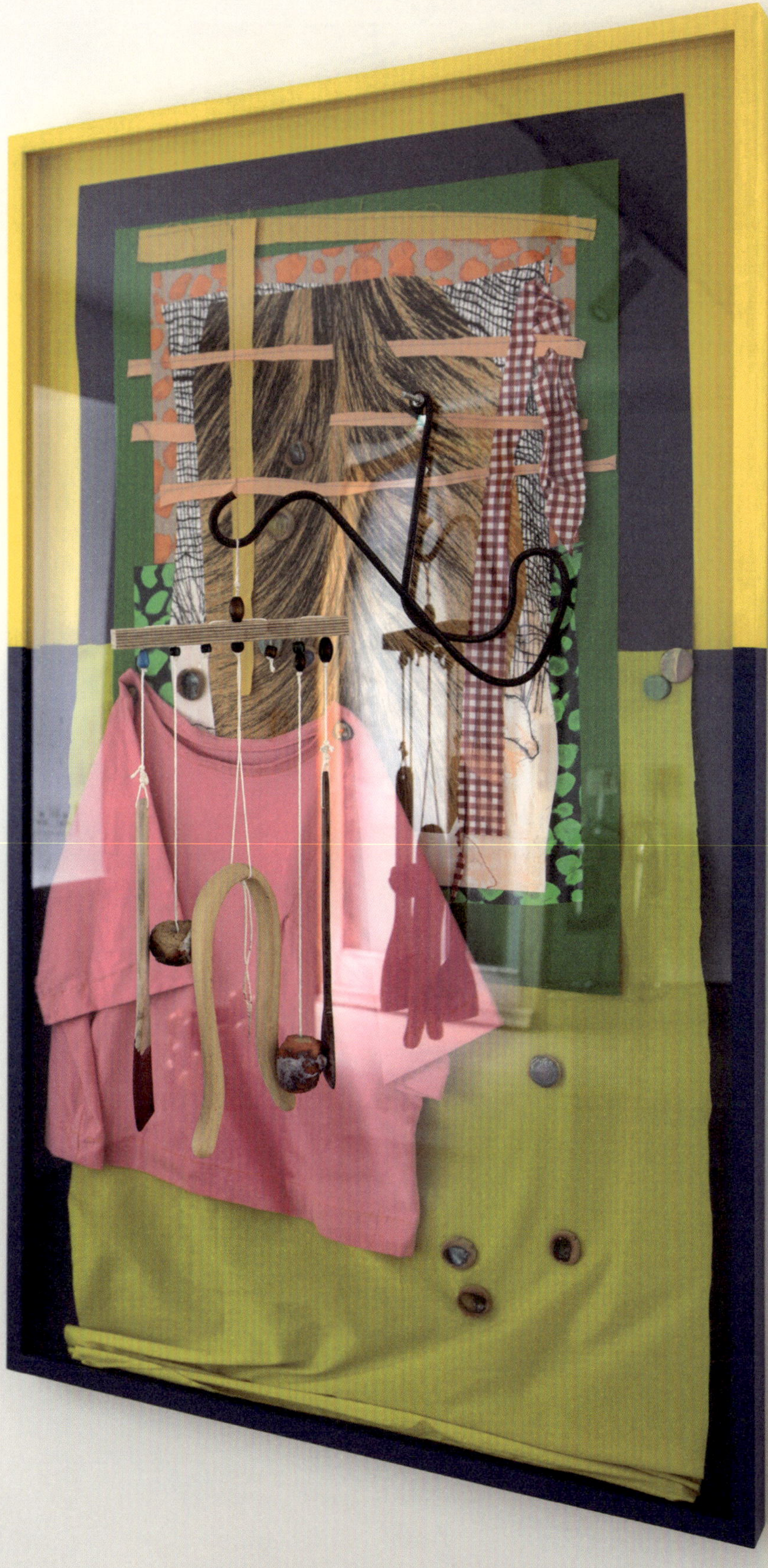

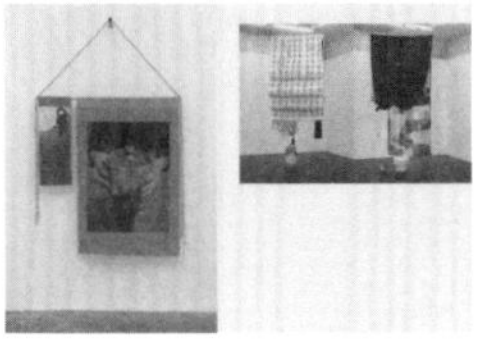

18
Holders (ah Dad), 2013
fabric, rope, dye, wood, metal, paint, 110 × 156 cm

19
(left)
Jerk, lug, paddle, pick, 2013
fabric, string, oil can, cement, metal, dye, 140 × 305 × 50 cm

(right)
Tear, tow, trail, truck, 2013
fabric, string, soda cans, steel, concrete, dye, 154 × 297 × 43 cm

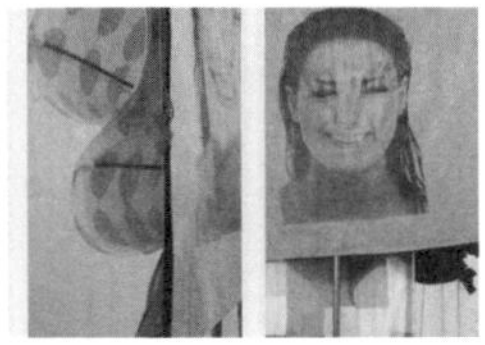

20
Jerk, lug, paddle, pick (detail), 2013

21
Tear, tow, trail, truck (detail), 2013

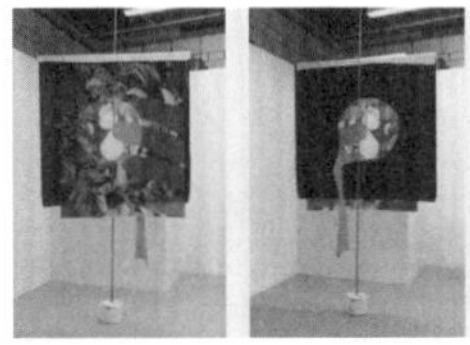

22–23
Physical Culture (touch, face, slip), 2014
fabric, wood, string, concrete, metal, 152 × 310 × 35 cm

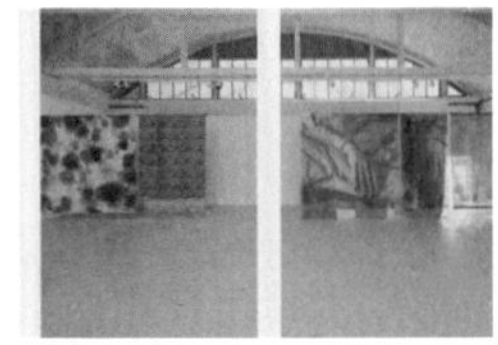

24–25
One to another, one-to-one, installation view, Passerelle, Brest, 2015

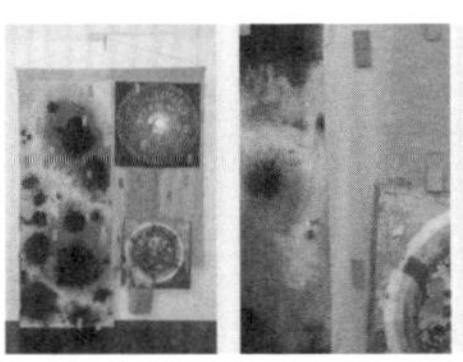

26
Round the outside (looking as a means of attachment), 2016
digital print on fabric, beach towels, dye, wood, and string, 180 × 304 cm

27
Round the outside (looking as a means of attachment) (detail), 2016

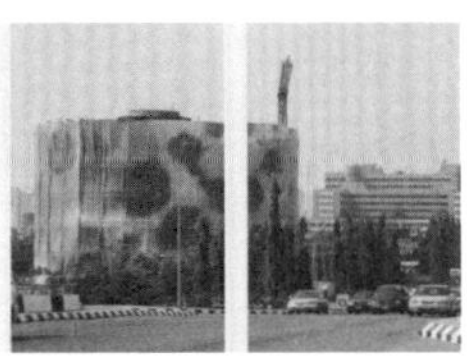

28–29
GO WOMAN GO!, 2016
digital printed fabric

installation view, Headquarters of Federal Ministry of Women Affairs & Social Development, The British Council, Abuja, 2016

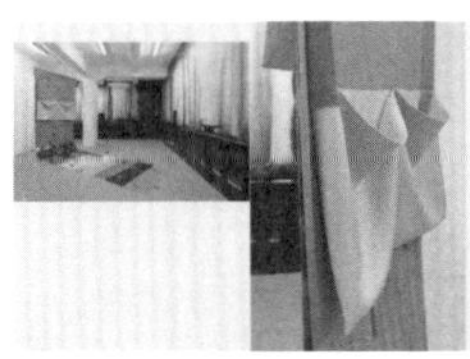

30
What noise is garden (block out, bring about, put together, turn out), 2018
fabric, acrylic, and dye, 180 × 285 × 320 cm

31
What noise is garden (block out, bring about, put together, turn out) (detail), 2018

installation view, Peles Empire, Berlin, 2018

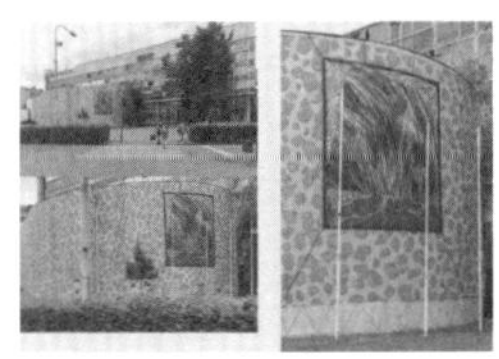

32–33
PHYSICAL CULTURE: Raise your vibration and stick this up where it will do some good, 2019
digital printed fabric and rope, 2000 × 500 cm

I am a Dependent Object, installation view, Biennale of Contemporary Art Brno, The Brno House of Art, 2019

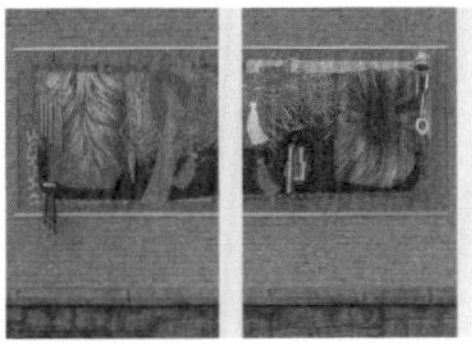

34–35
NO MATH METHOD, 2020
digital print on fabric with homemade wind chimes,
500 × 200 cm

installation view, Kunsthall Stavanger, 2020

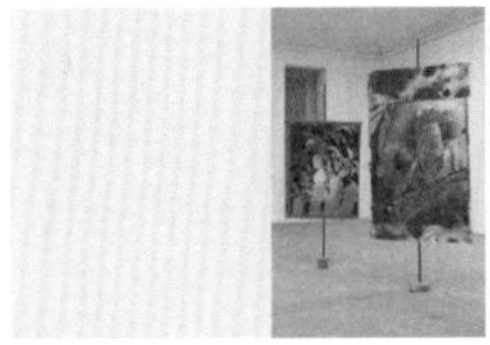

37
(left)
Physical Pink Pear Tree (touch face, slip), 2014
fabrics, dye, wood, metal, concrete,
140 × 270 × 30 cm

(right)
I'll tell you about it, because I am here and you are distant, 2014
fabric, towel, dye, wood, metal, concrete,
147 × 343 × 36 cm

DIDING – An Interior That Remains an Exterior?, installation view, Künstlerhaus, Graz, 2015

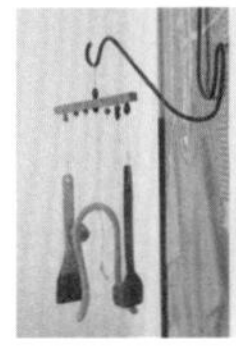

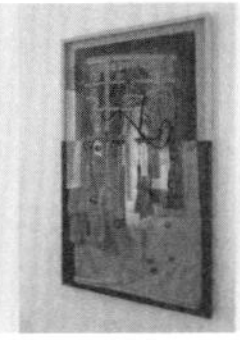

38
NO MATH METHOD (paper theory) (detail), 2021

39
NO MATH METHOD (paper theory), 2021
fabric, glazed stoneware, thread, wood, metal, and digital print on paper in artists custom frame,
146 × 86 × 45 cm

INSIDE ALL MY ACTIVITIES

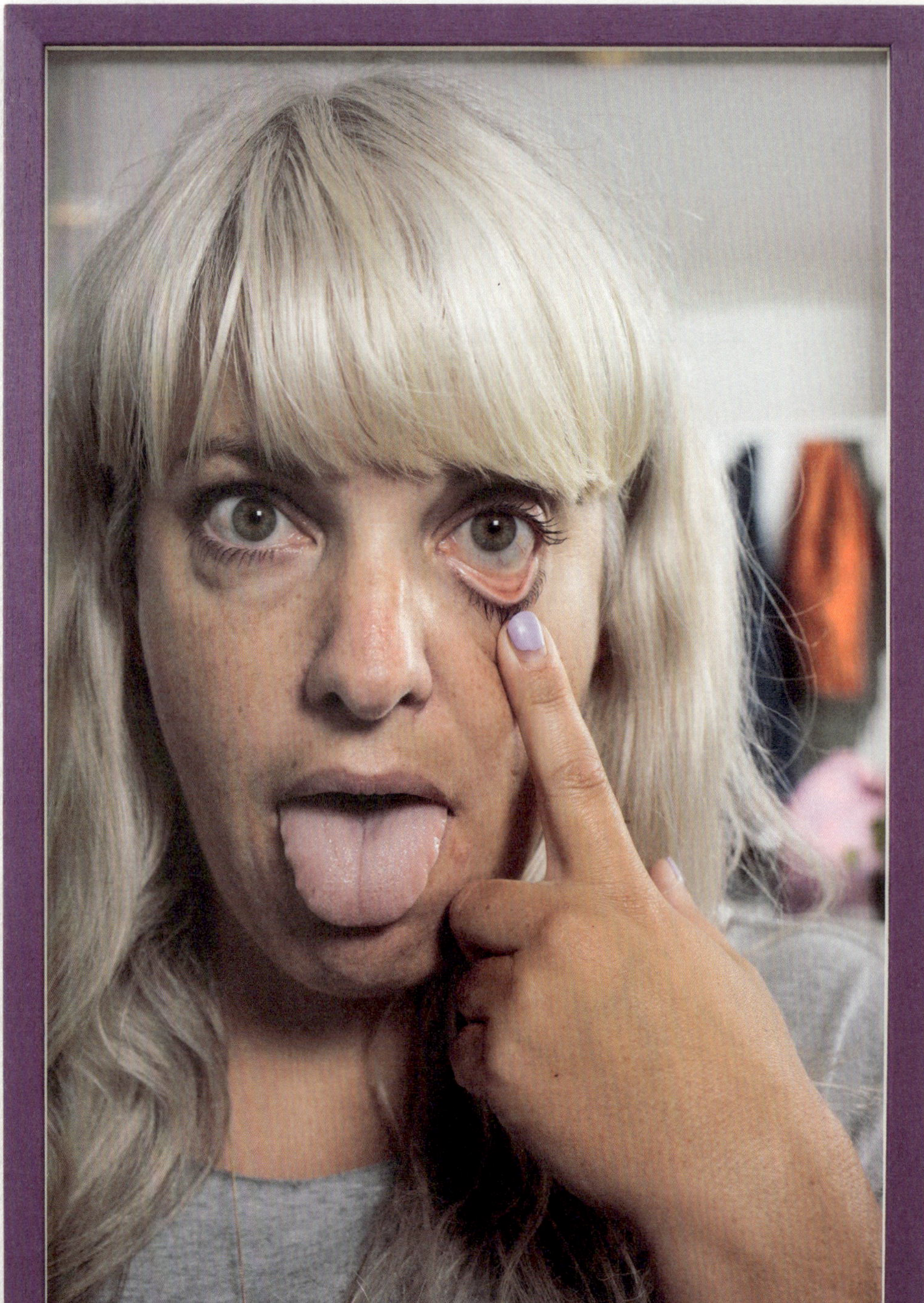

I'VE COME TO HATE MY BODY AND ALL THAT IT REQUIRES IN THIS WORLD

I want to be fully functioning

I can feel my body in relation to my mind

I can feel my body in relation to the floor

I can feel the floor in relation to the wall

CLOTHES ARE AN EXTENSTION OF THE BODY

THESE DAYS

I am becoming more aware of myself – body and mind. Confidence.

I hope I'm doing this for myself.

Enjoying my body. Letting others enjoy my body. Boys in the sand.

FAT IS A FEMINIST ISSUE

It is important to get your body out there in the public realm. I do this consciously sometimes. Showing different realities of yourself – Looking hot. Looking shit.

I don't want to be a body fascist. I just want to take pleasure in it

You are taught to be ashamed of your body, to reject pleasure

TAKING BACK OUR BODIES FOR OURSELVES

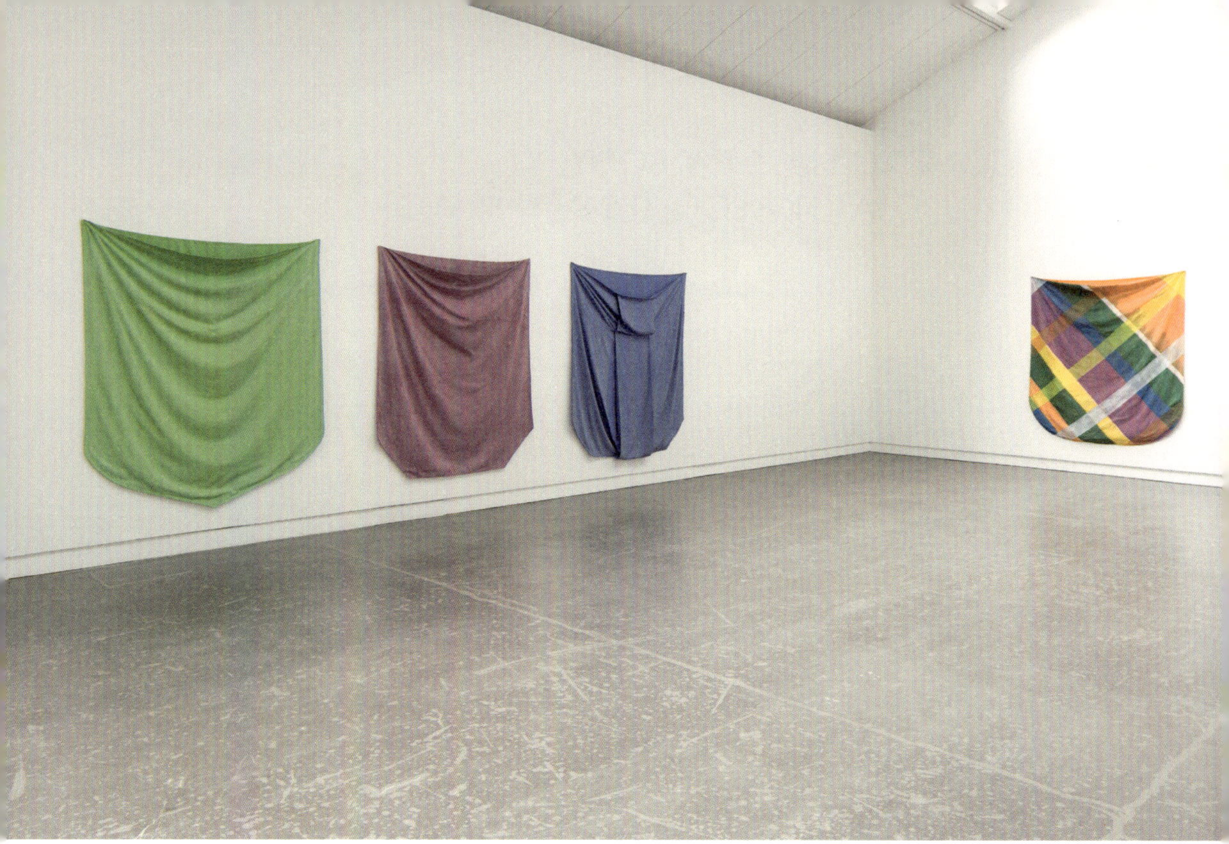

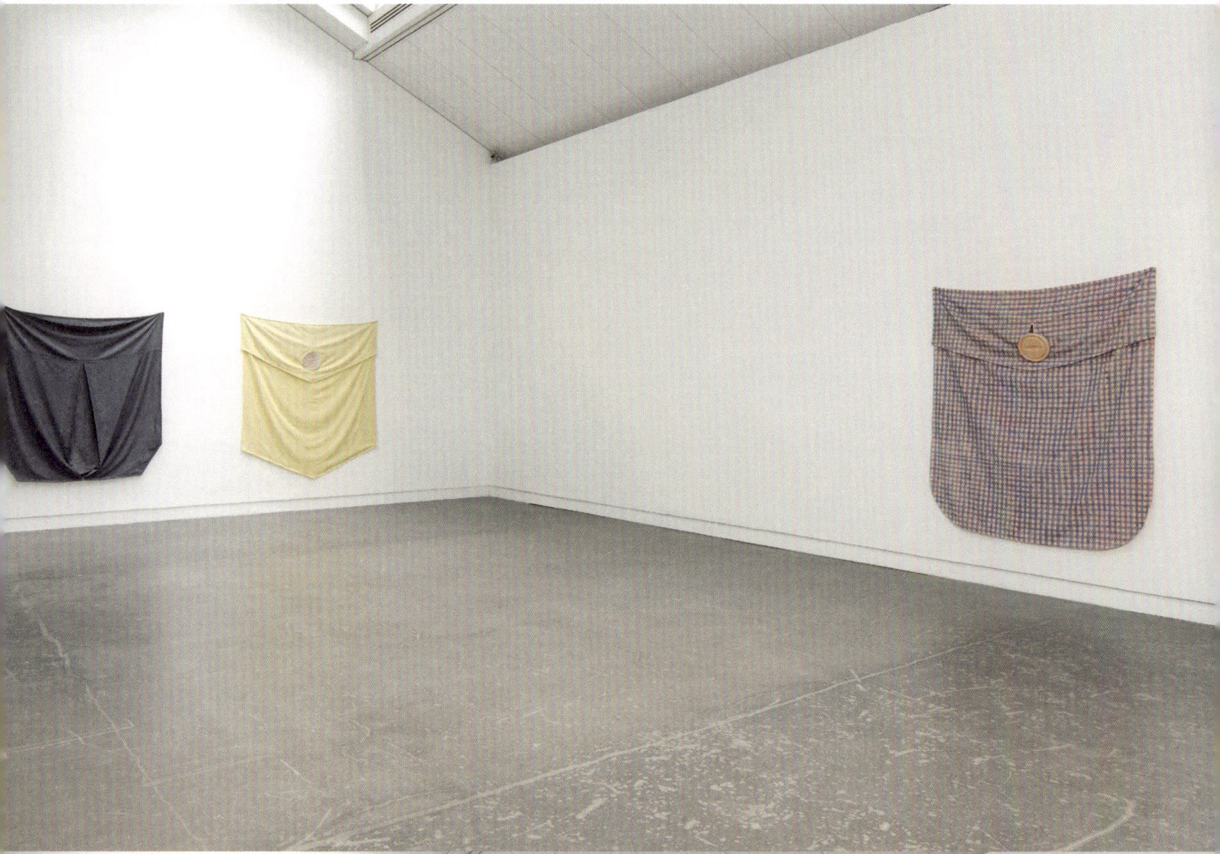

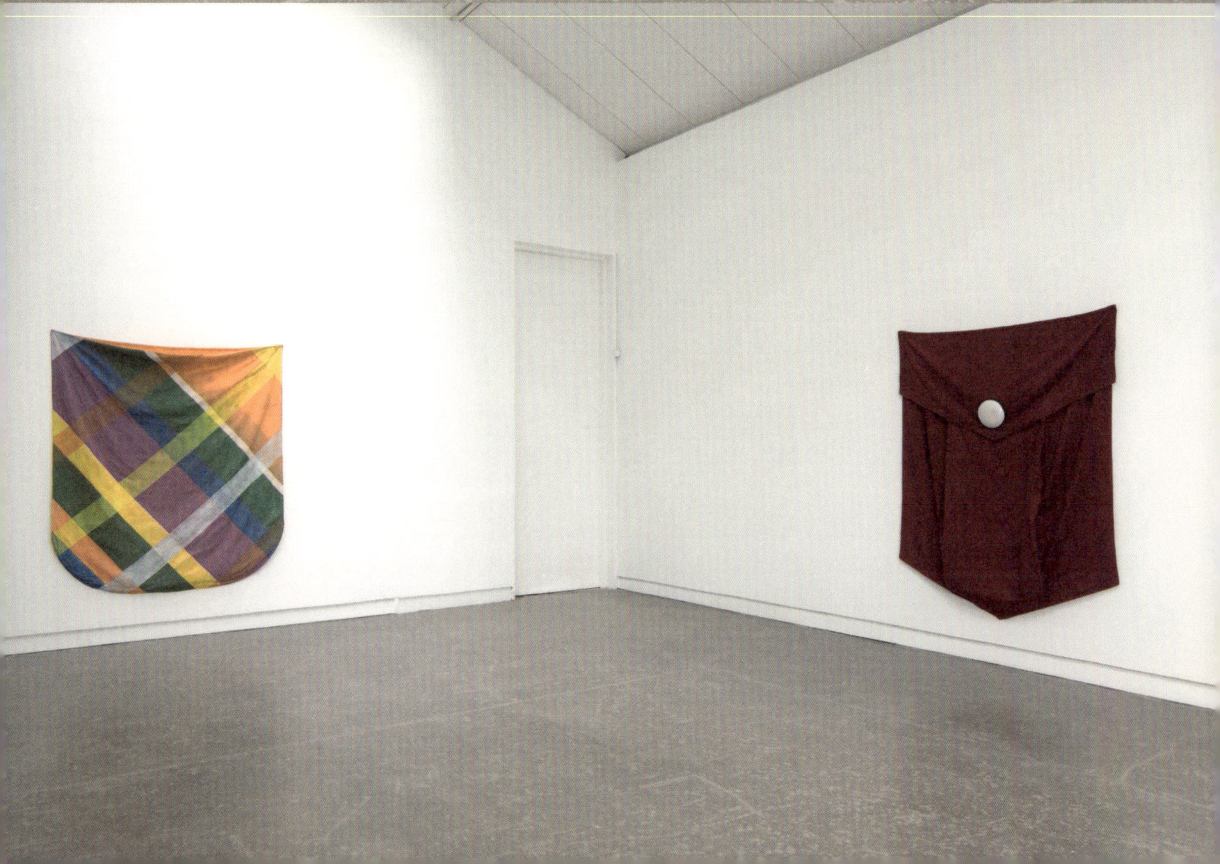

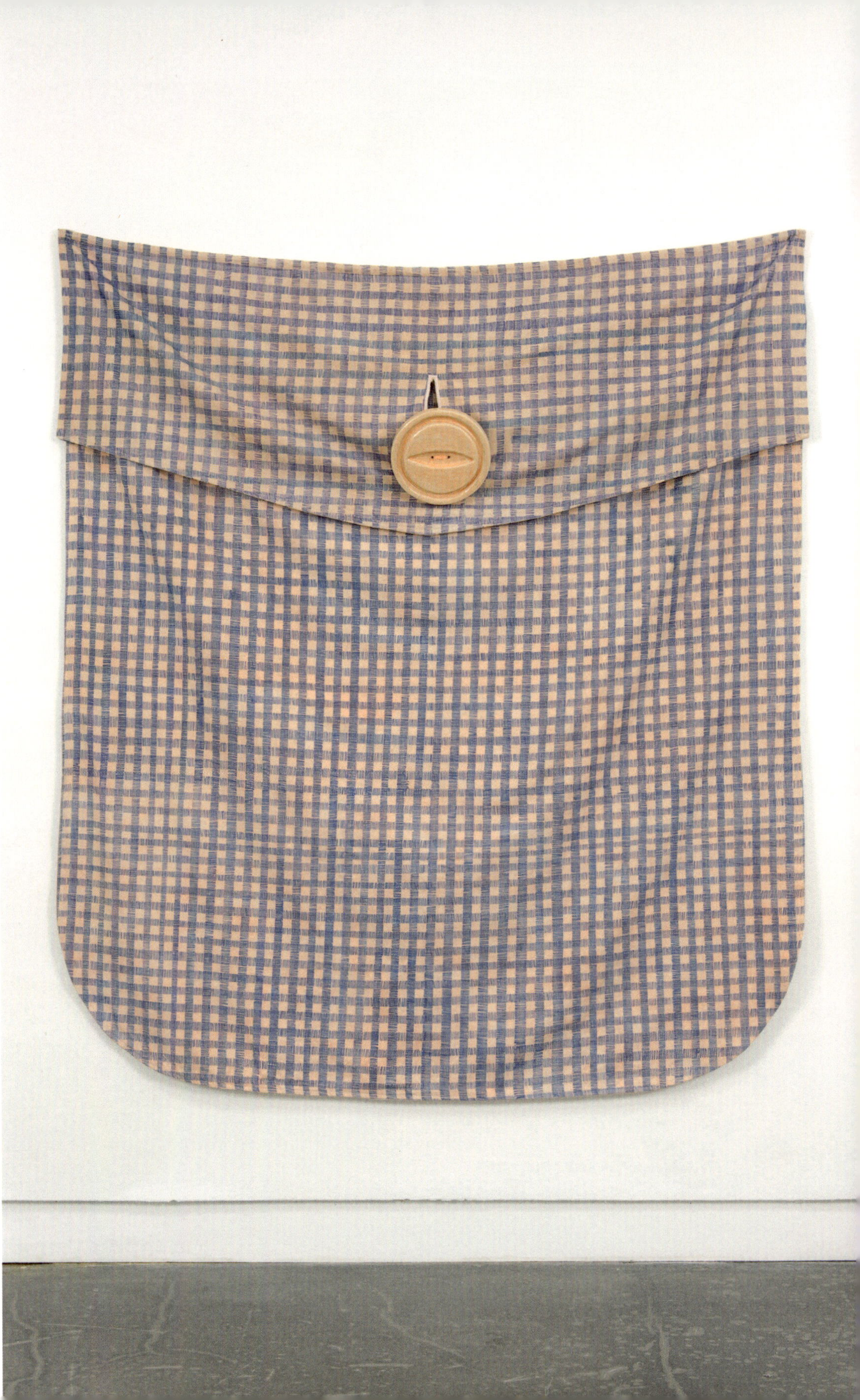

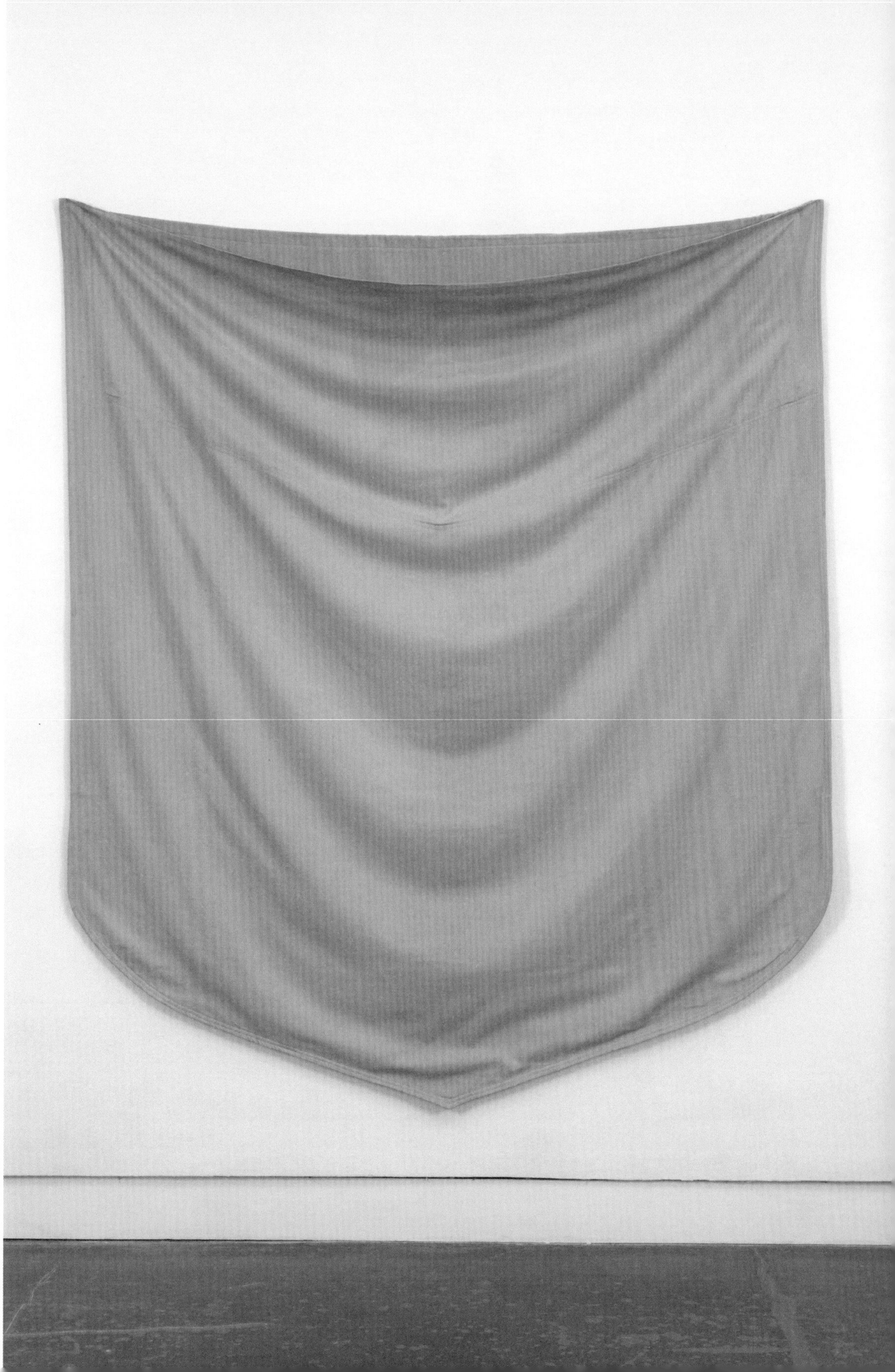

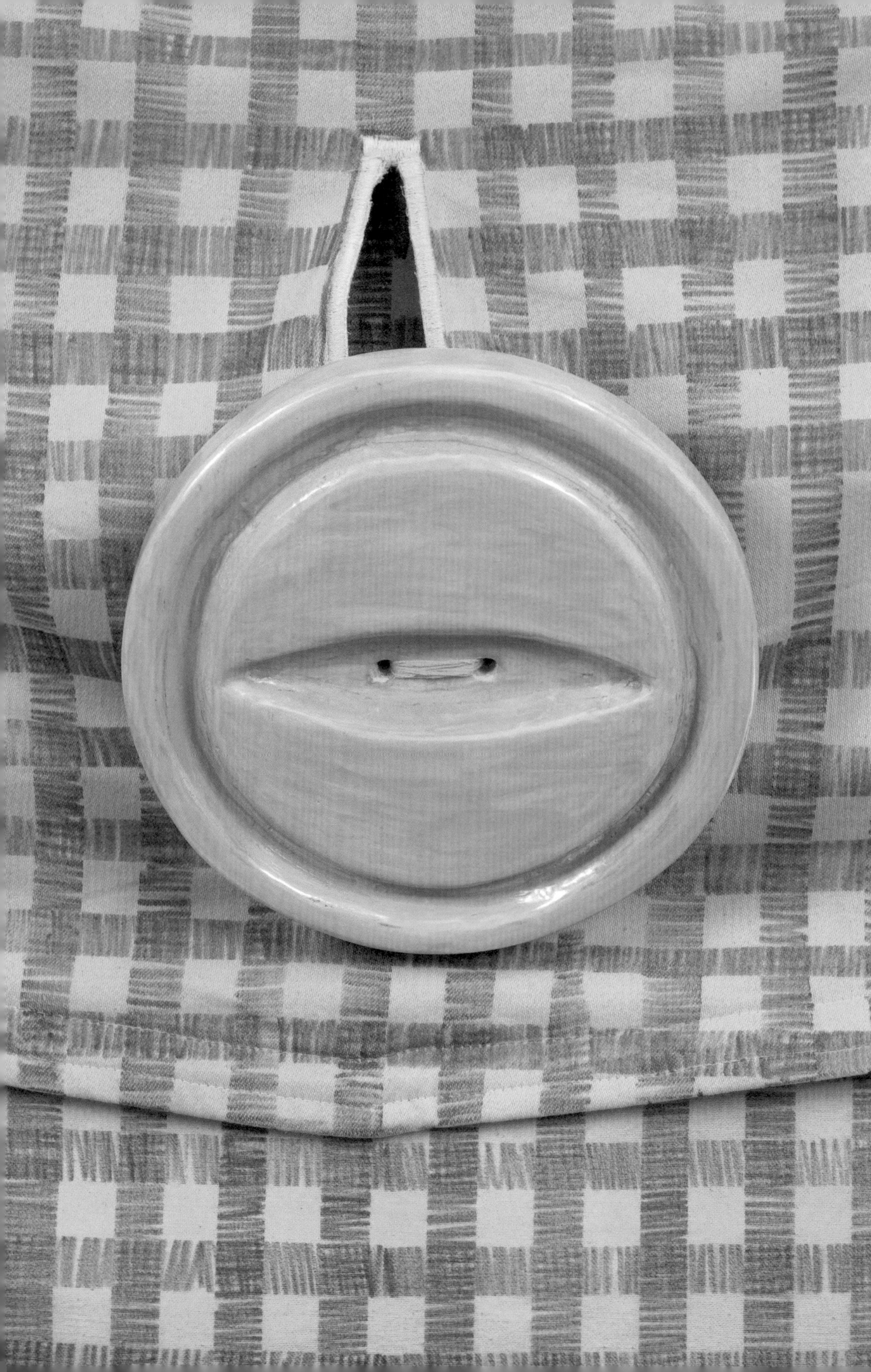

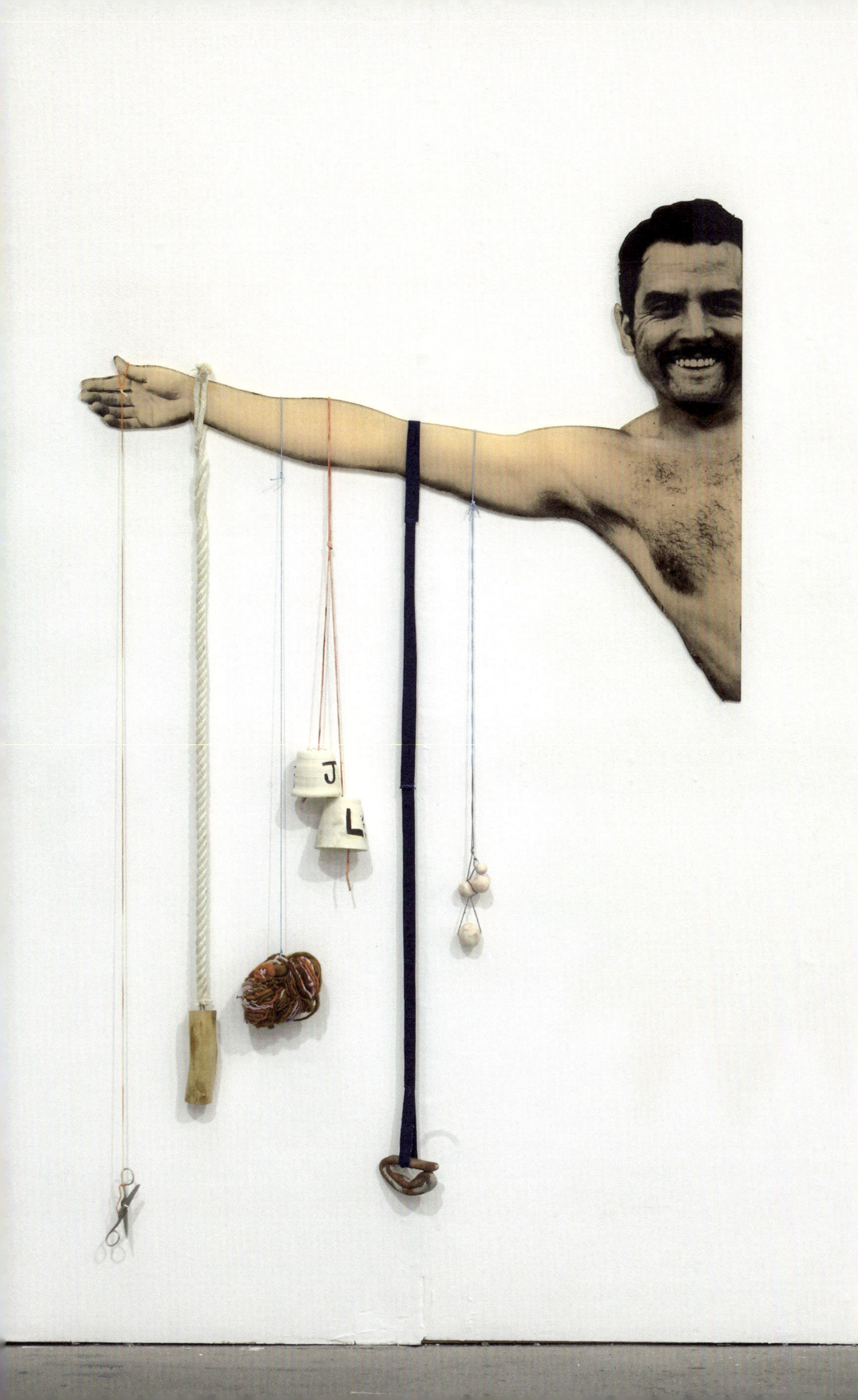

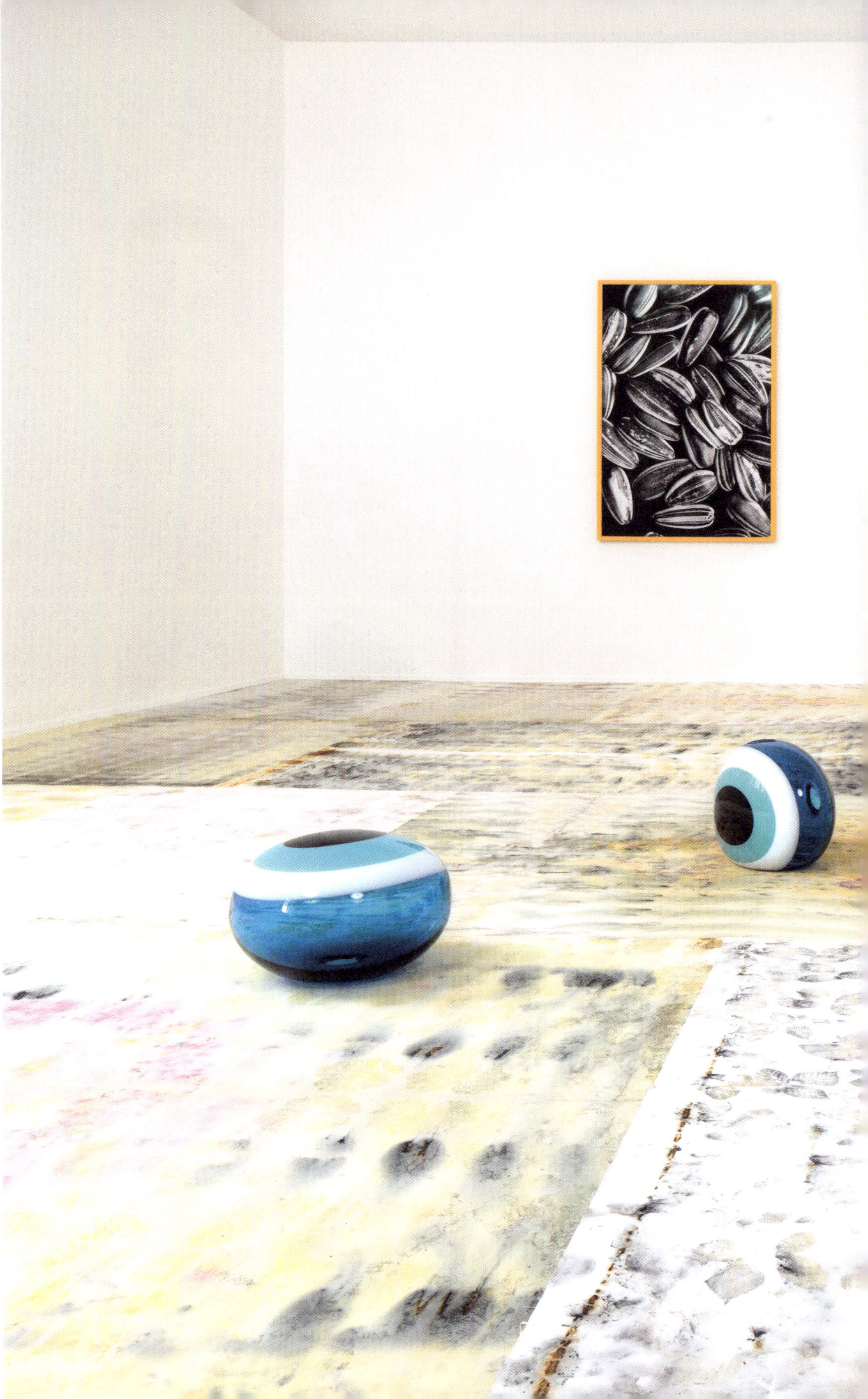

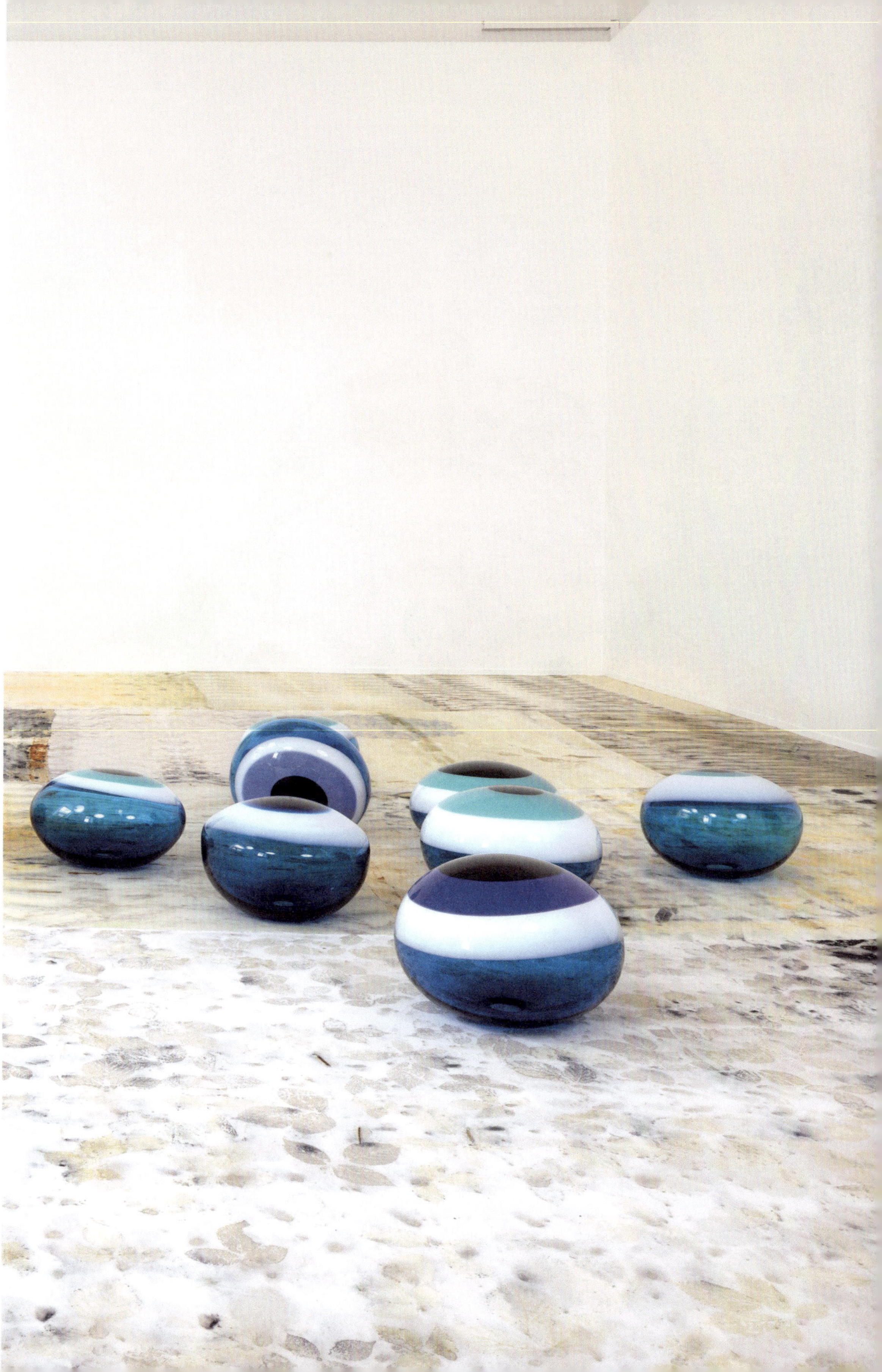

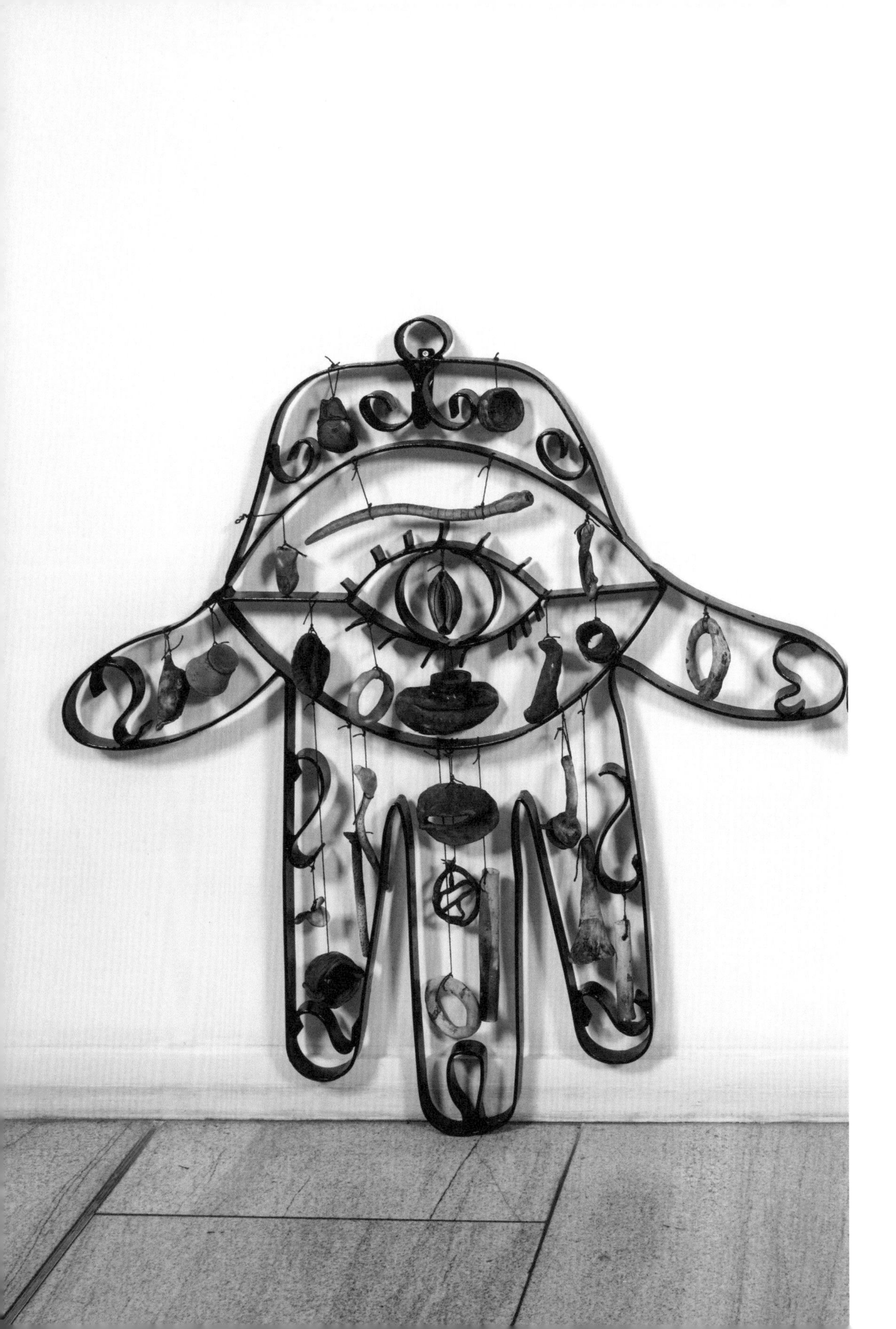

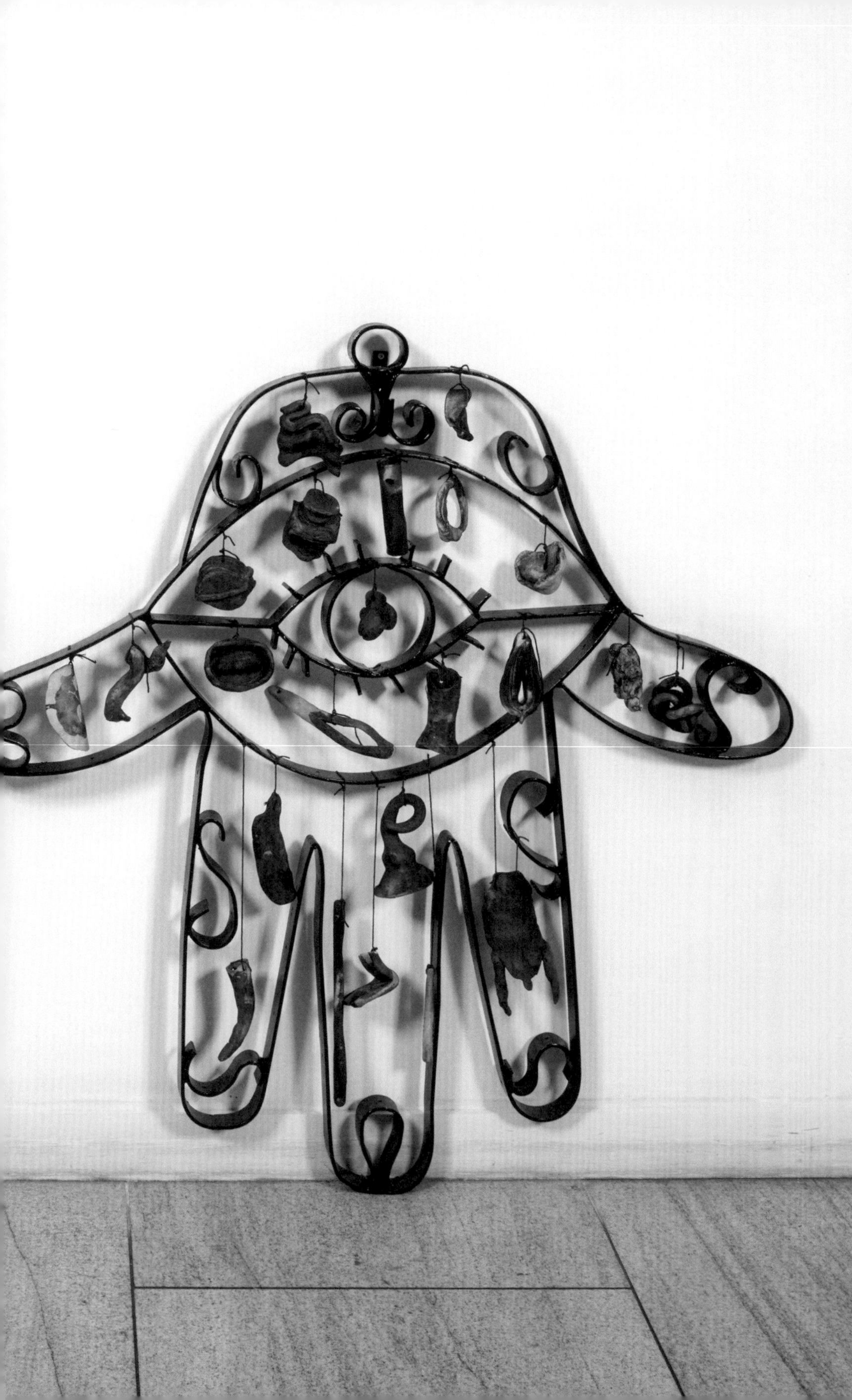

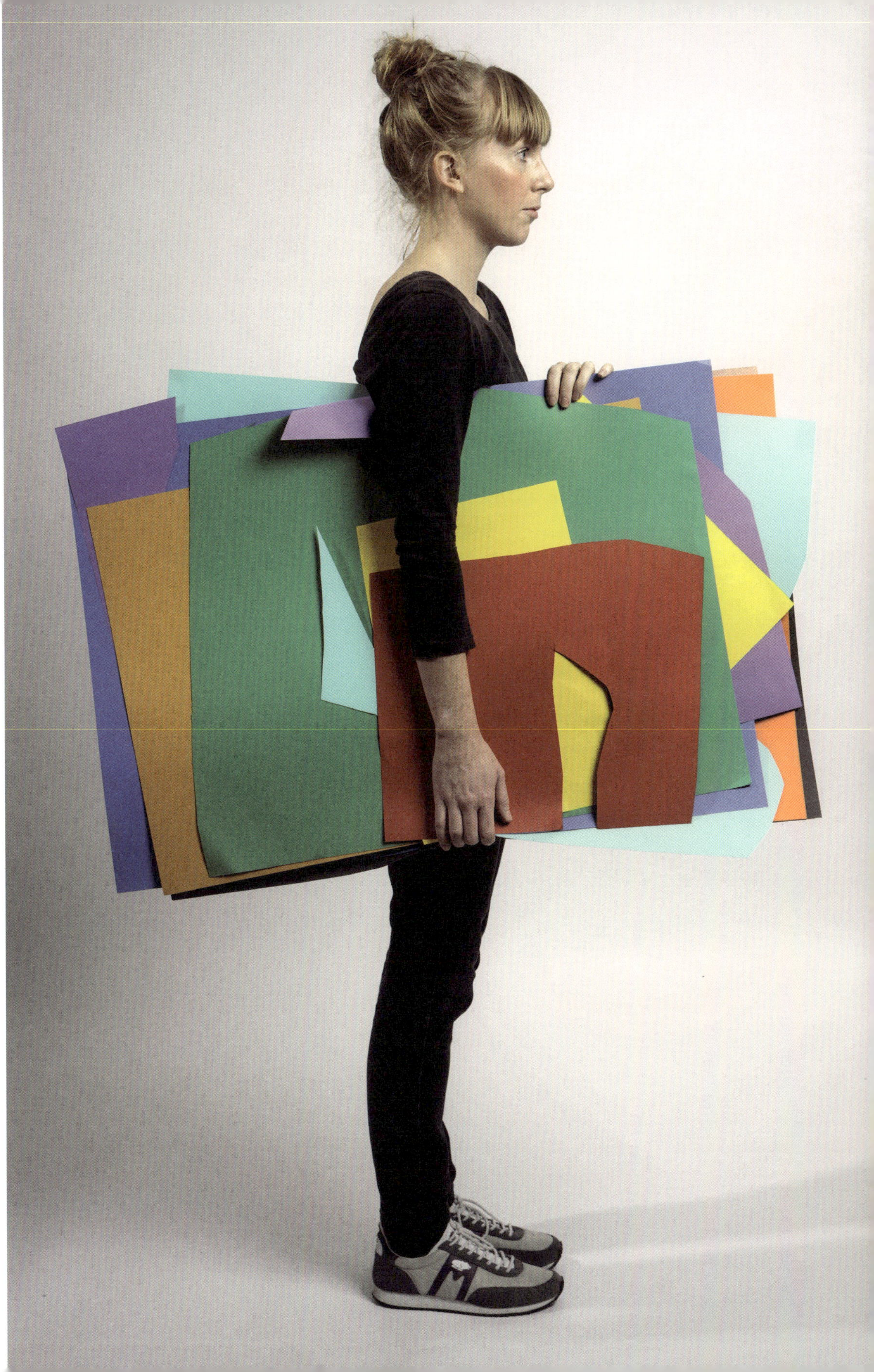

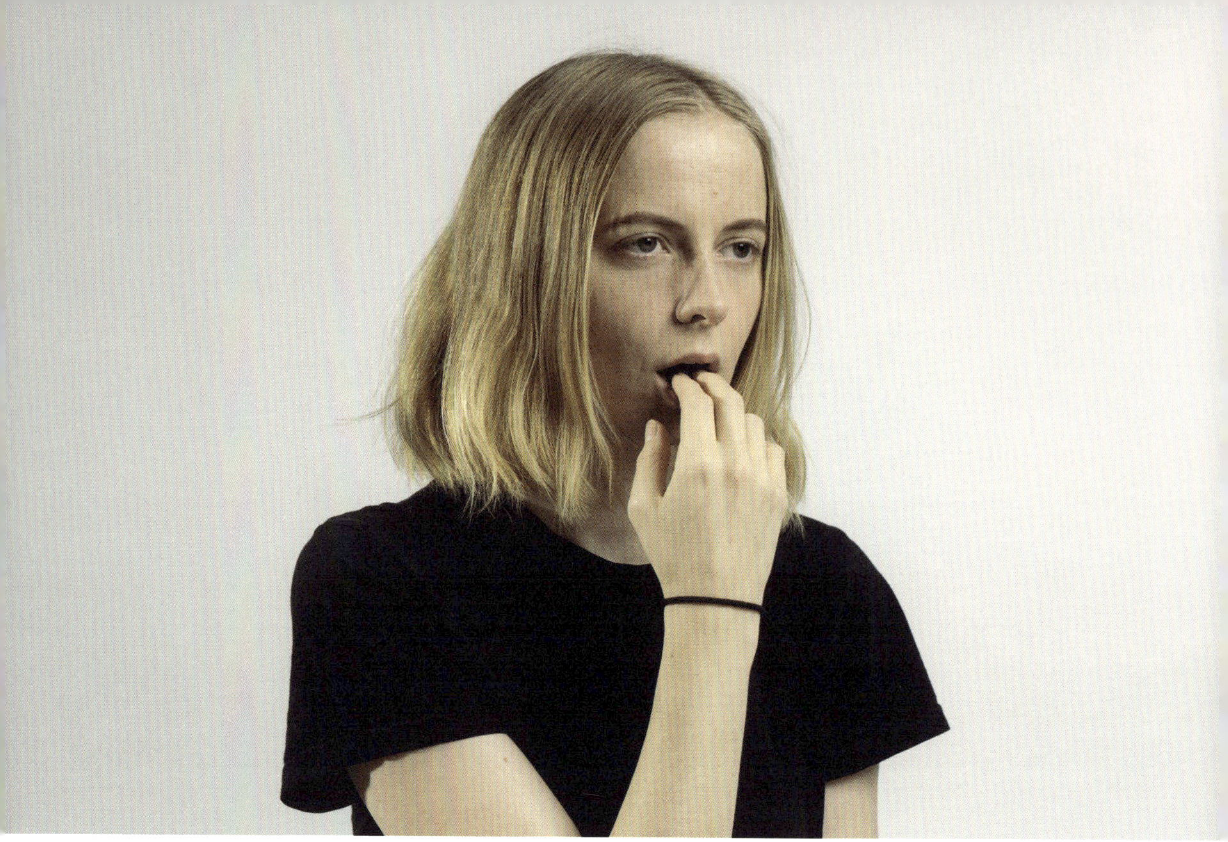

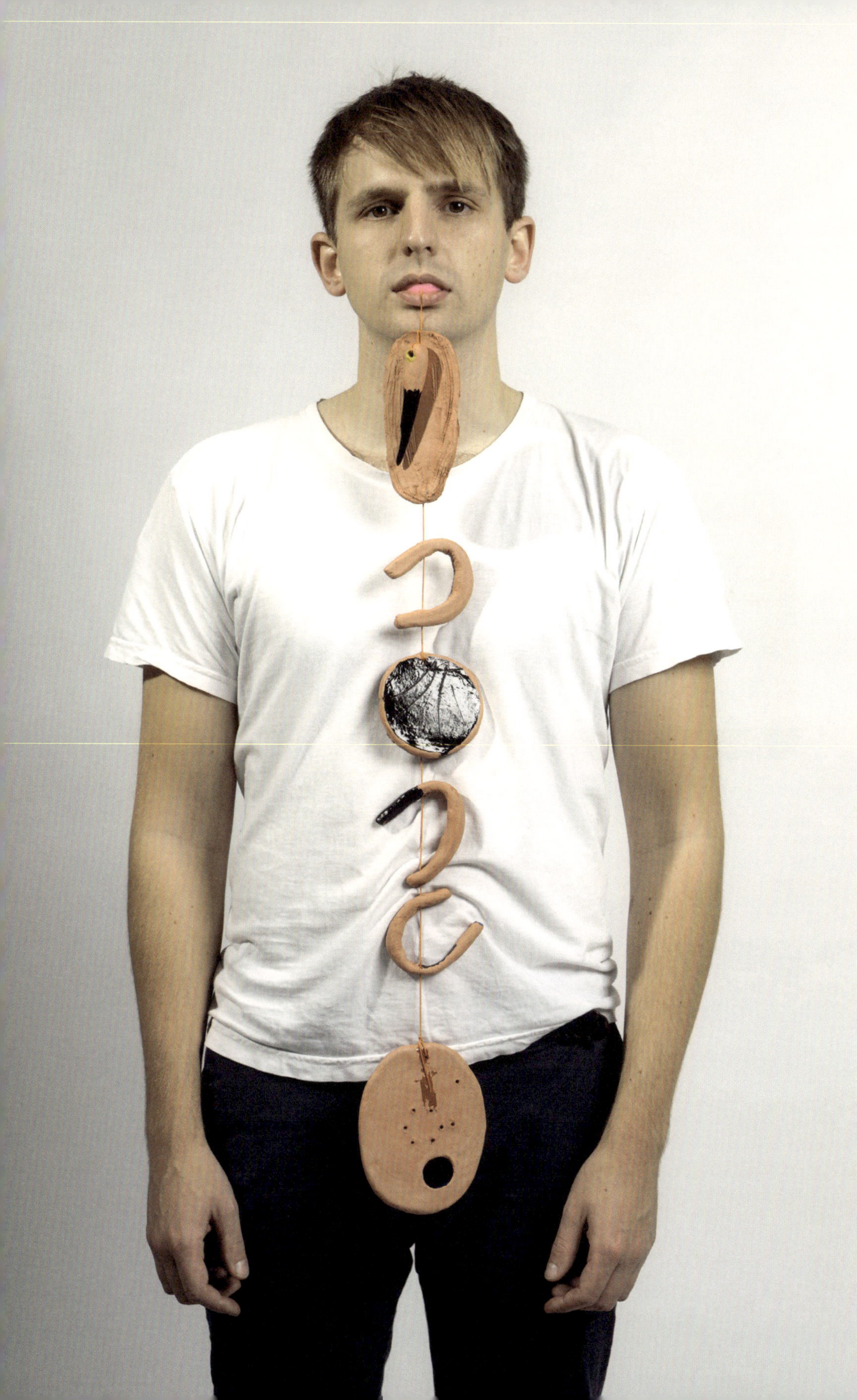

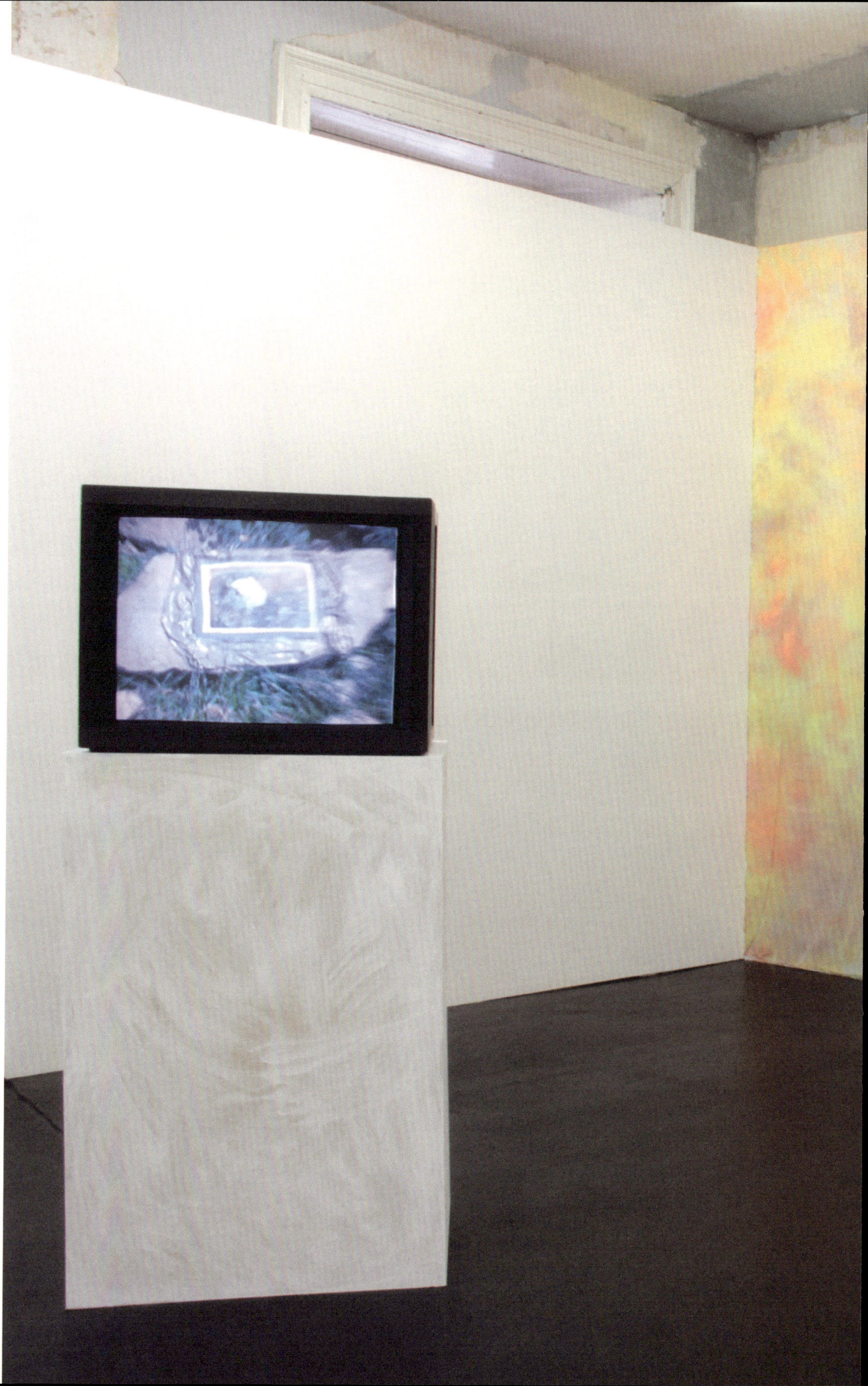

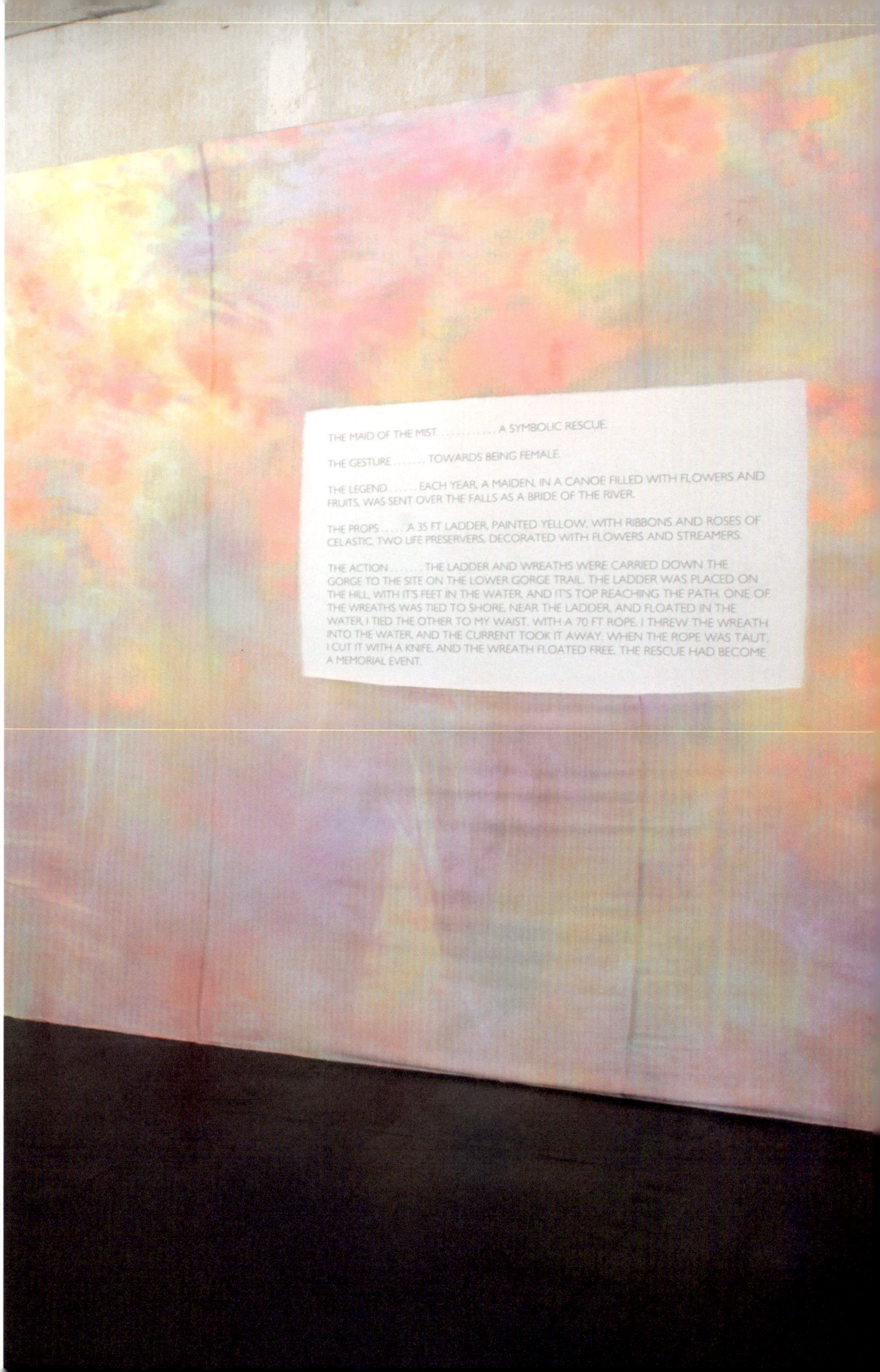
THE MAID OF THE MIST .... A SYMBOLIC RESCUE.
THE GESTURE .... TOWARDS BEING FEMALE.
THE LEGEND ...... EACH YEAR, A MAIDEN, IN A CANOE FILLED WITH FLOWERS AND FRUITS, WAS SENT OVER THE FALLS AS A BRIDE OF THE RIVER.
THE PROPS ..... A 35 FT LADDER, PAINTED YELLOW, WITH RIBBONS AND ROSES OF CELASTIC, TWO LIFE PRESERVERS, DECORATED WITH FLOWERS AND STREAMERS.
THE ACTION .... THE LADDER AND WREATHS WERE CARRIED DOWN THE GORGE TO THE SITE ON THE LOWER GORGE TRAIL. THE LADDER WAS PLACED ON THE HILL, WITH IT'S FEET IN THE WATER, AND IT'S TOP REACHING THE PATH. ONE OF THE WREATHS WAS TIED TO SHORE, NEAR THE LADDER, AND FLOATED IN THE WATER. I TIED THE OTHER TO MY WAIST, WITH A 70 FT ROPE. I THREW THE WREATH INTO THE WATER, AND THE CURRENT TOOK IT AWAY. WHEN THE ROPE WAS TAUT, I CUT IT WITH A KNIFE, AND THE WREATH FLOATED FREE. THE RESCUE HAD BECOME A MEMORIAL EVENT.

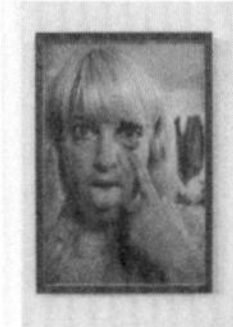

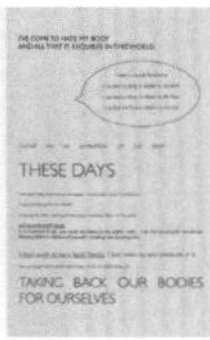

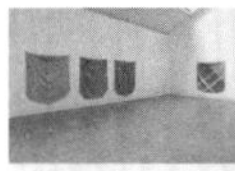

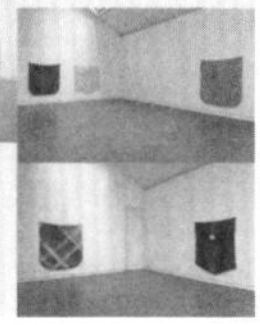

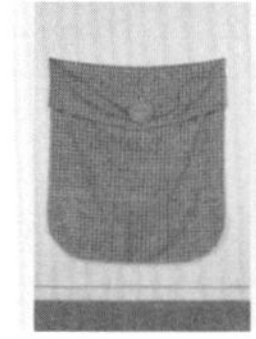

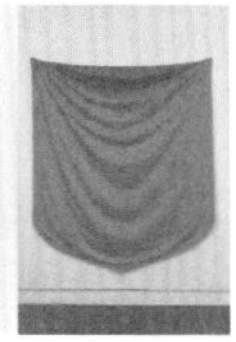

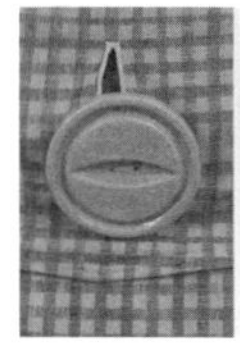

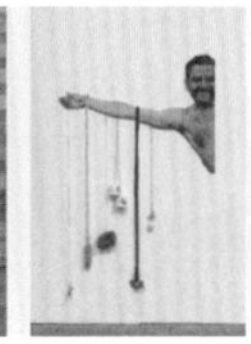

44
Today (myself), 2016
c-type photographic print, custom frame, 51.5 × 31.5 cm

45
Laura Aldridge & Joe Scotland, *THESE DAYS – Taking back our bodies (refund please)*, 2013
digital print on silk, 125 × 100 cm

46
Green Pane (with all the simple feeling, when I do it), 2012
transparent watercolour, dye on fabric, 160 × 180 cm

Cloudy (you are loved), 2012
transparent watercolour, dye on fabric, 162 × 183 cm

Blue Funk (gas lighting), 2012
bleach on fabric, 165 × 170 cm

Skin (welcome party), 2012
spray paint, dye on fabric, 165 × 180 cm

47
(top)
Light Black (I hope that your heart is open and your head is happy), 2012
transparent watercolour, dye on fabric, 150 × 165 cm

Yellowish (the grass has grown too long, and I can't find my roller skates), 2012
transparent watercolour, dye on fabric, 160 × 180 cm

Humanity Rose (paint the objects and not the atmosphere), 2012
transparent watercolour, dye, fabric pens on fabric, polystyrene, 160 × 180 cm

(bottom)
Skin (welcome party), 2012
spray paint, dye on fabric, 165 × 180 cm

Passionate Cherry (her autistic tendencies), 2012
corduroy, polystyrene, and felt, 165 × 180 cm

Underside, backside, inside, even, installation views, CCA Glasgow, 2012

48
Humanity Rose (paint the objects and not the atmosphere), 2012

49
Green Pane (with all the simple feeling, when I do it), 2012

50
Humanity Rose (paint the objects and not the atmosphere) (detail), 2012

51
Performance and Party (we can communicate through those cups, ok?), 2014
screen print on Perspex, string, ceramic, scissors, fabric, 95 × 157 × 5 cm

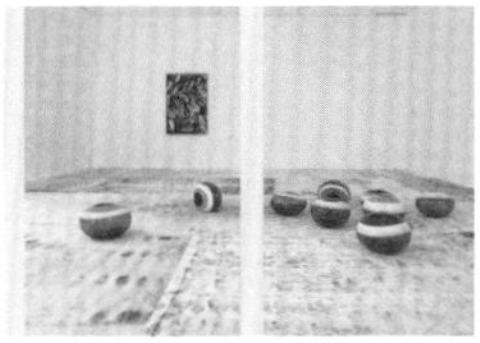

52–53
(wall)
Four weeks ago (seeds), 2016
giclee print on cotton, custom frame, 123 × 83 cm

(floor)
Signals and Get Wet (1–10), 2016
hand blown glass, dimensions variable

Inside all my activities, installation view, Koppe Astner, Glasgow, 2016

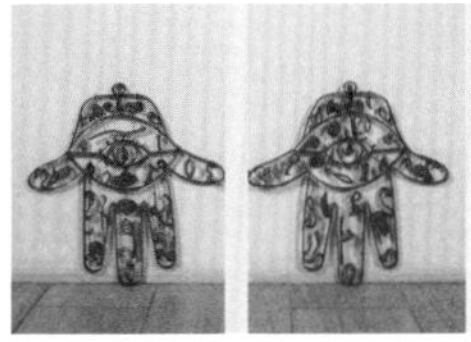

54–55
Anna Mayer & Laura Aldridge, sculpture from *OPENARIES II (Vaginas and snakes)*, 2014
metal, ceramic, string, fire, iron oxide, banana skins, wind, 230 × 120 × 50 cm

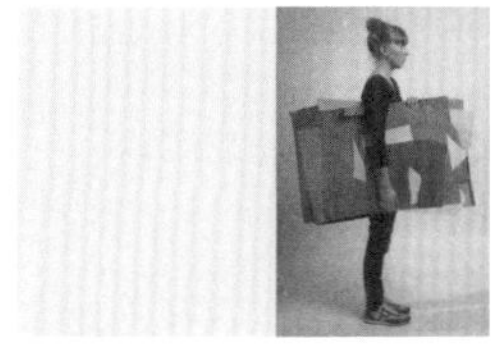

57
Seemingly (holding), 2015
digital print on Perspex, 190 × 135 cm

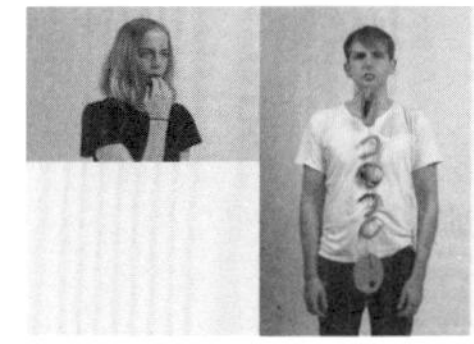

58
Seemingly (pushing), 2015
digital print on Perspex, 195 × 130 cm

59
(still) Radical Facial Jewellery (Simon), 2015
digital print on Perspex, 190 × 135 cm

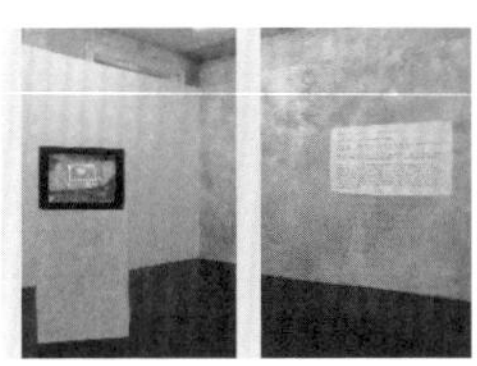

60–61
(plinth)
Ree Morton, *Regarding Landscape: The Maid of the Mist*, 1976
8mm film transferred to digital (colour, sound), 11:17 min.

(wall)
Untitled, 2011
fabric, watercolour, Ree Morton text, vinyl, 567 × 300 cm

LAYING DOWN AND KISSING THE LOVE IN THE MIST Part 1 - Ree Morton, installation view, Kendall Koppe, Glasgow, 2012

JOE SCOTLAND

Joe Scotland is Director of Studio Voltaire, London.

IN CONVERSATION WITH LAURA ALDRIDGE

JS
Hi, Laura.

JS
I've been thinking about how your work has continuously made use of textiles. It feels like a core element running throughout your practice. Tell me a little about the decision to use textiles and why you keep returning to them.

JS
It's interesting you should say that; you originally studied painting when you were doing your BA at Wimbledon College of Art. How do you think that influenced your approach to materials?

L A
Hiya, Joe.

L A
I started actively working with fabric while on a residency in Amsterdam.[1] I quickly tuned in to the abundance of textiles throughout the city's fabric shops and markets, both new and second hand. You could buy old hotel linens for practically nothing, so it felt natural to start buying up piles of fabric. In part, the reason was cost—it was cheaper than paper—but predominantly, I responded to how it was already *something*.
Fabric didn't have the same blankness as a piece of paper or a sheet of wood; it already felt imbued with its own "life." By that, I mean fabric comes with its own history and social significance. The fabrics I was buying appealed to me because they felt like a kind of readymade, and my use of them was another step in their production.
Significantly, fabric offered a direct relationship to tactility, either through a connection to the hands of the maker or the functional uses of textiles. Fabric represents an open-ended medium, possessing a particular kind of physicality that I gravitate toward. I think I use fabric in the way a painter might use oil paint.

L A
I studied painting without ever actually making one. I feel my time on that course has meant that I approach sculpture from a painterly perspective. Fabric hovers between being both a flat two-dimensional surface and a three-dimensional object, and I am interested in the tension of that duality. Fabric's potential for soft construction and robust flexibility appeals to me. In the studio, it allows for a certain kind of lightness that suits my approach to making. I can assemble things provisionally before committing to pinning them down. I can unpick, work over, and reshape things until I settle on something, as you might do when you make a toile for a dress. Even then, there is a feeling of the work being in flux, that it is never finished, or that I could cut it up or add another layer.
Equally, the language surrounding textiles informs my practice. Words like *material*, *thread*, *weave*, and *fabric* have multiple uses dependent on context. Textiles are full of possibilities.

JS

Textiles often seem to be the poor cousin to other materials, and I wonder if its ubiquity partly leads us not to give it the value it deserves?

JS

Last year there was a slightly sentimental piece on Radio 4 where someone was describing the connections between touch, loss, and sadness in relation to their cat. I can't recall the wider context for the piece, but there was a point where she spoke about crying into her cat's fur and how it would absorb her tears and emotions—she described it as being almost like a filter. I liked the sense of how materiality might absorb or encourage certain feelings, and in relation to fabric, how it has the ability to absorb things, physically and otherwise. Does this resonate with you?

JS

There is something particular about how fabric absorbs light and how different colours appear. Could you tell me a bit more about fabric, colour, and absorption?

LA

It really is everywhere, all around us. We are all in contact with fabric—we sleep in it, sit on it, wear it, sweat in it, wash it, iron it, dry our bodies with it, blow our noses on it. It is part of the fabric (no pun intended) of our daily lives. Our identities and emotions are in part constructed through the garments that we wear. Often what we use most we tend to overlook.

LA

Yes, it really does. It's an incredible explanation of pets, their tactility and our physical experience of that. In particular, it reminds me of the show I did with you at Studio Voltaire in 2011, in which the series *Hand Extended* featured disembodied hands holding cats among plaster knots.

This also resonates with the sensory workshops I lead with Artlink.[2] Working with people with complex needs has meant I have had to develop a material vocabulary as another method of communication, where I am often thinking about both the physical and emotional qualities of materials. This has heightened my awareness of the relationships between sight and touch—that we see, hear, and feel texture in equal measure. We can see *crunchy*, not just hear or feel it.

Eve Kosofsky Sedgwick's book *Touching Feeling* explores the complexities of both texture and touch. There's a line from it that I have repeatedly copied down. I write it in my sketchbooks, I add it on "to do" lists, I have written it on my studio wall: "There is no such thing as textural lack."[3]

LA

The haptic qualities of colour are very important to me. Thinking about how colour gets places is fascinating—how it can sit embedded into a material, be applied over a surface or soaked in. You can paint with it, dye using it, add and take it away, and it can change drastically when light shines through it. Colour is at once both simple and incredibly complex. Wittgenstein's *Remarks on Colour*[4] has been a formative book for me. Through a set of notes and propositions, he scrutinises our perceptions

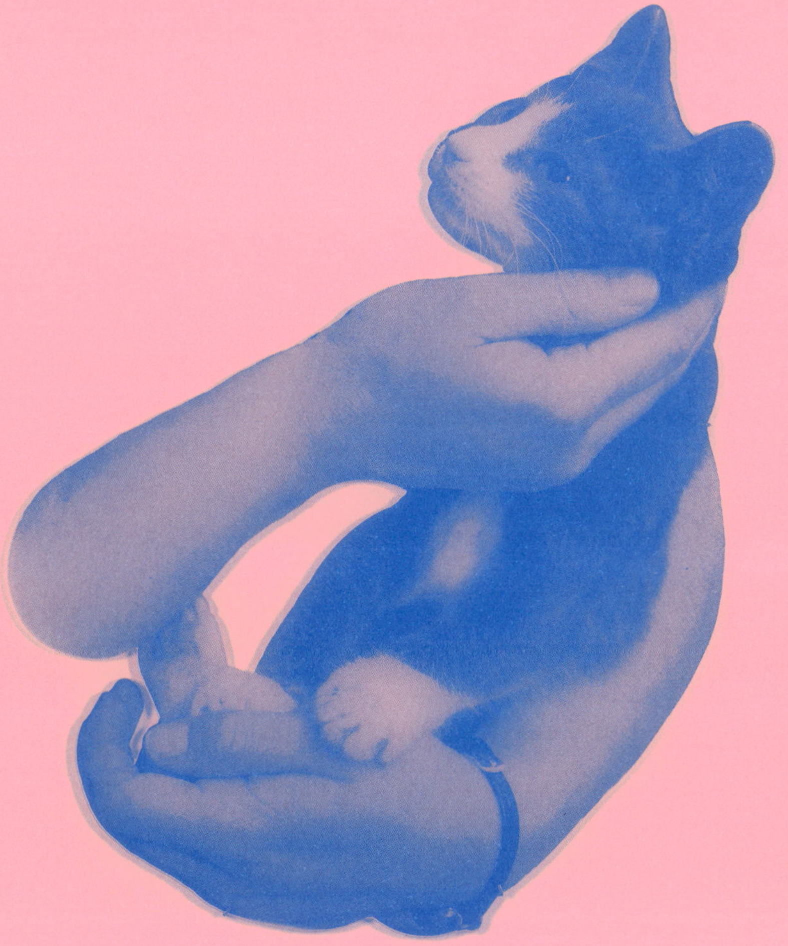

Hand Extended (II), 2010, screen print on Perspex, 70 × 60 cm

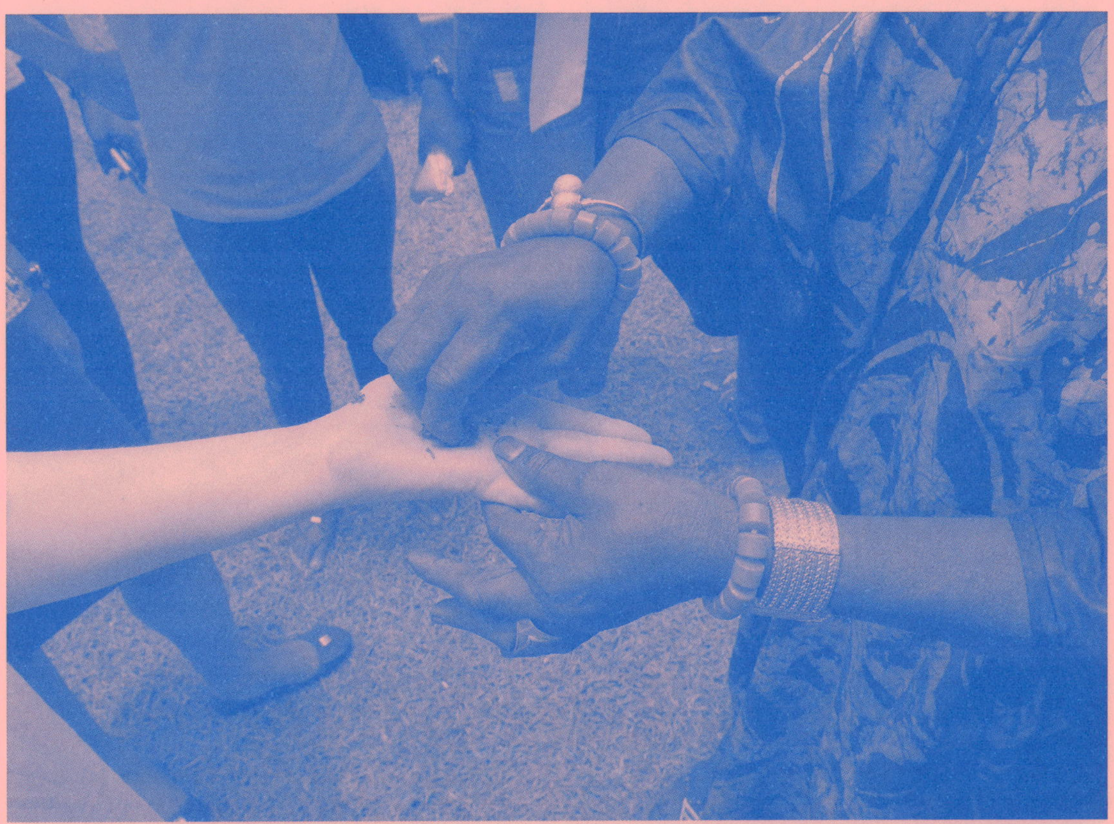

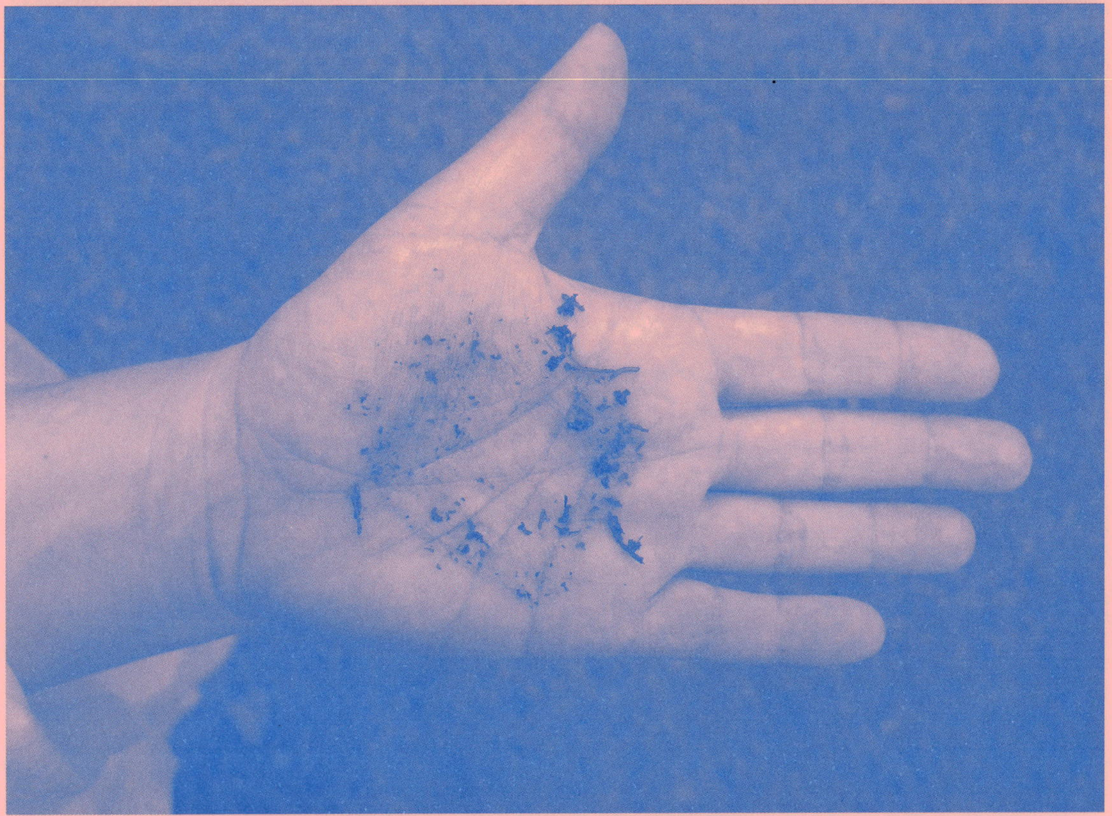

Dyeing workshop at Nike Outdoor textile studio, Abuja, 2015

JS

How did you come to the title *Things that soak you*? Were you particularly thinking about absorption?

JS

This makes me think about the fabric works you started making after your trip to Nigeria in 2015.[5] There was a shift in how you worked toward using plant-based materials to imprint and dye fabric. Tell me about that process. It feels linked to notions of absorption.

of colour and dismisses the idea that colour is a singular, instantly perceivable and fixed notion.

I see colour as a material to engage with. I have an ongoing series of works called *Things that soak you* (2016–present), which came from my desire to hold up colour directly in various forms. Colour absorbed is my material and my palette in the same way a painter might squeeze out some red or blue paint.

LA

It is a bit of found language that resonated with what I was thinking about at the time. I recognised something of my own approach to making in the phrase that, when applied to my work, opened up a new way of understanding what I am trying to do. There is a level of ambiguity to the phrase that is important—I never want the words I use to be labels, or directional. The text I took the title from was talking about rain, but I want to point to other things that can soak you with feeling—like colour, pattern, and texture.

LA

I was researching mordants for a project as I needed to fix the dyes I was playing with more permanently, and I wanted to better understand the science behind what makes dye "bite" the material. Along the way, I came across the work of India Flint, a textile artist from Australia who is known for her approaches to eco printing. Eco printing is a kind of contact print process, where steam is used to extract the pigments from plants and objects onto paper or fabric.

This research coincided with a small residency at an outdoor textile studio in Abuja. I went to Nigeria to learn, and without a language in common, knowledge was shared with me through demonstrations and repeated actions. One morning, one of the teachers was eager to show me something, and she rubbed leaves from an indigo bush on my hands. I didn't think much about it until I looked at my hand an hour or so later, and it had turned blue.

It was inspired, and it aligned with how I was thinking about colour and where it comes from, what its origins are, and the effects that colours may carry. Eco printing or eco-dyeing seemed like a good approach to demonstrate these ideas. I have often been drawn to processes where the material itself determines the outcome, so its unpredictability also appealed to me. Unlike most dyeing methods, eco-dyeing does not focus on strict replication of results, because there are many variables that can affect your outcomes. Different times of the year produce different pigment concentrations in plants, as do the conditions of the water you are using, the fabric you use, the mordants, et cetera.

JS
Thinking back to the fabrics you would buy in Amsterdam and now these eco-dyed fabrics, do you feel there is tension between the readymade aspect of the material and the more natural, hand-laboured process?

JS
This attentiveness with your materials and engaged actions makes me think of the practice of deep listening.

It was fascinating to me that you could also use different metals to push out the colours held within the plant material. For example, if you wrapped your plant and fabric bundle around a copper pipe, it would push out the greens, but if you placed several iron nails near your plant matter, it might give you black, all from the same plant. The alchemy of dyeing suddenly became much more interesting and understandable to me. I really used this process to school myself into dyeing fabric. The level of detail you can achieve is also incredible. Sometimes the prints look almost photographic, whereas other times you will just get a very soft diffusion of colour, allowing something quite abstract to butt up against something realistic. I think this goes back to the idea of fabric being able to hold so much information within itself, be it emotional or physical.

LA

For me it is about the conversations between materials and approaches, allowing the work to discuss and emphasise strategies of making and reception through specific choices. The push and pull between dualities such as synthetic versus natural, object versus subject, inside versus outside runs throughout my practice and prevents the meaning of an artwork [from] becoming prescriptive.

This way of working allows for a kind of language of comparison. It affords me space to articulate my interests in a way that doesn't pin down the work or explain it away; rather, it provides me with a framework to take risks within the practice.

It's not so easy to be able to say what something is doing while you are doing it, but as long as I am inside that tension you're speaking of, I know I am onto something.

LA

Yes, have you heard of Pauline Oliveros? She was a composer and musician, and coined the term *deep listening* as a way to describe a practice of radical attentiveness. I often listen to her music in the studio when I'm making, in particular her album *Accordion & Voice* (1982). It helps me to get somewhere else in myself, where I feel removed from language. These alternate modes of learning and experiencing have been crucial to me and my relationship to making.

I think the lockdown has affected a lot of our haptic experiences, and we started to notice things we might not normally pay attention to. It feels like there has been time to go more slowly and pay attention in new ways, particularly at the beginning. Not so much during the most recent lockdowns, but at the start, when all the cars stopped, the planes were grounded, and you could hear more outside. I mean in terms of

JS

I remember working together as invigilators at the Serpentine in the early 2000s when they had a Blinky Palermo show; we have previously spoken about how important this exhibition was for the both of us. It was the first time I had ever come across his work. I remember being really underwhelmed when the exhibition opened, but one of the few privileges of invigilating the galleries is that you spend so much time with the work, hours and hours of just looking. This process of extended looking and feeling the work really opened it up to me.

JS

Do you ever give much thought to how a viewer will respond to your work? How important is pleasure for you, and to what extent do you consider this when you are thinking about audiences?

the sounds from wildlife returning but also that you could literally hear more, including oneself.

LA

I often think of that show and Palermo's *Stoffbild*, or "fabric paintings," in particular. I had just finished my undergraduate when I experienced the work, and yes, like you say, at first sight it was so underwhelming. It took a lot of time and looking—I just wasn't ready to see that work out of nowhere. It felt so out of step with both what I had been shown at art school and with what was being shown in galleries at that time. We were both students during *Sensation* at the Royal Academy of Arts (1997), and that kind of work was just *everywhere*.

I remember a similar response from us both when we saw work by Hayley Tompkins (whose practice I have come to admire) for the first time at *Beck's Futures* at the Institute of Contemporary Arts in 2004. You had to climb stairs to a meeting room where she had installed these tiny abstract watercolours. I was furious, I just couldn't see what the work was, but in hindsight I know that I was just seeing the work and not *looking* at it. My understanding now is that I just wasn't ready for work like that, I had no register for it. Looking back, I feel that there was this really big gap in my art education. We didn't look at artists like Blinky or Hayley, it was predominantly focused on object-based Conceptualism and how we arrived there.

LA

I don't think of an audience when I am making work but rather when I am making exhibitions. I can't give consideration to whether a viewer is experiencing pleasure from my work because pleasure is such a subjective and individually formed experience. I can think about the pleasure, joy, or drive I experience when resolving and making the work, and the importance of that, but that is mine. I would hope that if the work elicits a form of pleasure from a viewer, this sensation [can] be given the same reference as an intellectual or conceptual response. I try to give equal weight and understanding to these emotive and instinctual responses to the artwork. Emotions are a driving force in all our daily lives, and both pleasure and repulsion are a significant part of how we experience the world around us. A viewer may experience my practice and be repulsed yet still like

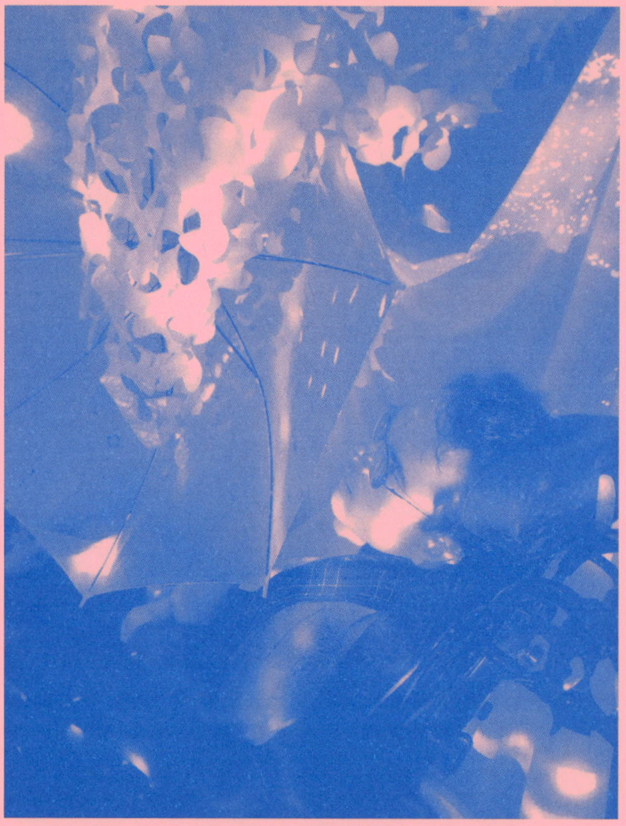

Sensory workshop for Artlink at Cherry Road Learning Centre, Midlothian, 2020

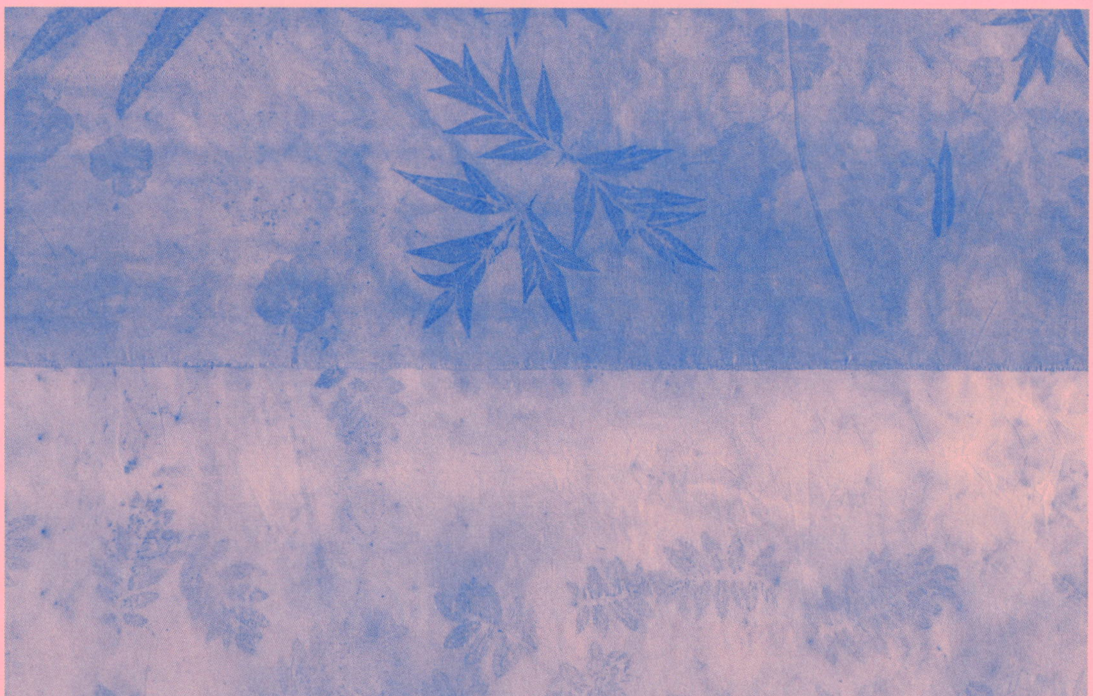

DISPLAY SCAPE #5: DROP. CLOTH (REMOVE SHOES AND COLLAPSE YOUR METONYMIC IMPULSE, REPLACE IT WITH A REFRESHED SENSE OF HOW WE RELATE TO THE THINGS AROUND US), 2016
plants, nails, fabric, copper, steel, hairpins, and Meabh's keys, dimensions variable

the work. That reaction wouldn't surprise me because these experiences are incredibly nuanced. I like the idea that someone would love something yet be repulsed by it—it's that push and pull, that tension we talked about earlier. The significance of pleasure in experience and art should not be moot.

1
Scottish Arts Council, Amsterdam live/work residency, 2009.
2
Artlink is an Edinburgh-based organisation that supports and promotes the involvement of disabled people in the arts. Workshops take place at the Cherry Road Resource Centre, Bonnyrigg, for artists with profound and multiple learning disabilities.
3
Eve Kosofsky Sedgwick, *Touching Feeling: Affect, Pedagogy, Performativity* (Durham, NC: Duke University Press, 2003).
4
Ludwig Wittgenstein, *Remarks on Colour* (Oxford: Blackwell, 1979).
5
Residency as part of the British Council UK/Nigeria 2015–16 season, in collaboration with the Nike Centre for Art and Culture, Abuja.

sumVIGOUR

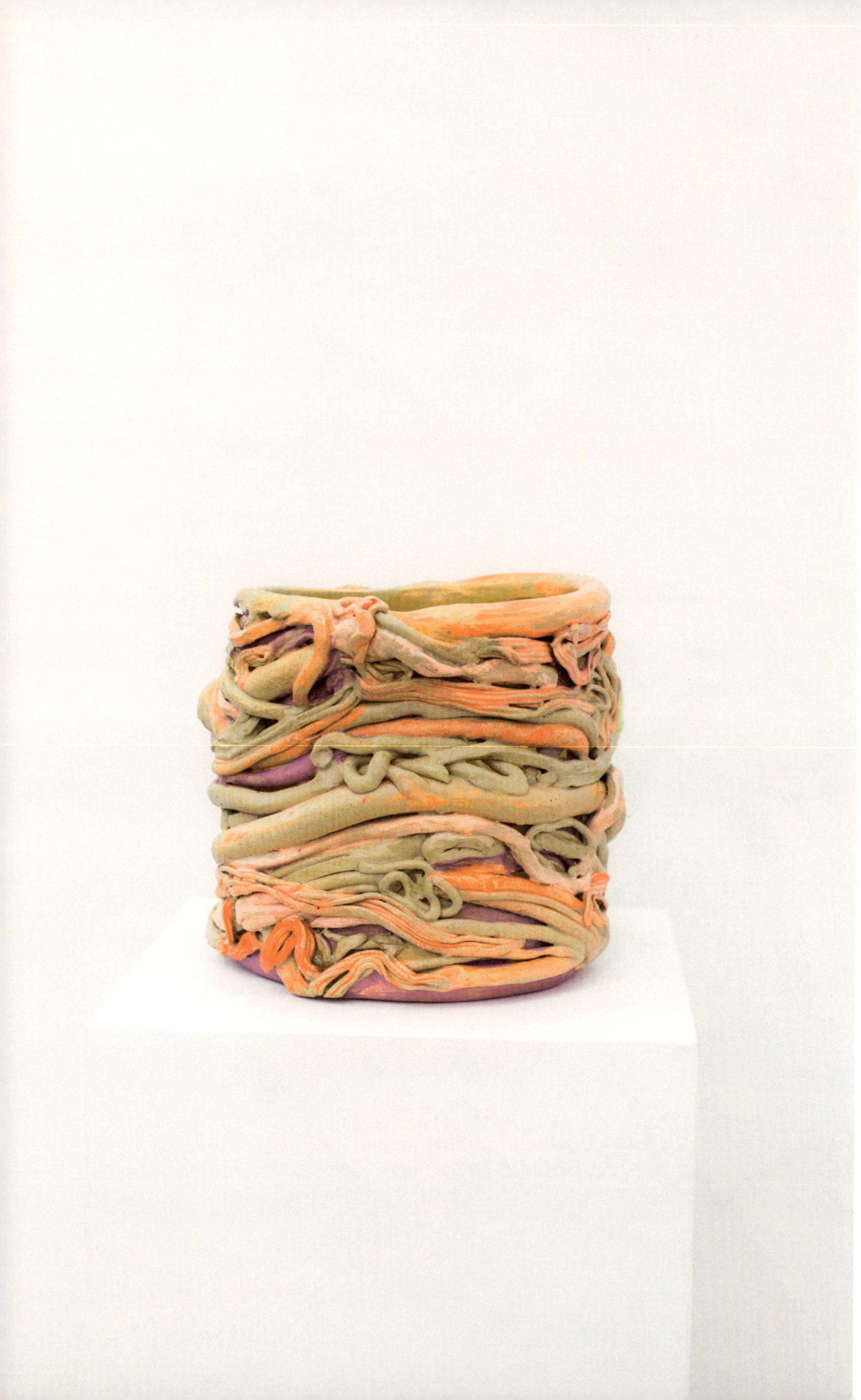

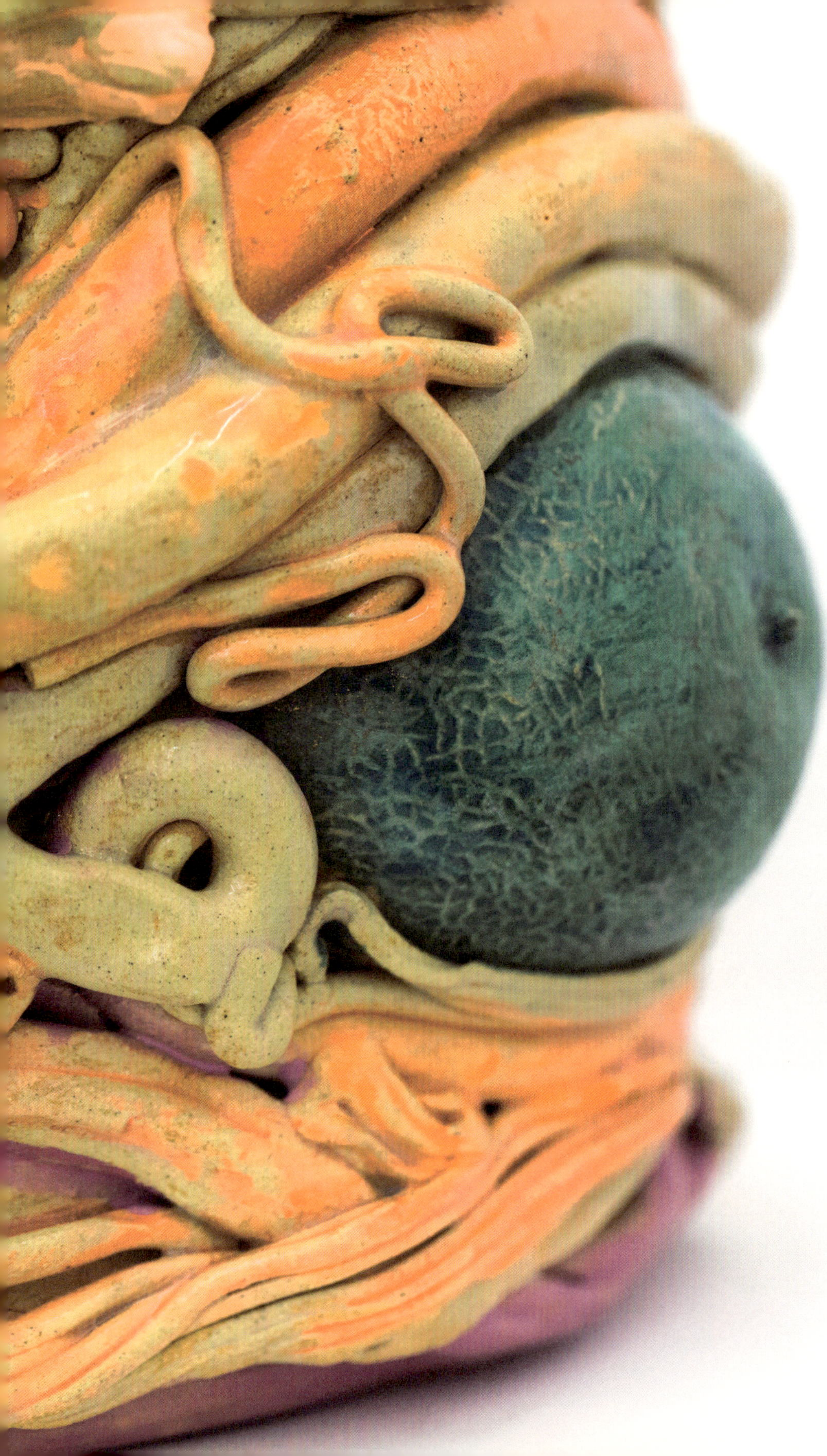

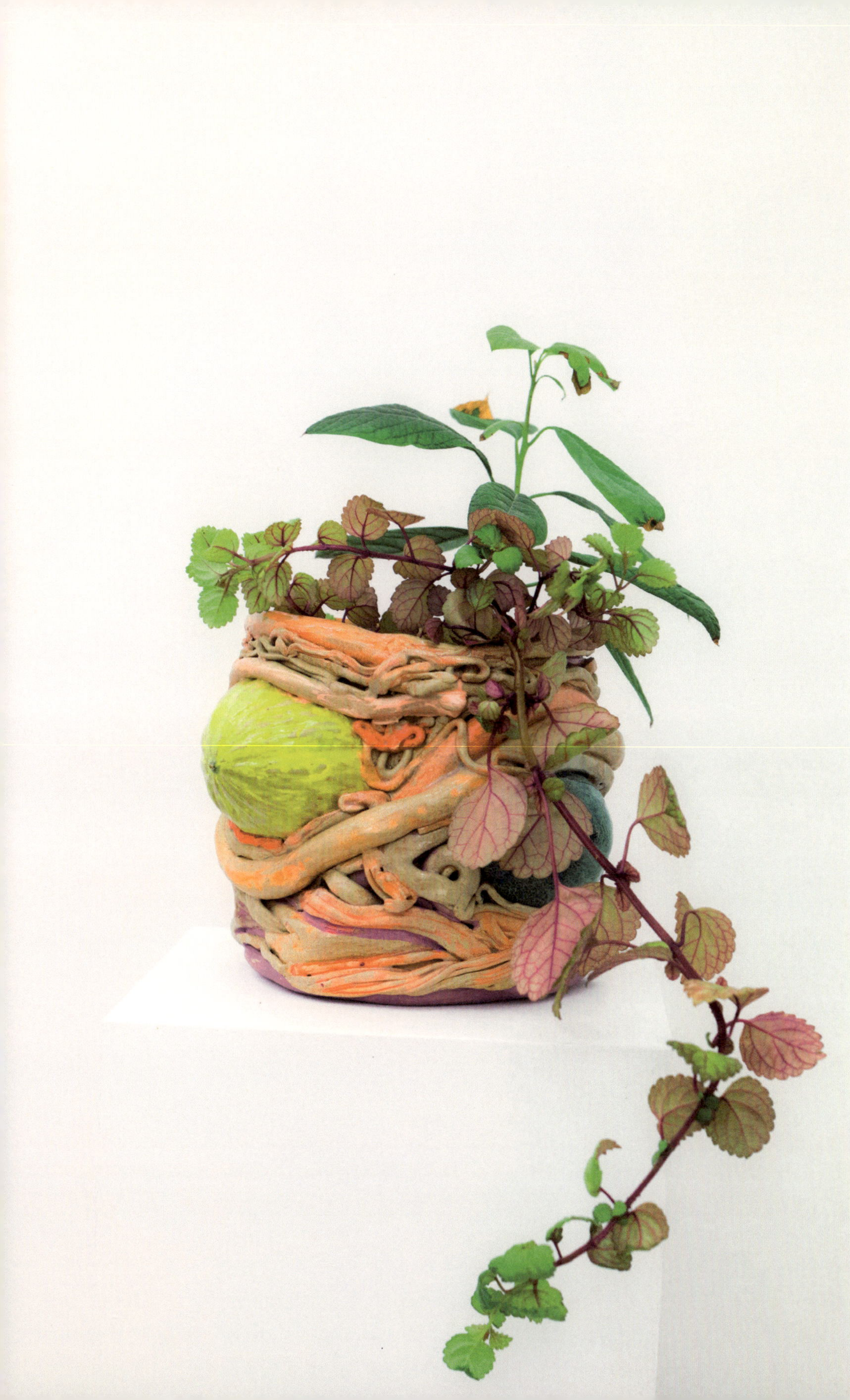

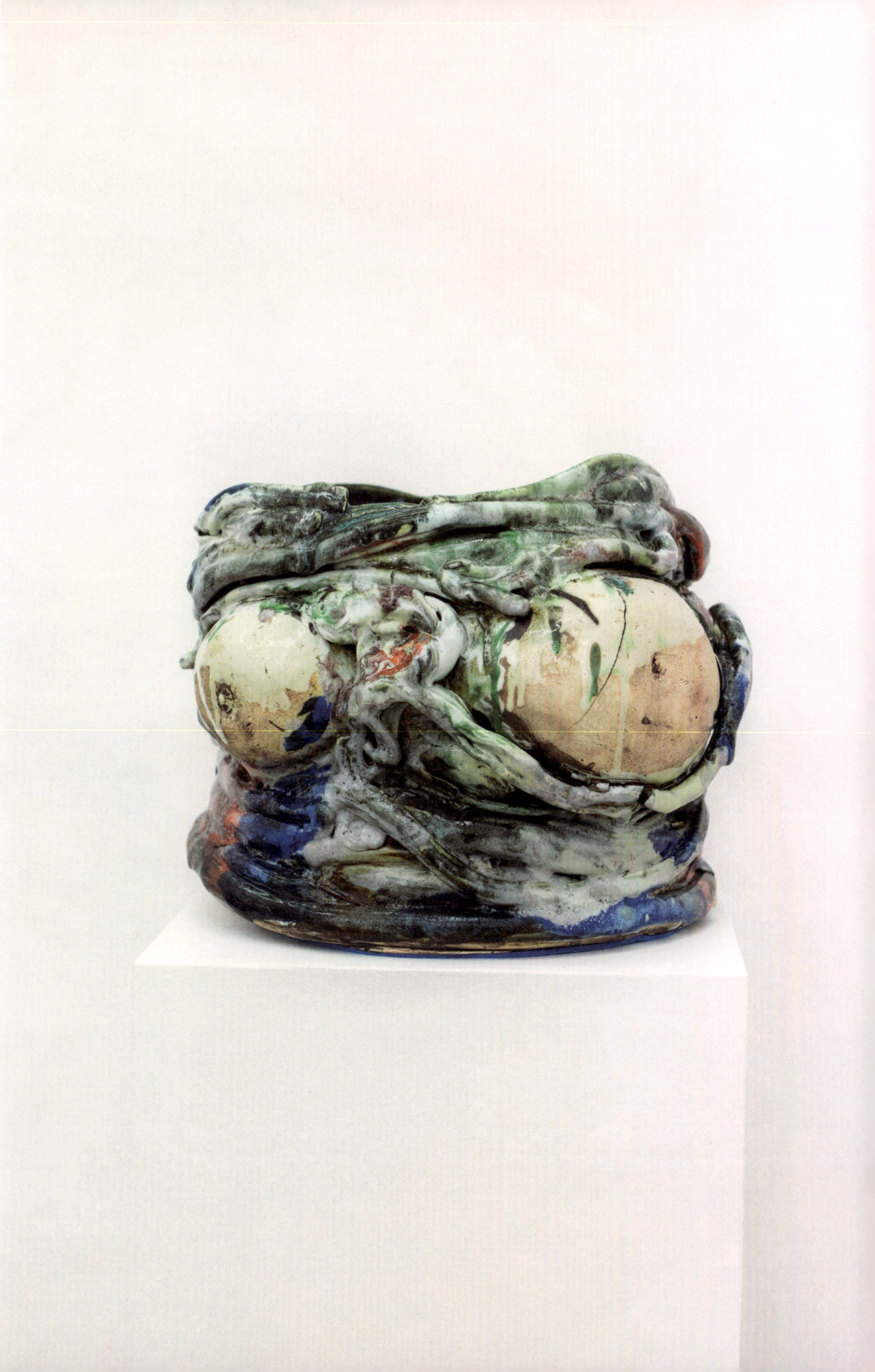

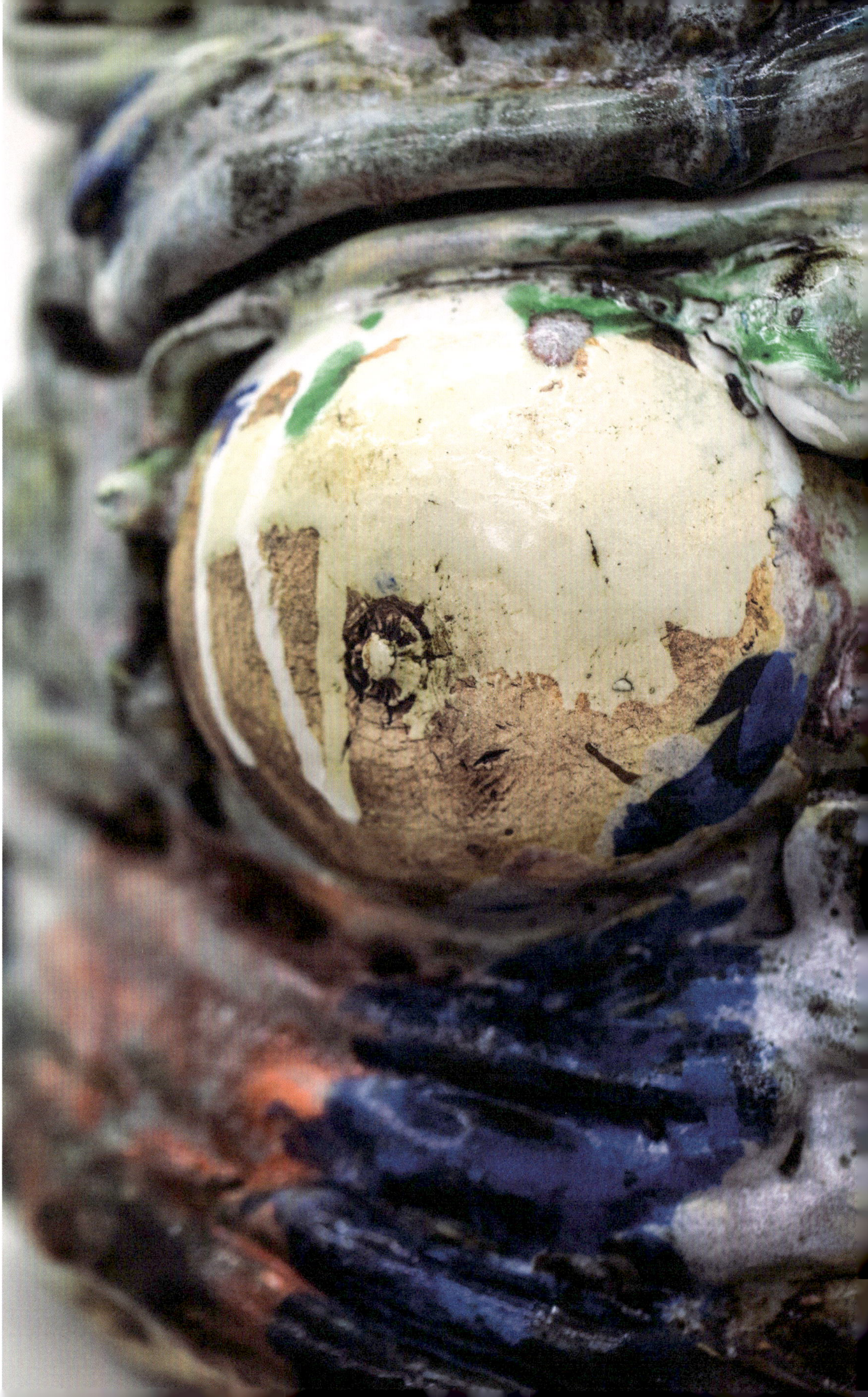

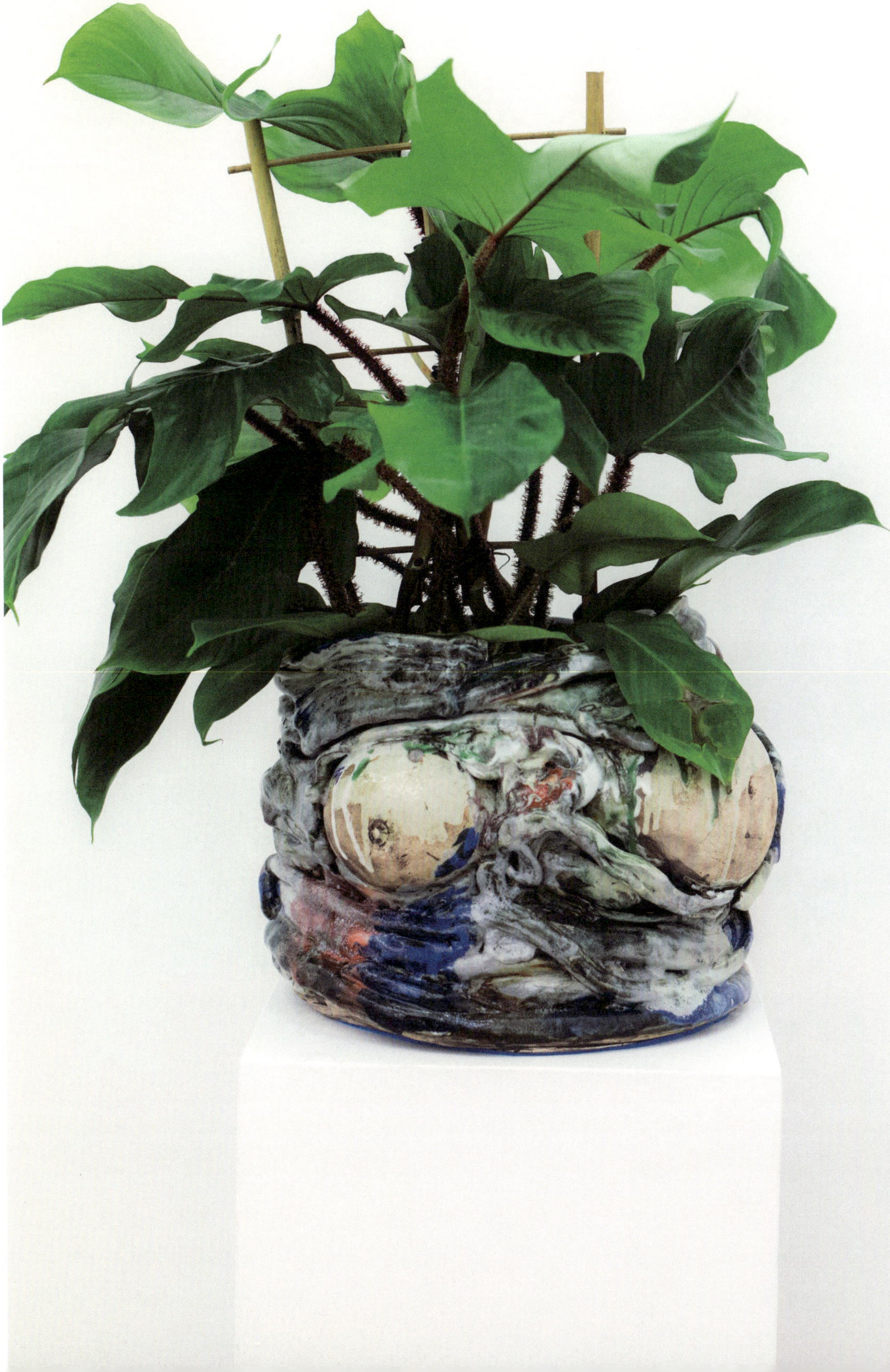

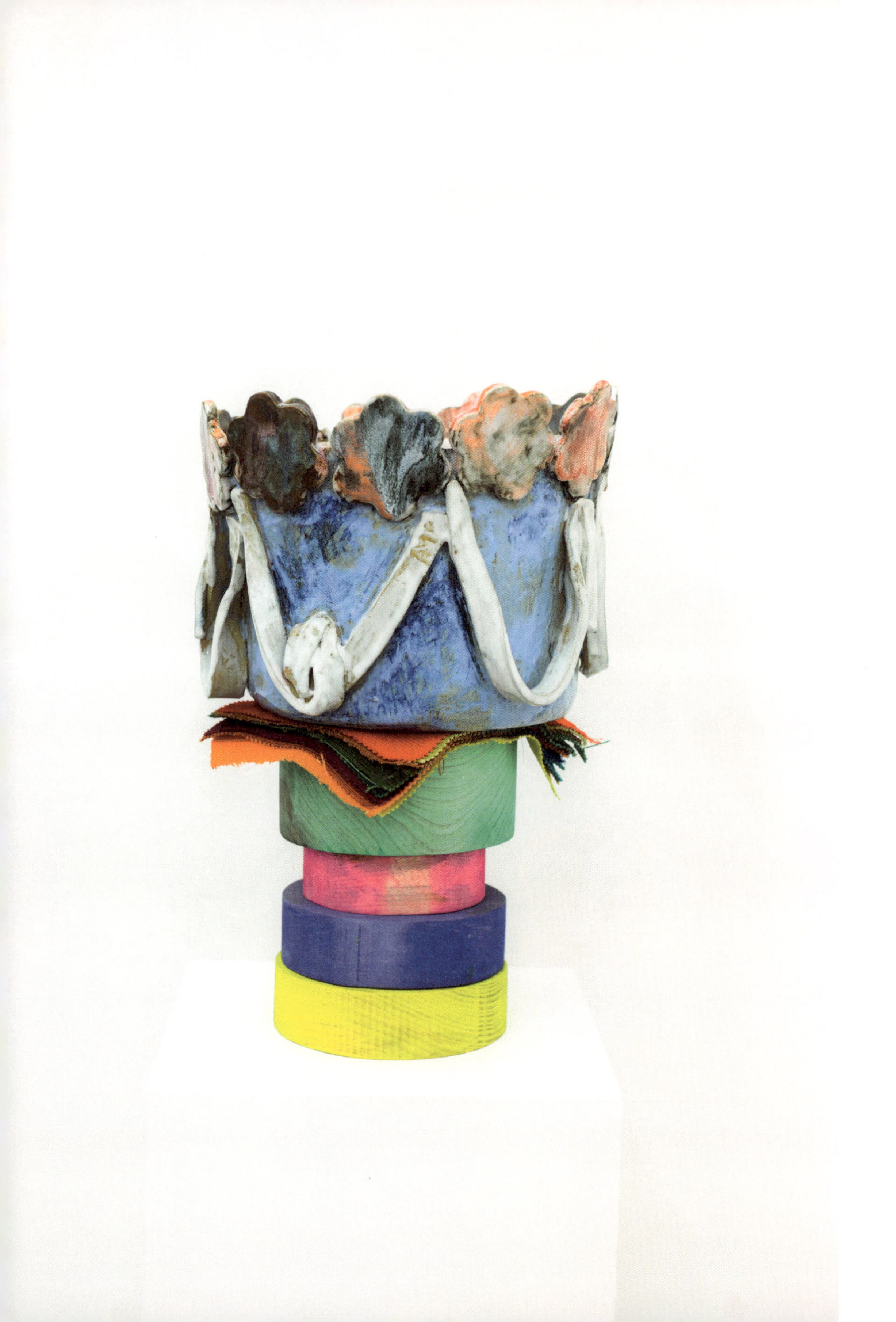

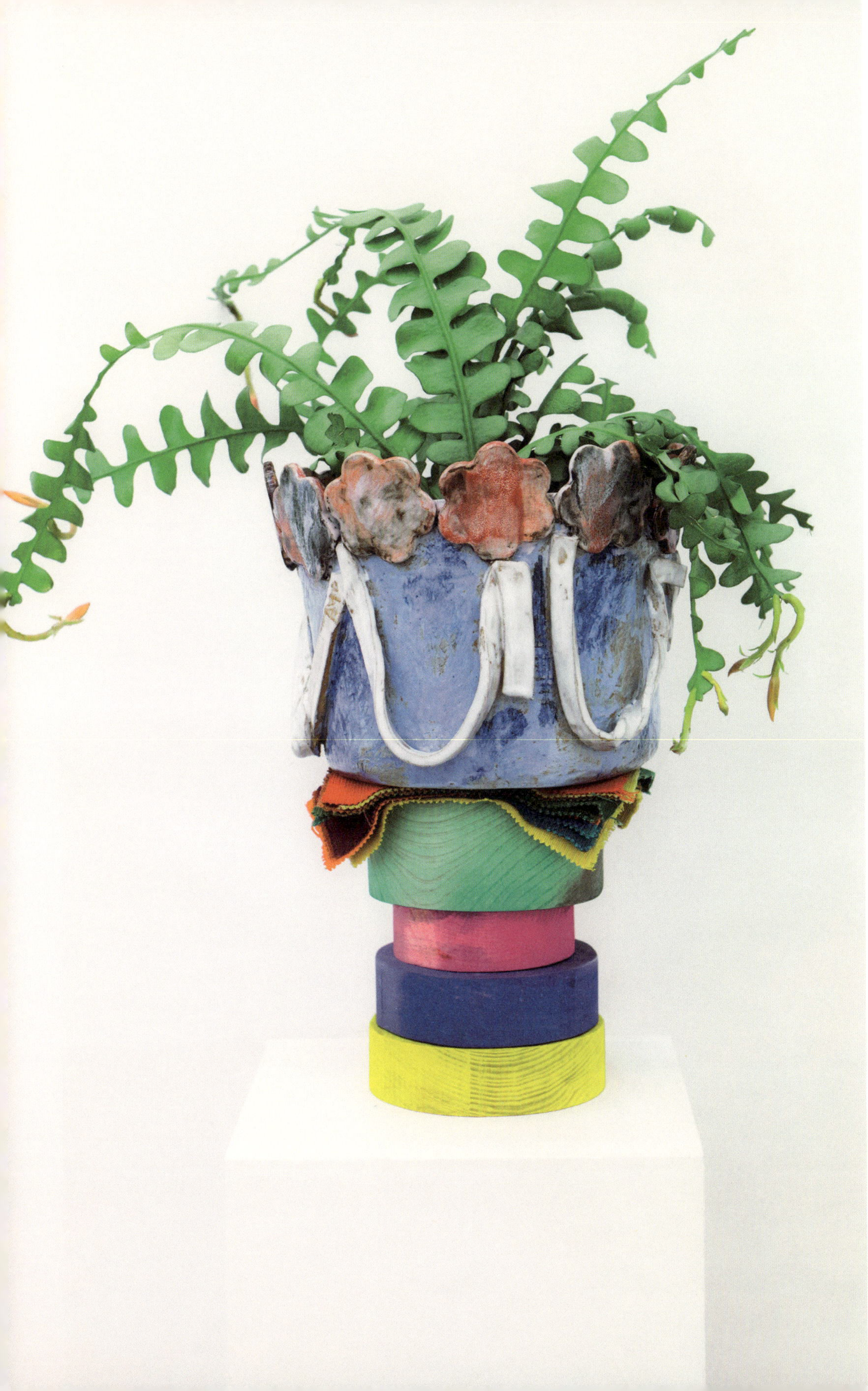

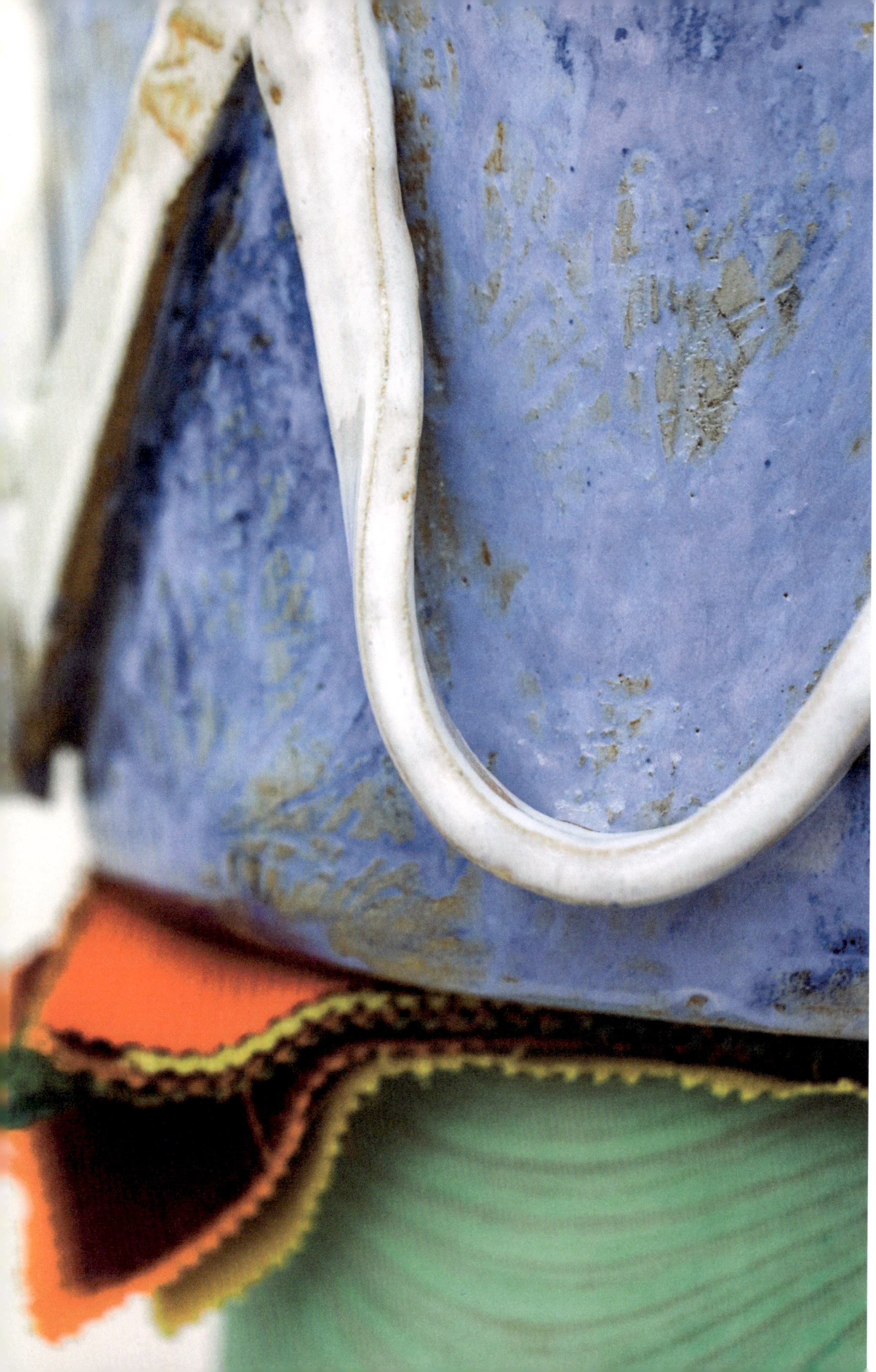

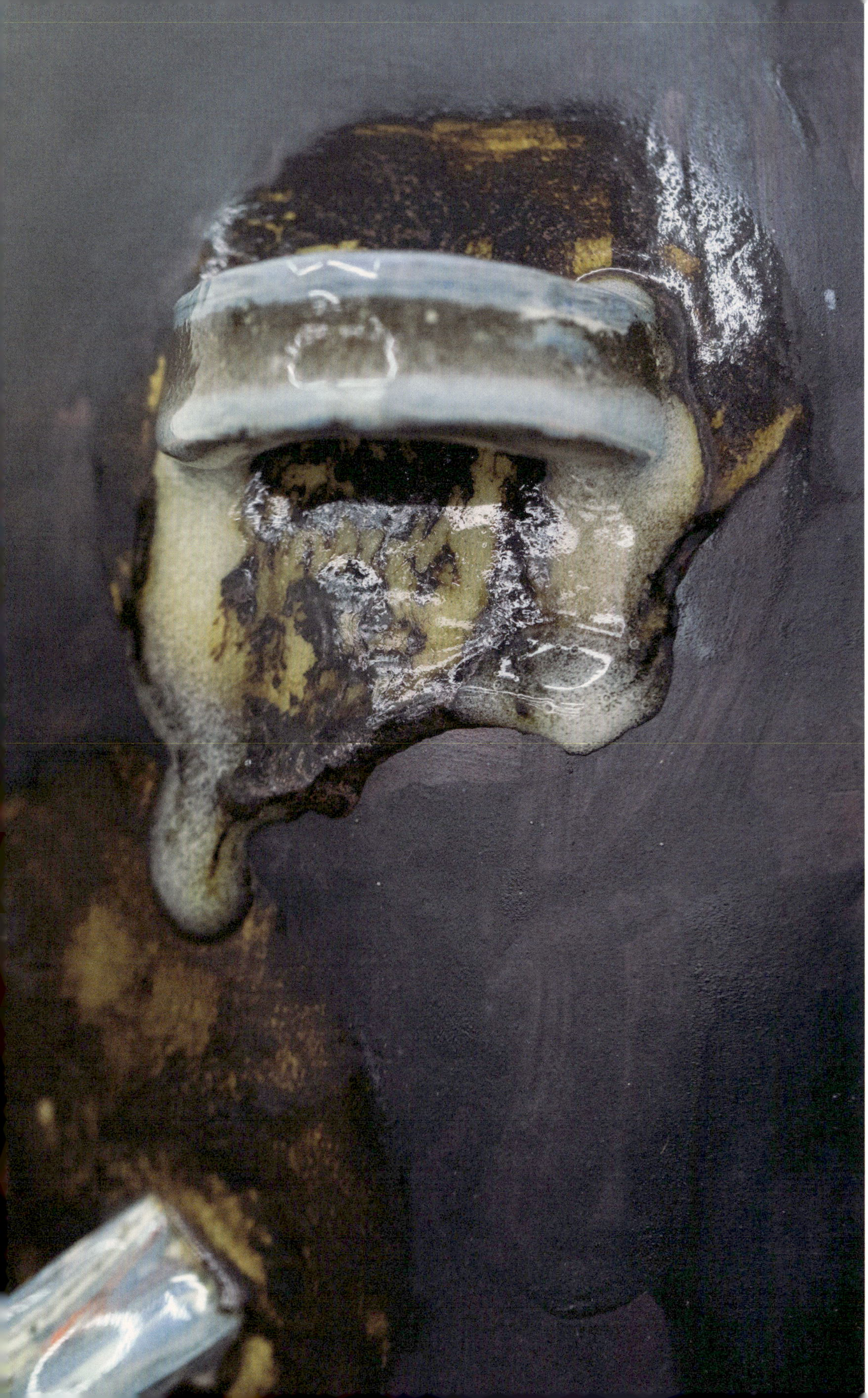

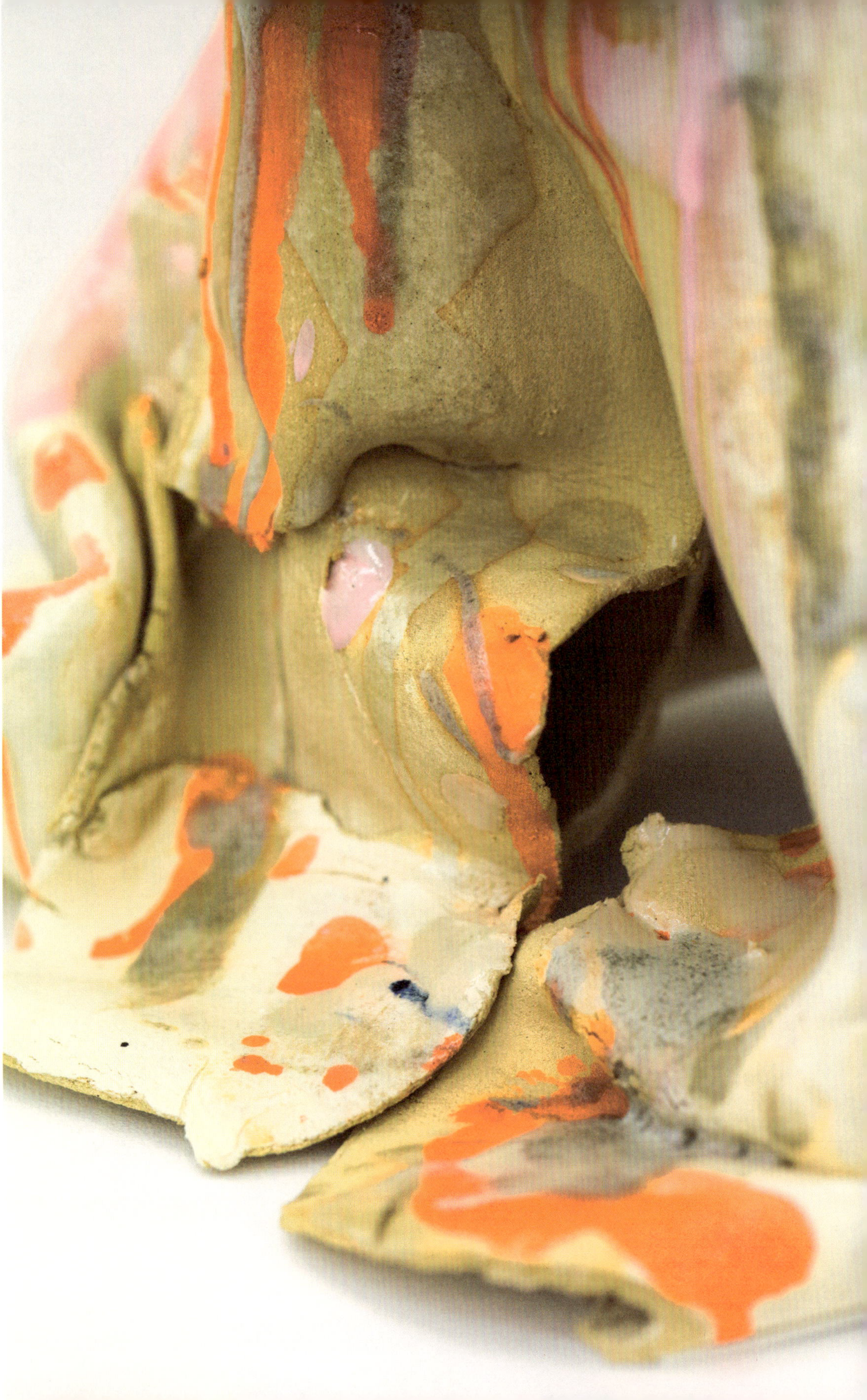

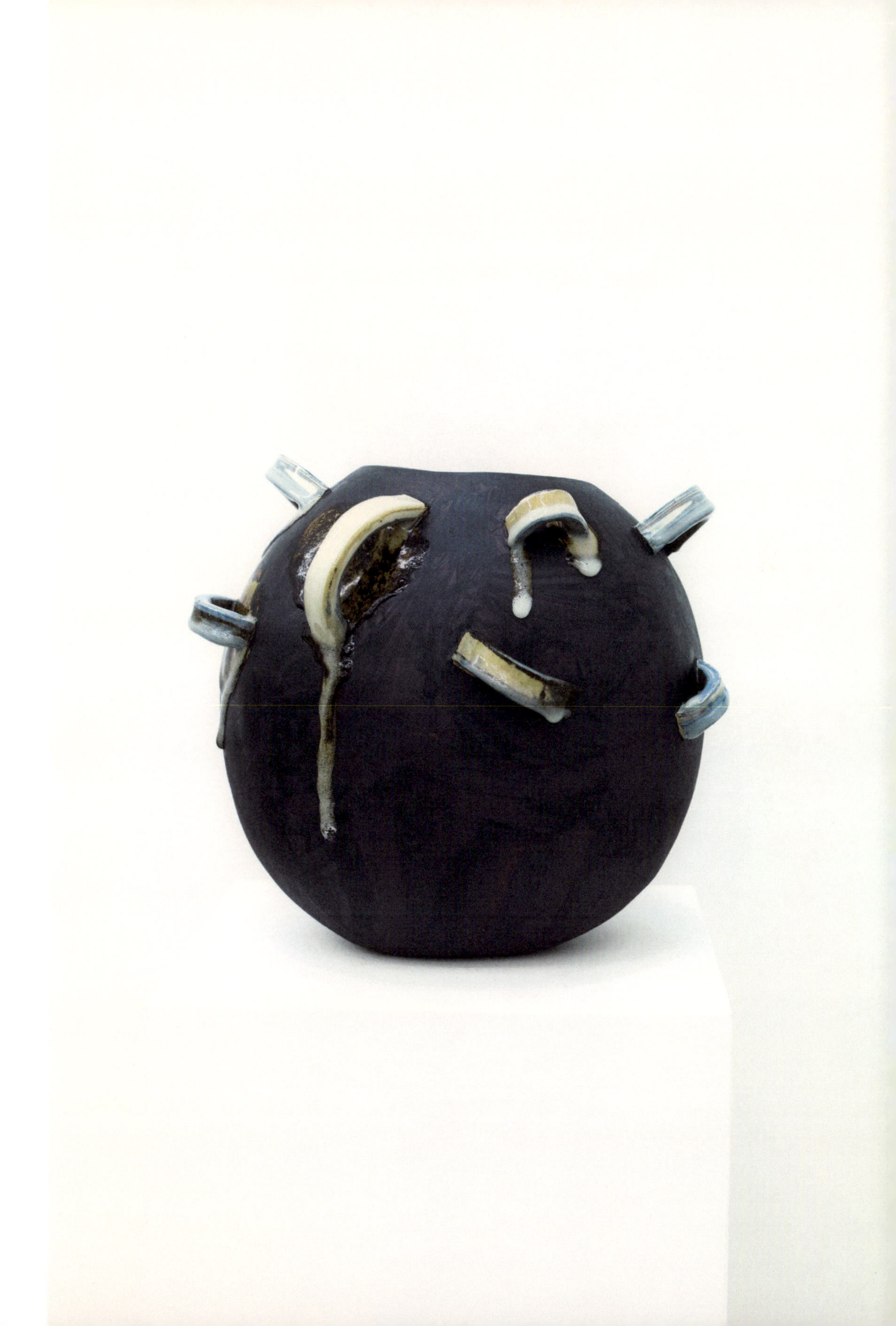

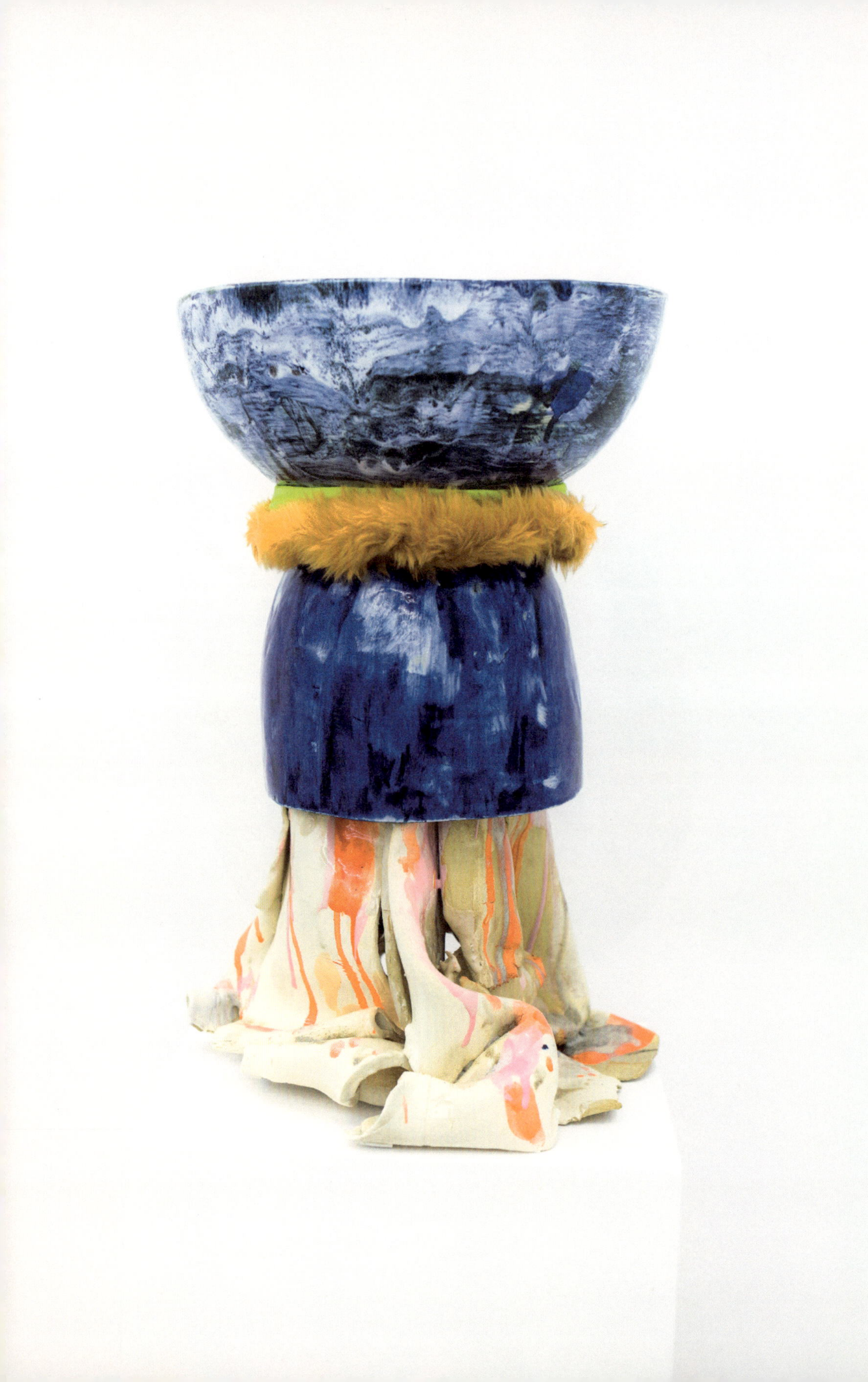

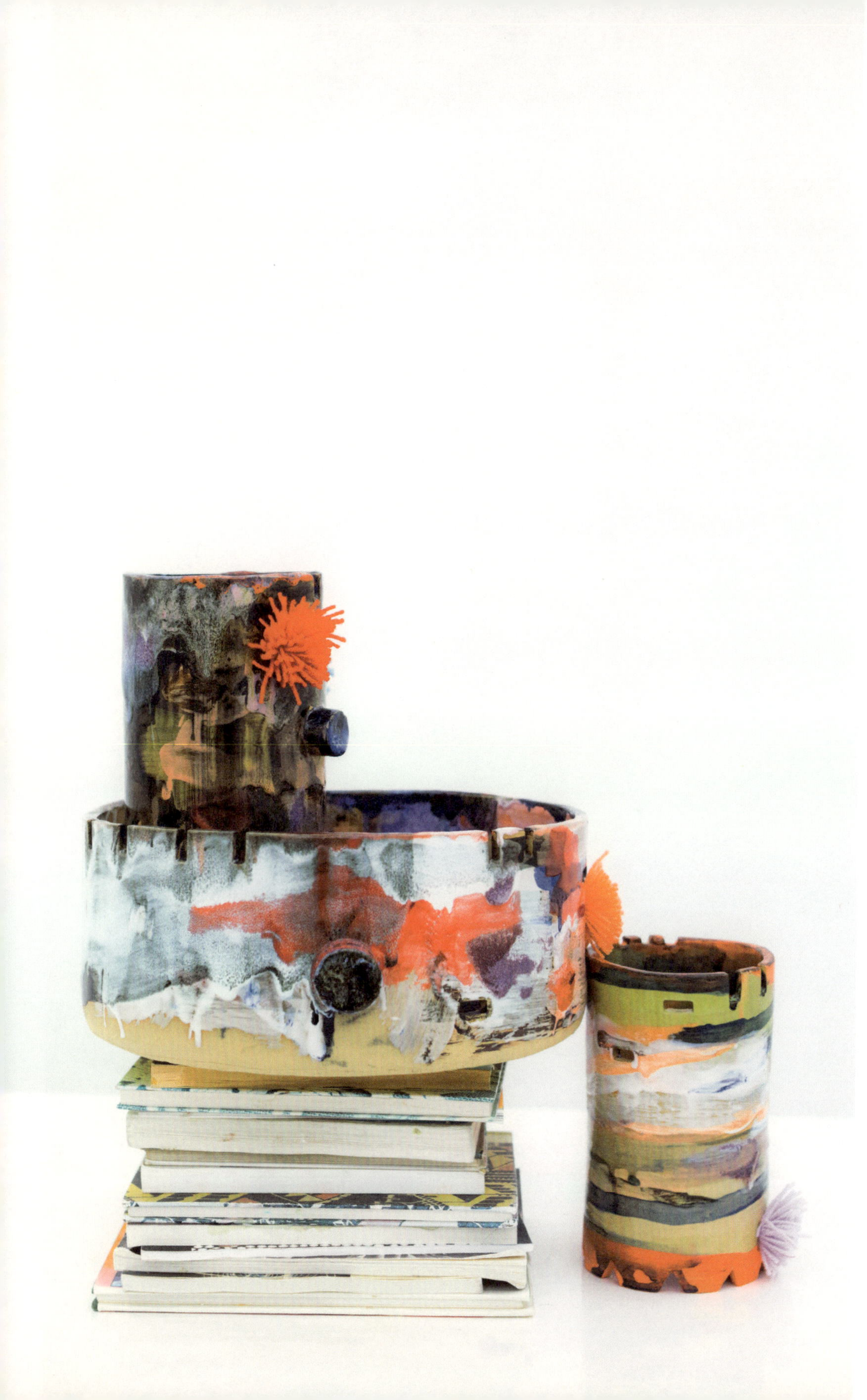

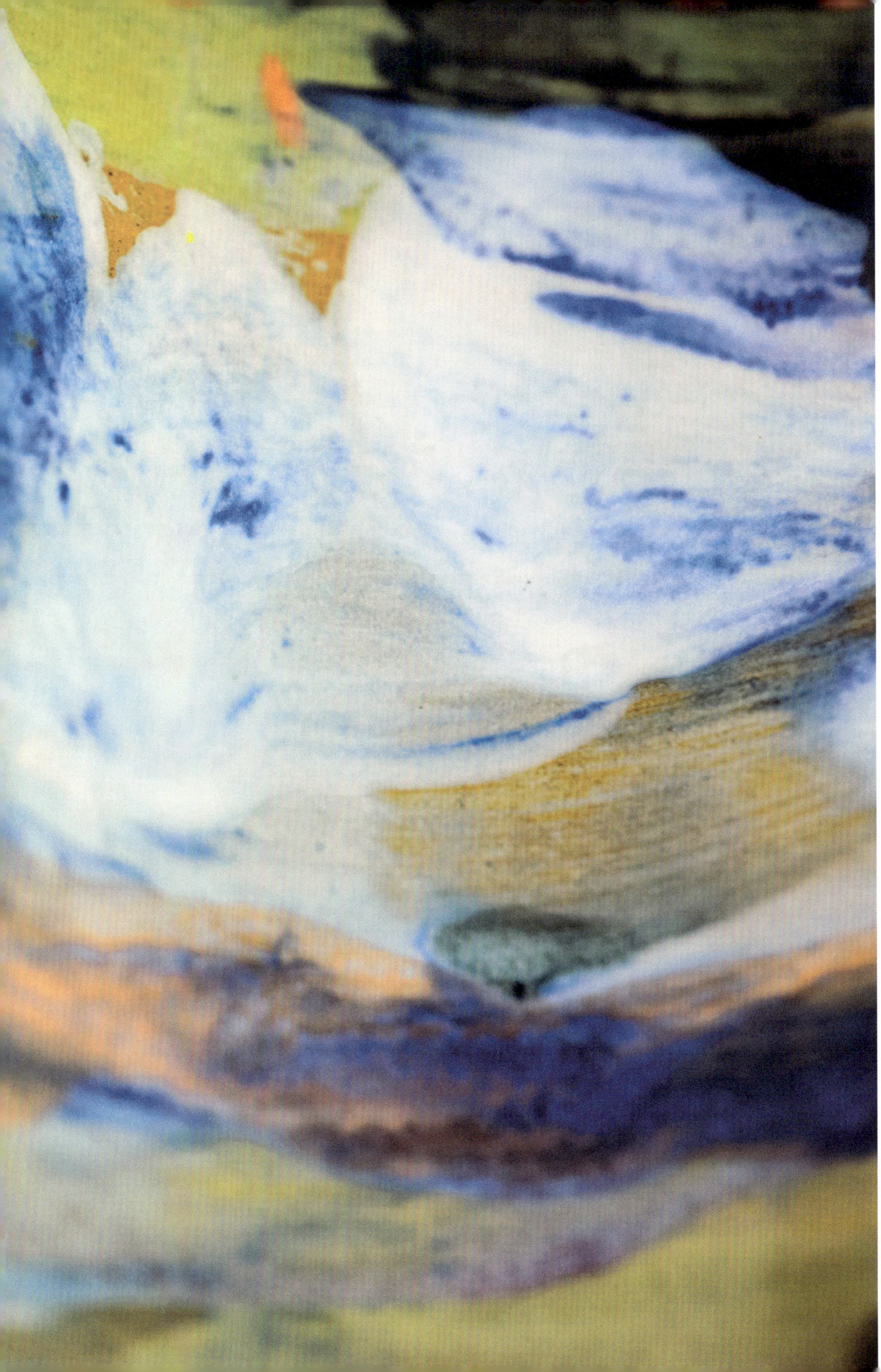

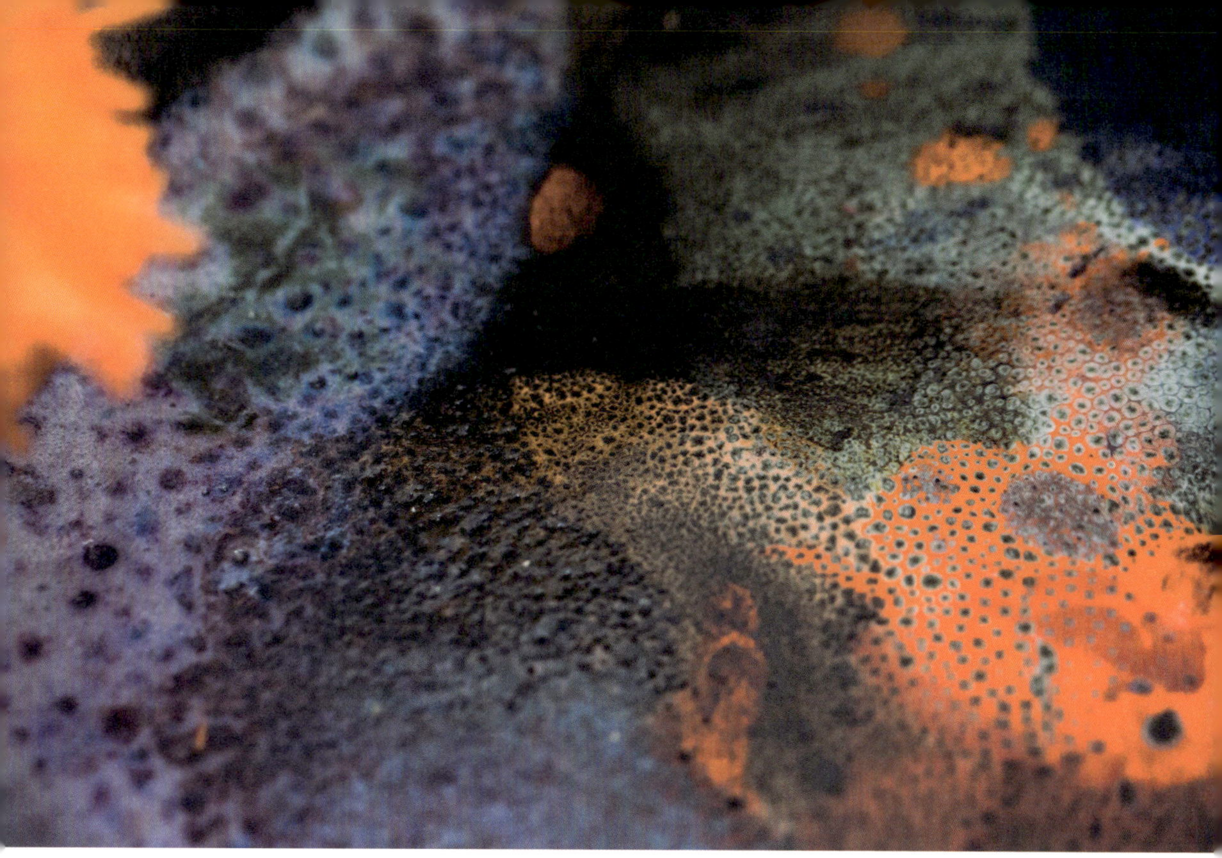

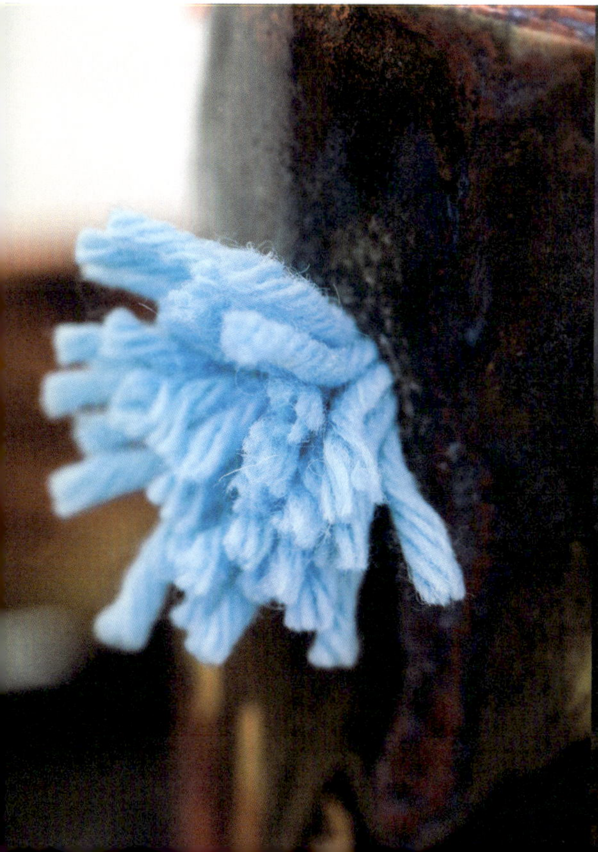

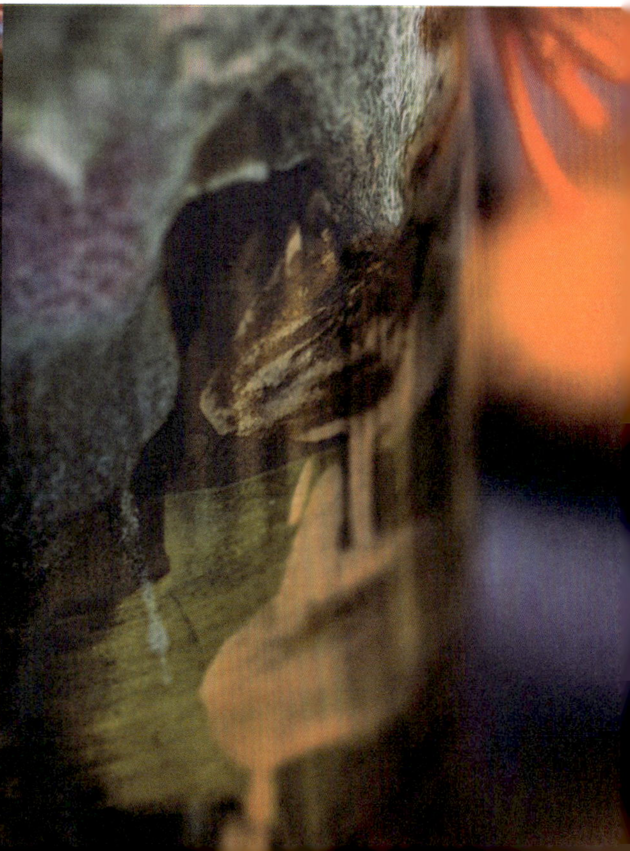

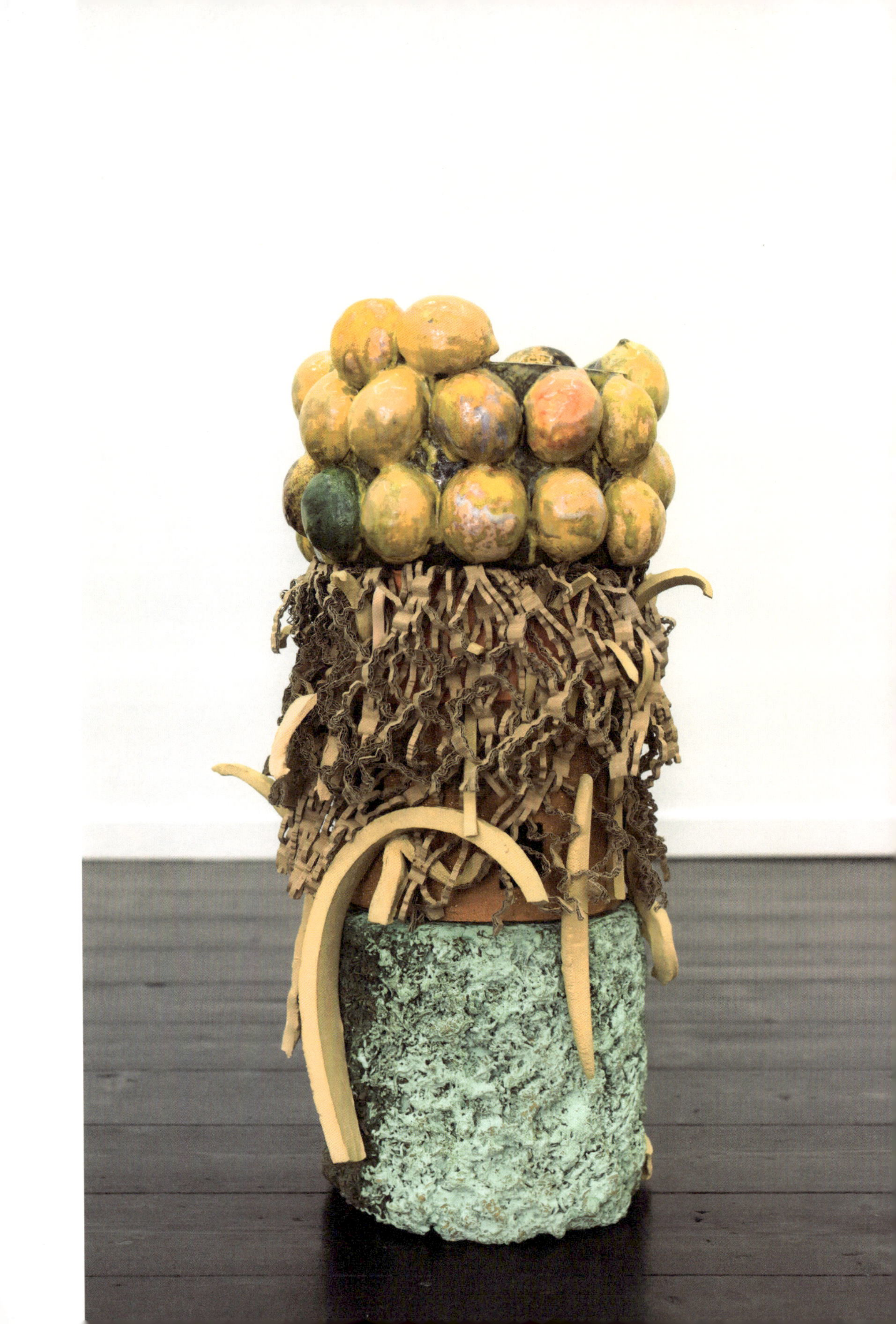

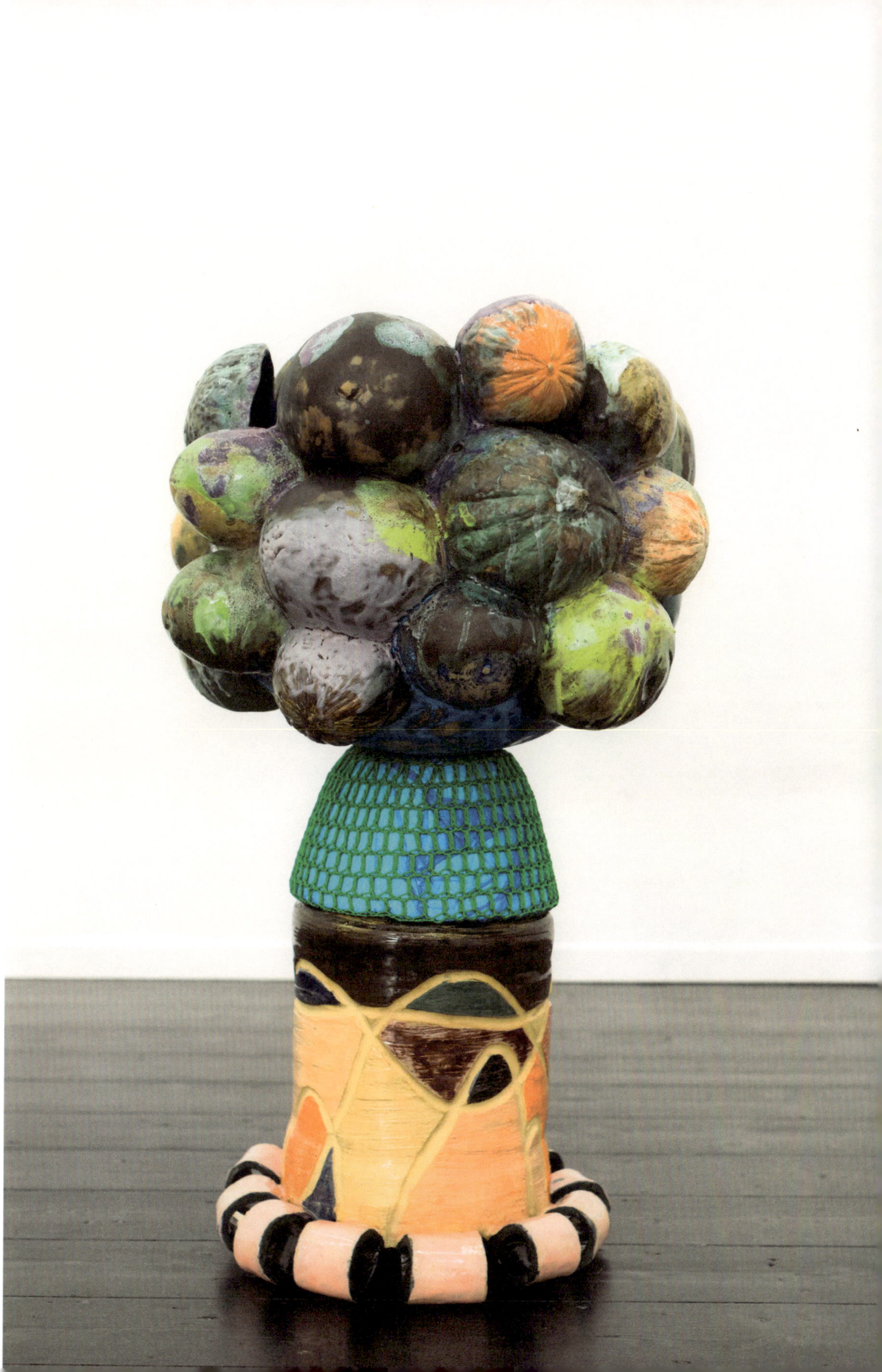

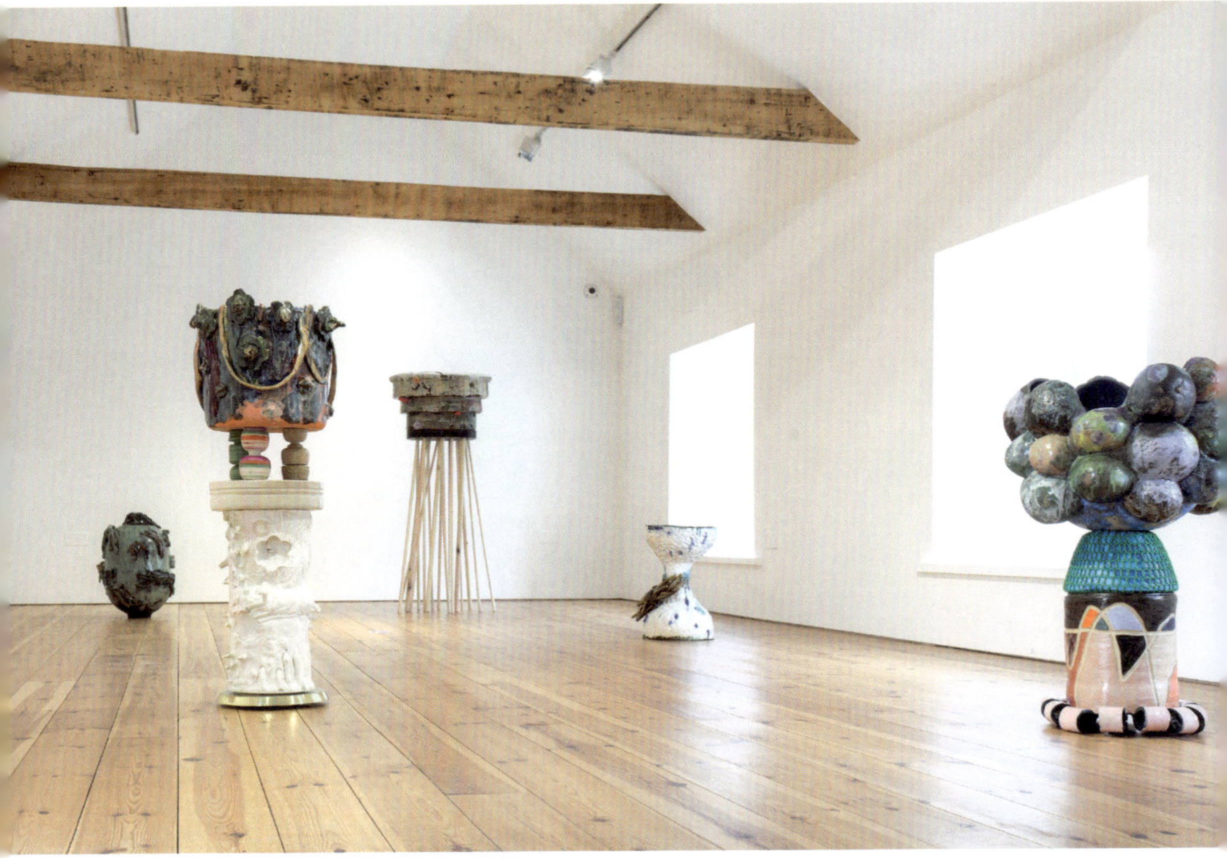

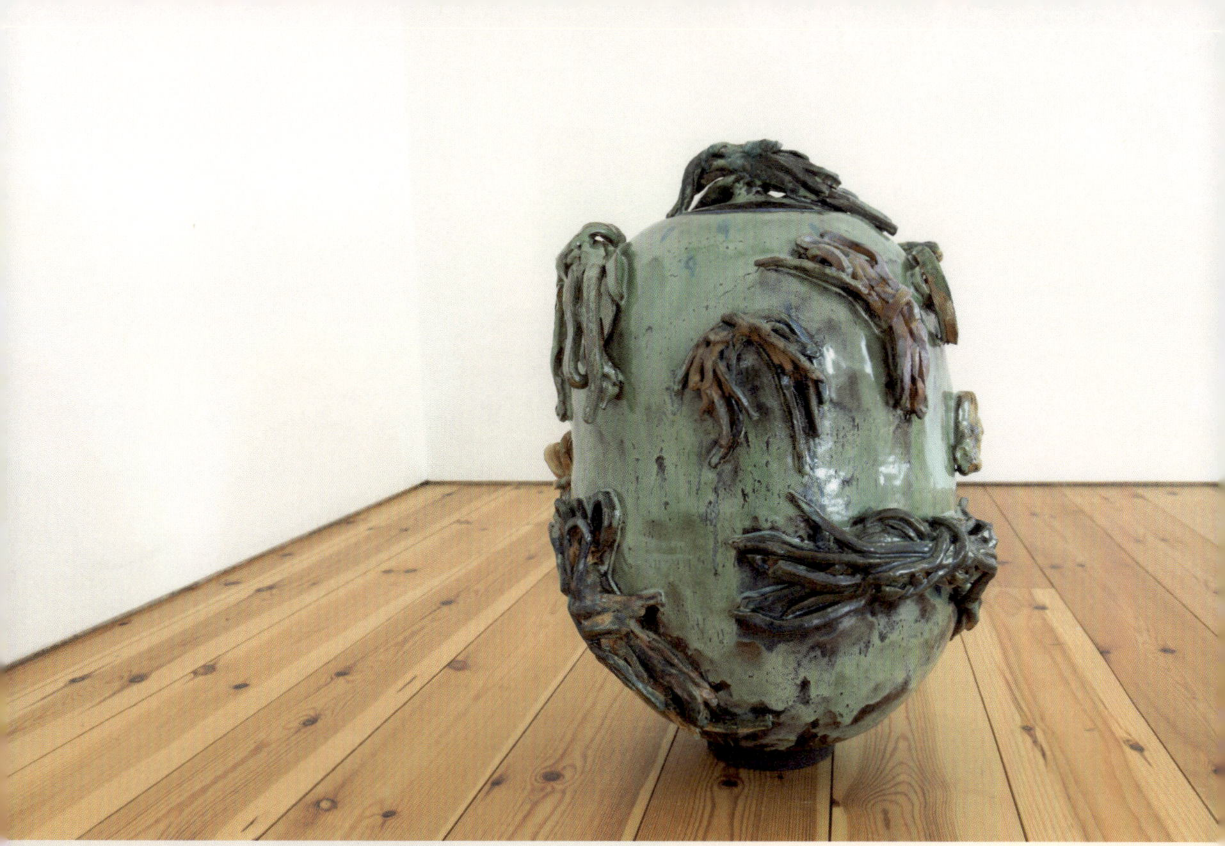

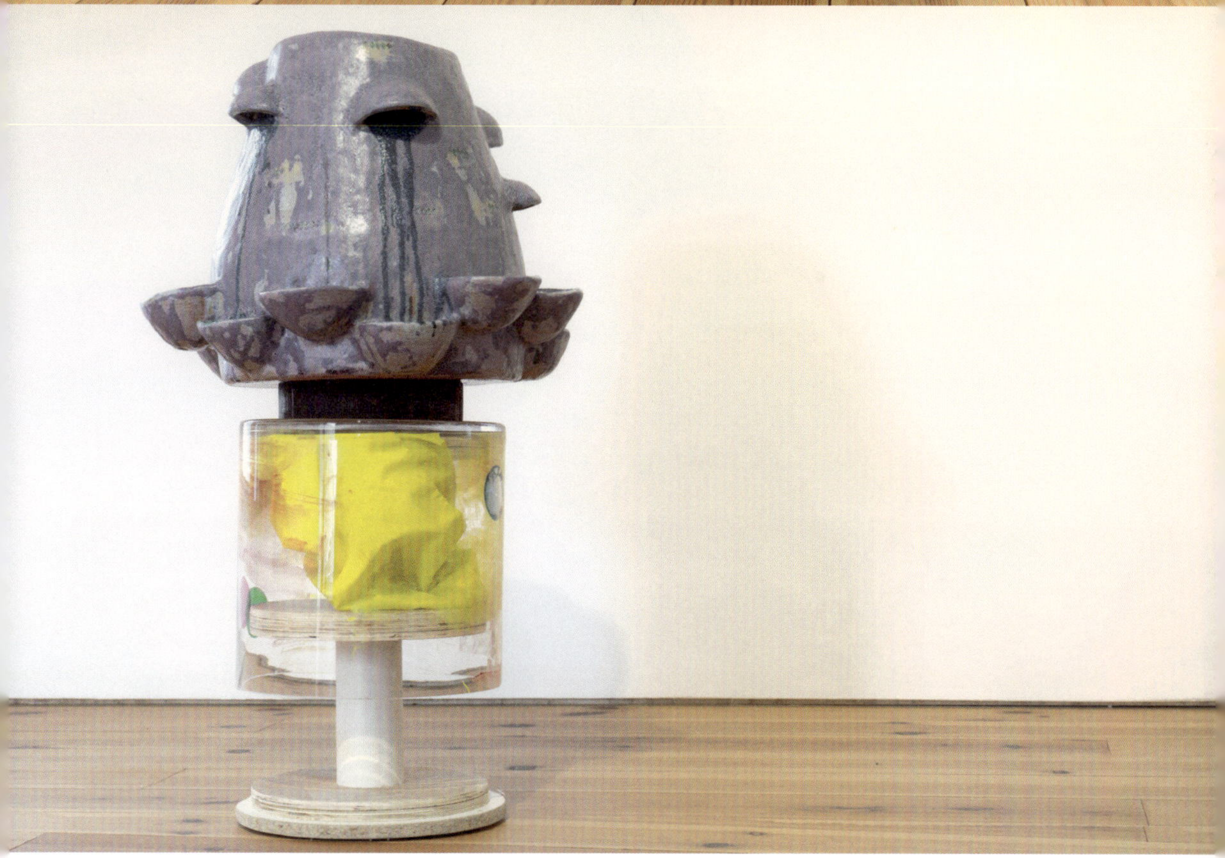

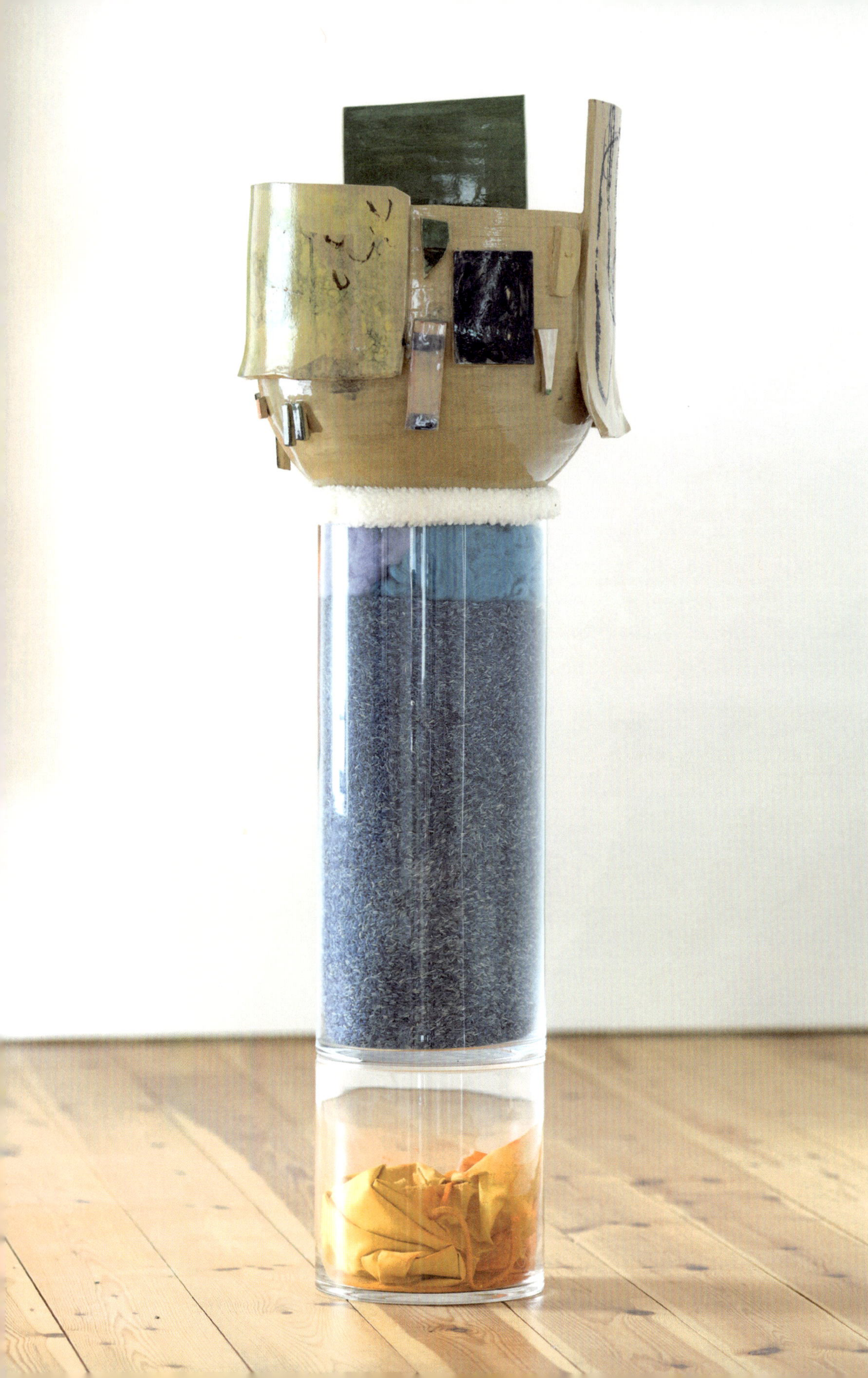

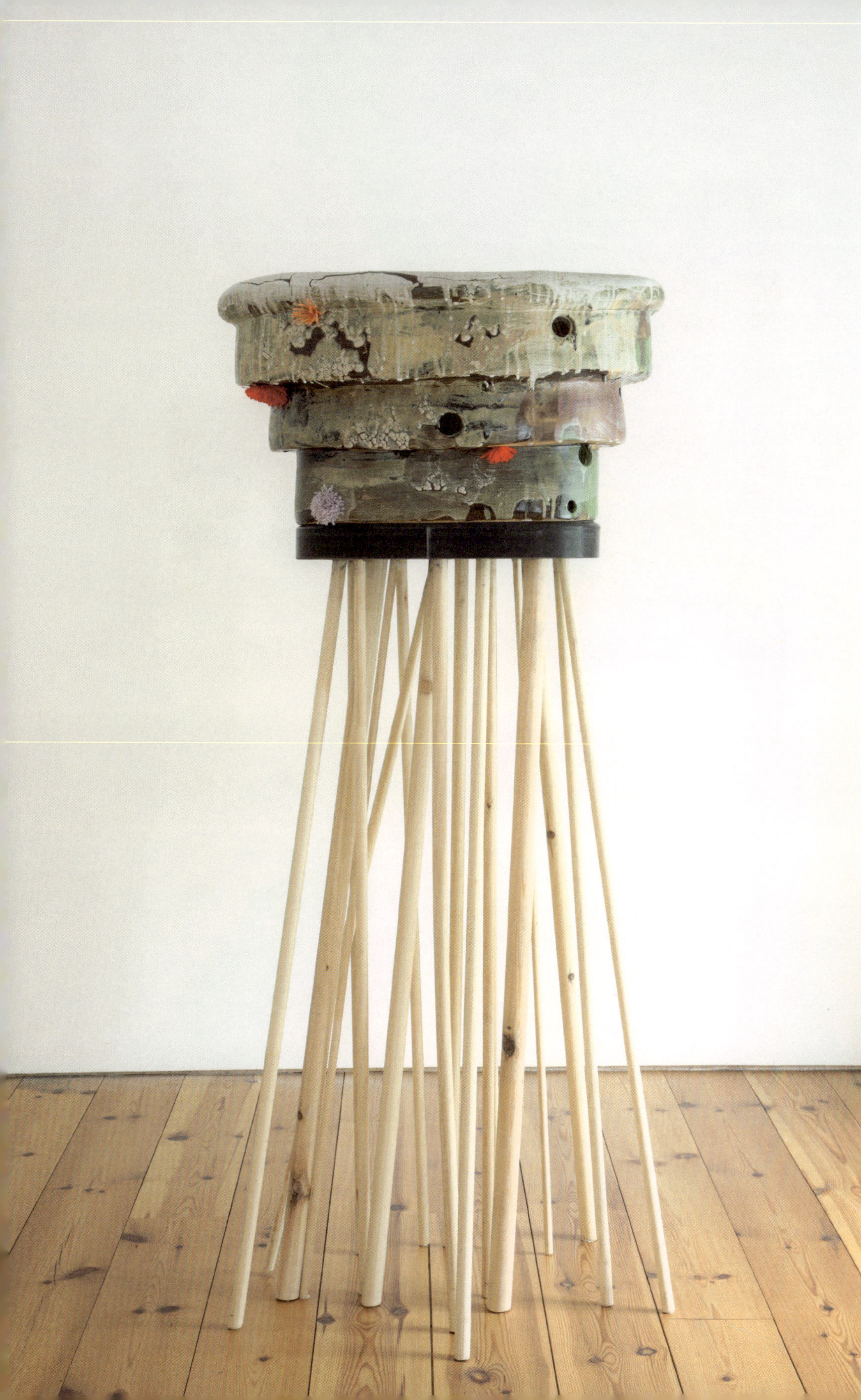

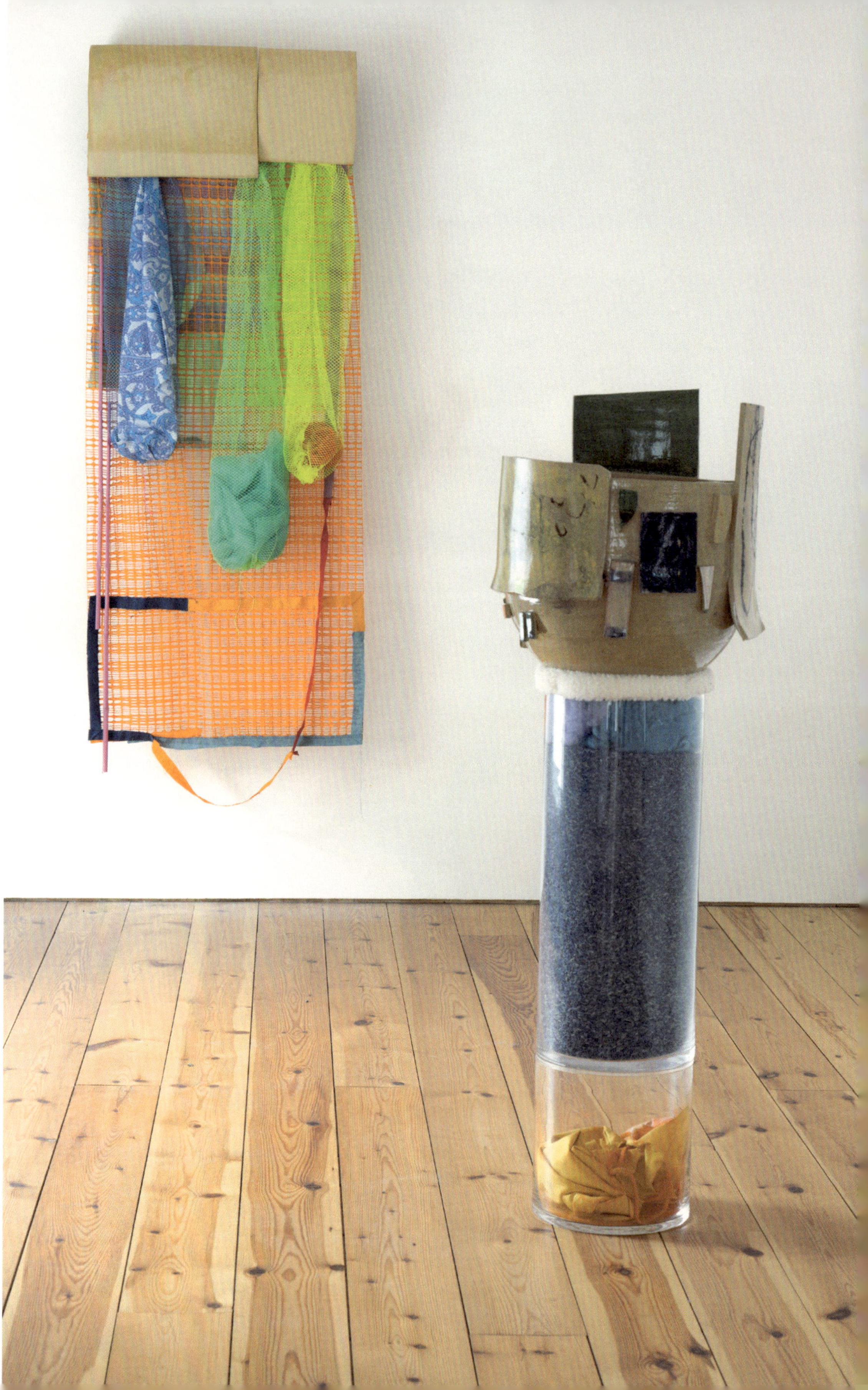

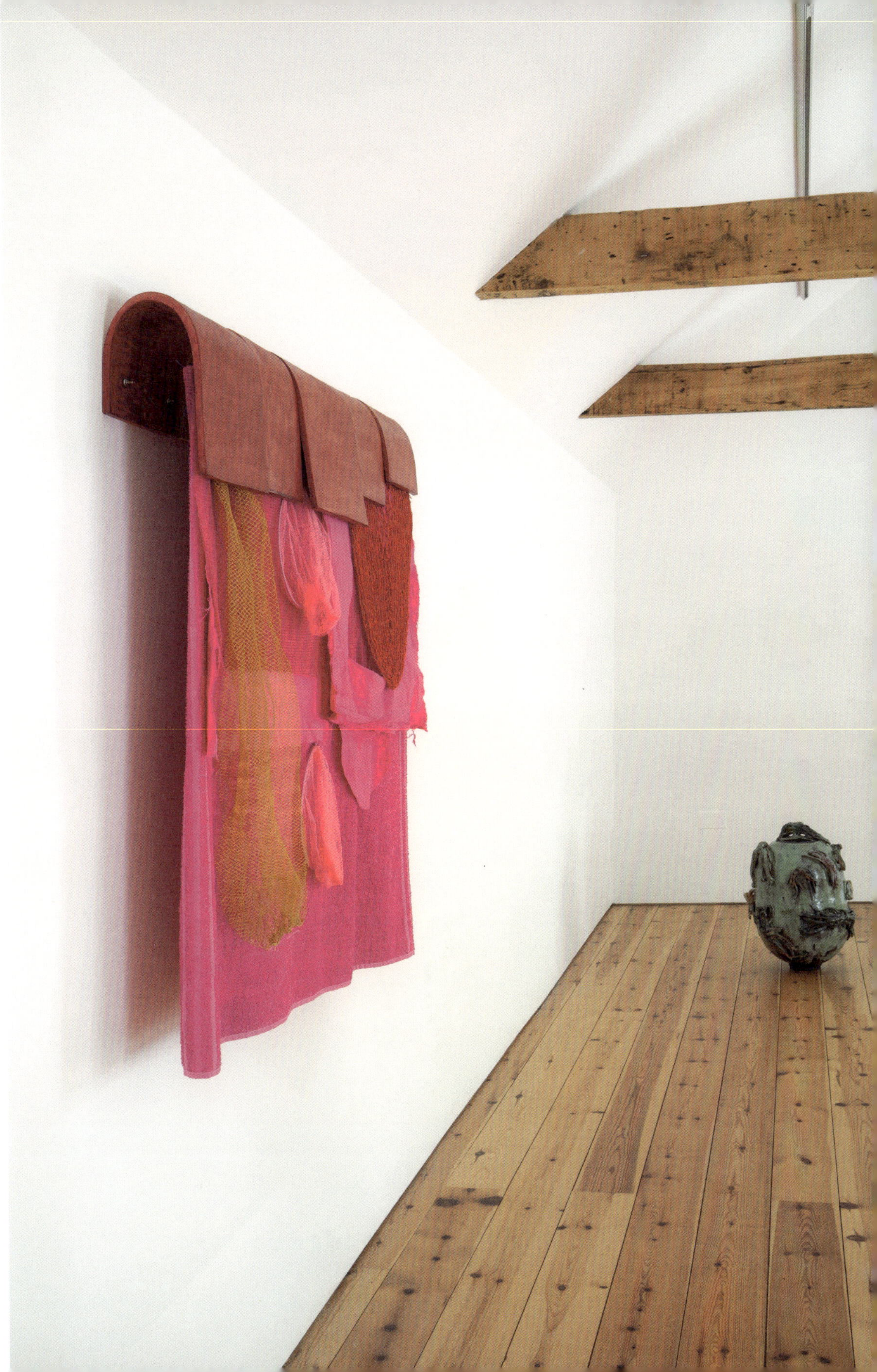

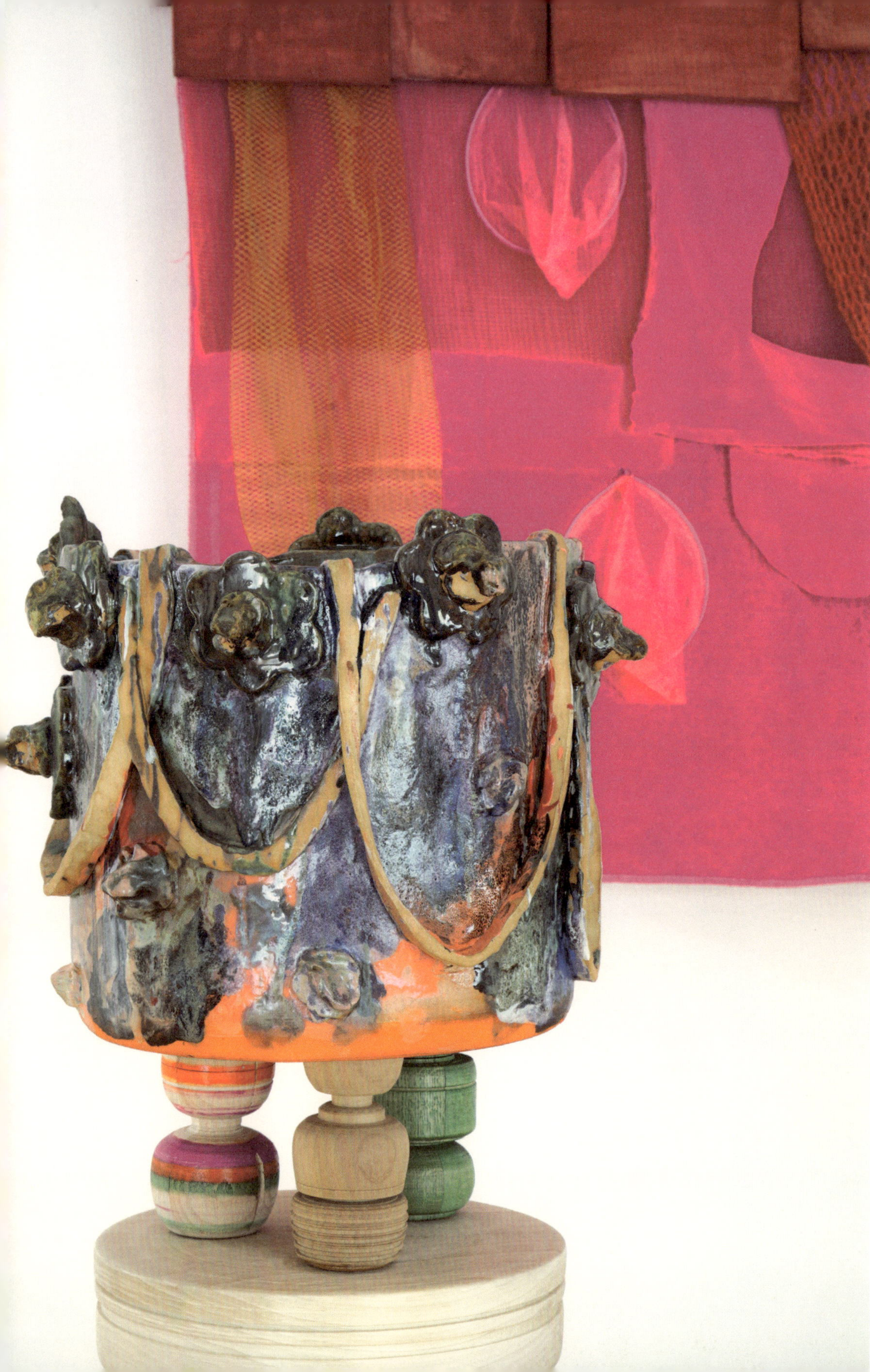

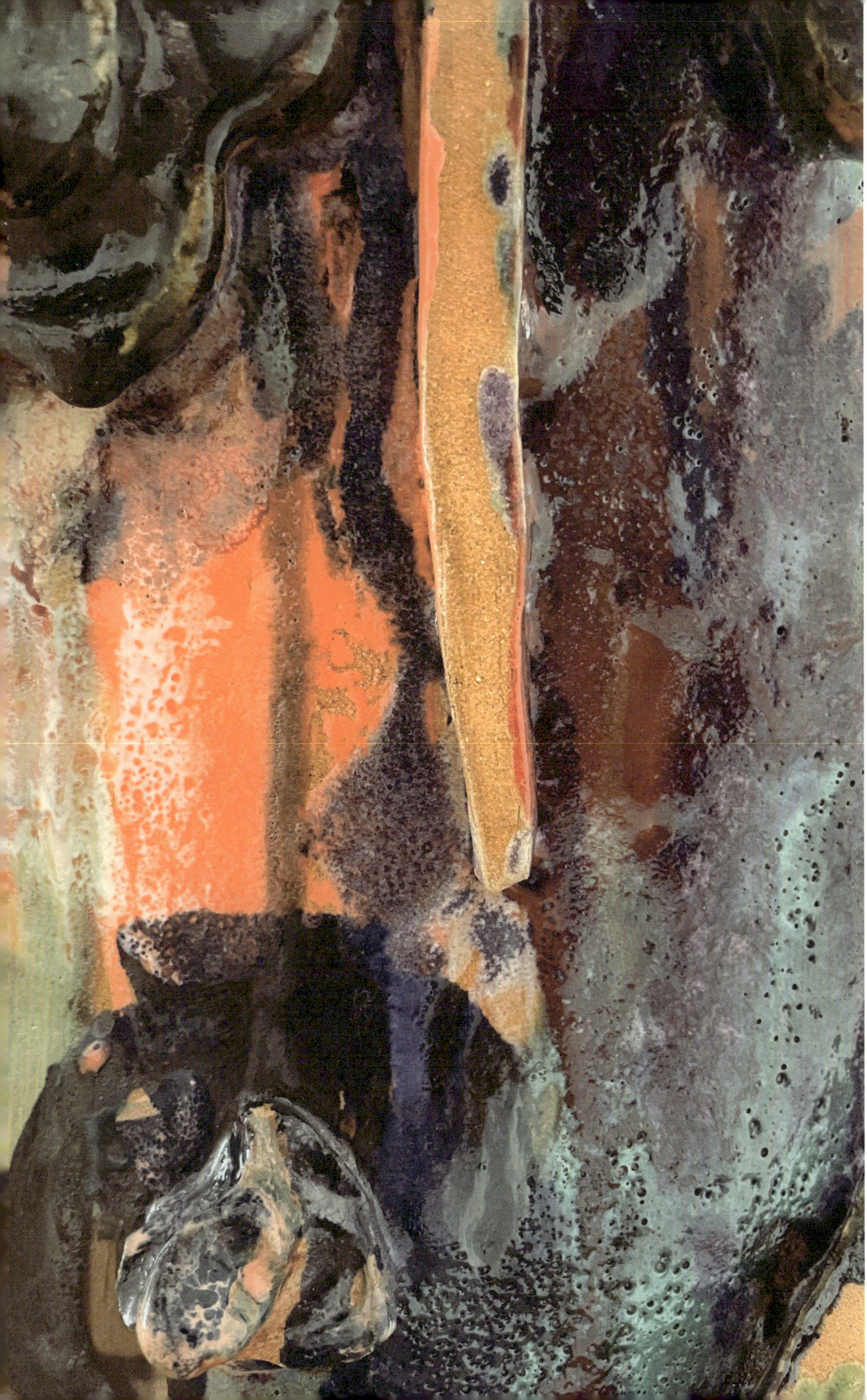

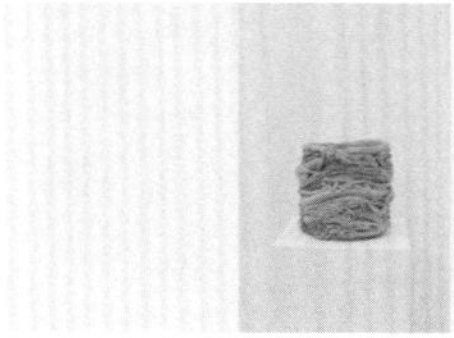

83
TWO, 2020
glazed stoneware,
35 × 35 × 42 cm

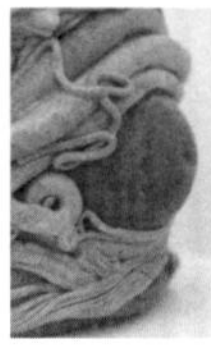 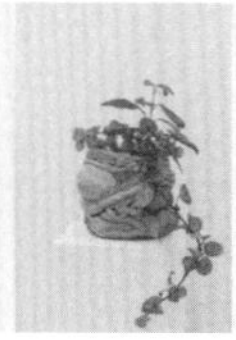

84
TWO (detail), 2020

85
TWO, 2020

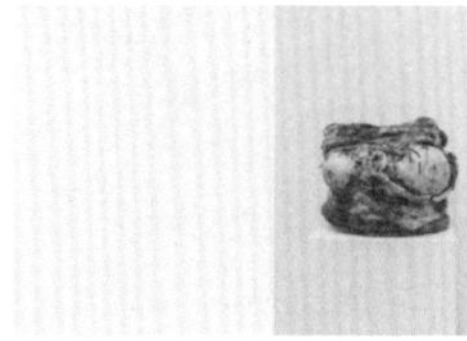

87
THREE, 2020
glazed stoneware,
47 × 47 × 50 cm

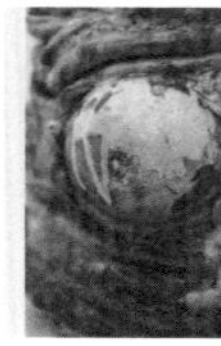 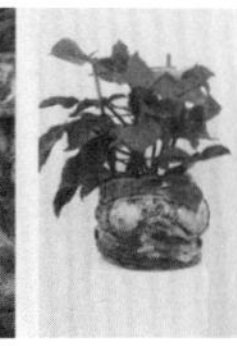

88
THREE (detail), 2020

89
THREE, 2020

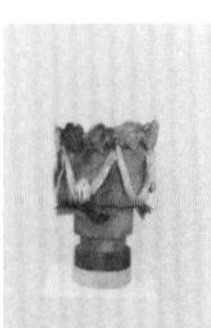 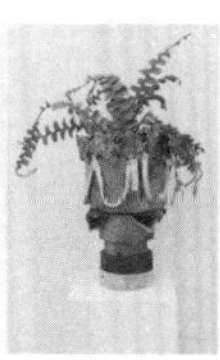

90
ONE, 2020
glazed stoneware, fabric,
wood, dye, 45 × 45 × 67 cm

91
ONE, 2020

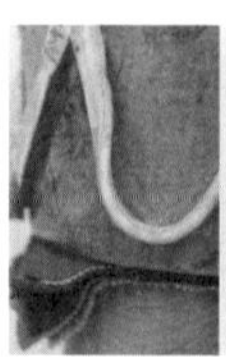 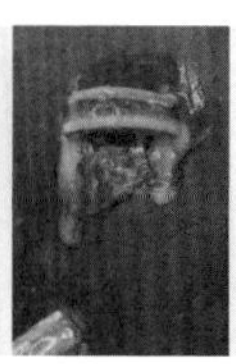

92
ONE (detail), 2020

93
FOUR (detail), 2020

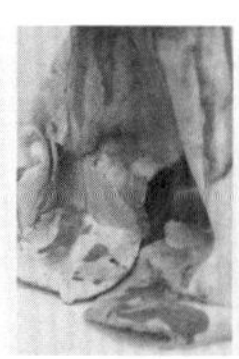 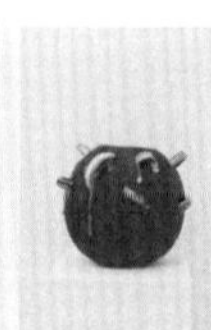

94
FIVE (detail), 2020

95
FOUR, 2020
glazed stoneware,
38 × 38 × 42 cm

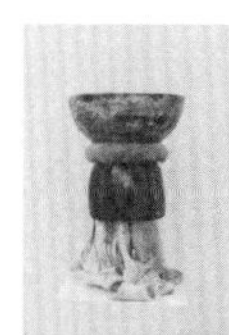 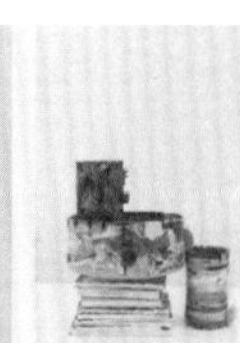

96
FIVE, 2020
glazed stoneware and fabric,
38 × 38 × 57 cm

97
SEVEN, 2020
glazed stoneware, wool,
books, 48 × 30 × 54 cm

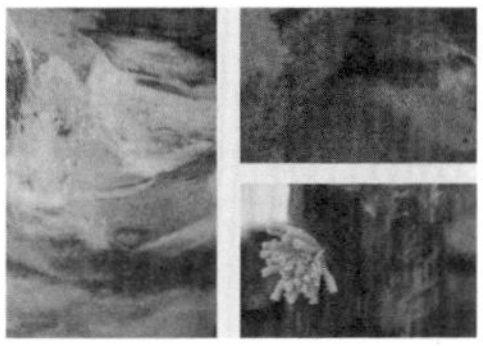

98
SEVEN (detail), 2020

99
SEVEN (details), 2020

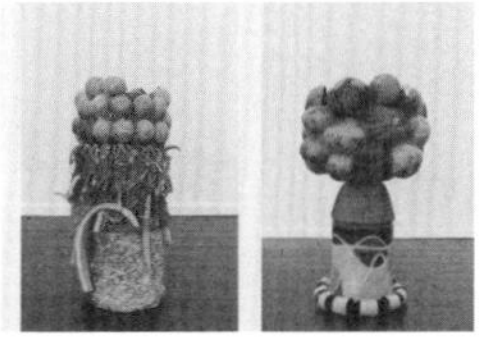

100
NINE, 2021
glazed stoneware, fabric, cardboard, epoxy resin, 65 × 25 cm

101
Comparing my insides to other people's outsides (that's your freedom), 2021
glazed stoneware, plastic bag, hairnet, 91 × 54 cm

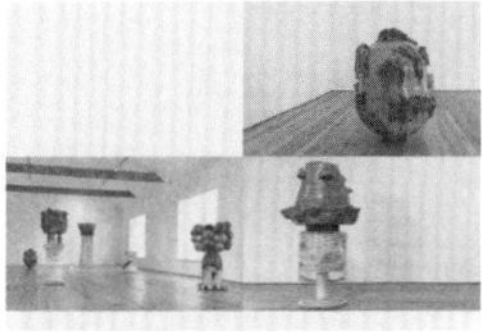

102
Walking Bundles (lamp-shades, waistcoats and book covers), 2021
glazed stoneware, 52 × 52 × 60 cm

Ennobled Objects, 2021
glazed stoneware, turned wood, plaster, brass tray, dye, epoxy resin, 47 × 47 × 149 cm

Libretto-ah!, 2021
glazed stoneware, wool, jesmonite, wooden dowel, 148.5 × 64 cm

TEN, 2021
glazed stoneware, epoxy resin, 45 × 70 × 45 cm

Comparing my insides to other people's outsides (that's your freedom), 2021

sumVIGOUR, installation view, CAMPLE LINE, Dumfries, 2021

103
(top)
Walking Bundles (lamp-shades, waistcoats and book covers), 2021

(bottom)
Handle/relief, 2021
glazed stoneware, wood, glass vase, rainbow filter, fabric, 48 × 48 × 89 cm

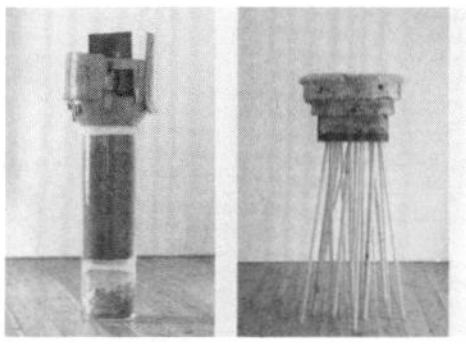

104
Make an image an act (don't take it peripersonally), 2021
glazed stoneware, dyed rice, wool, glass vases, rope, wool, pigment, fleece, 40 × 40 × 157 cm

105
Libretto-ah!, 2021

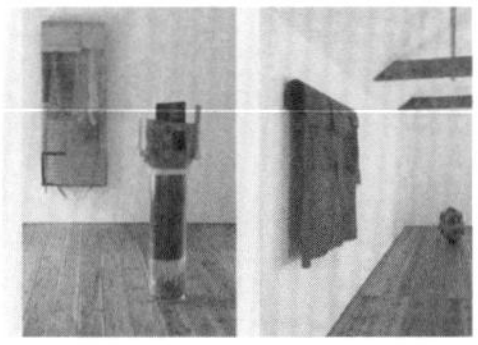

106
(left)
Things that soak you (XIV), 2021
stoneware, netting, fabric, plastic sheet, pigment, bamboo cane, 190 × 64 × 17.7 cm

(right)
Make an image an act (don't take it peripersonally), 2021

107
(wall)
Things that soak you (XV), 2021
stoneware, dye, netting, fabric, towel, 124 × 112 × 18.5 cm

(floor)
Walking Bundles (lamp-shades, waistcoats and book covers), 2021

sumVIGOUR, installation views, CAMPLE LINE, Dumfries, 2021

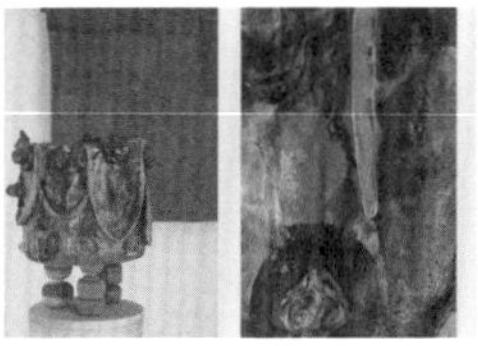

108
Ennobled Objects, 2021

109
Ennobled Objects (detail), 2021

THINGS THAT SOAK YOU

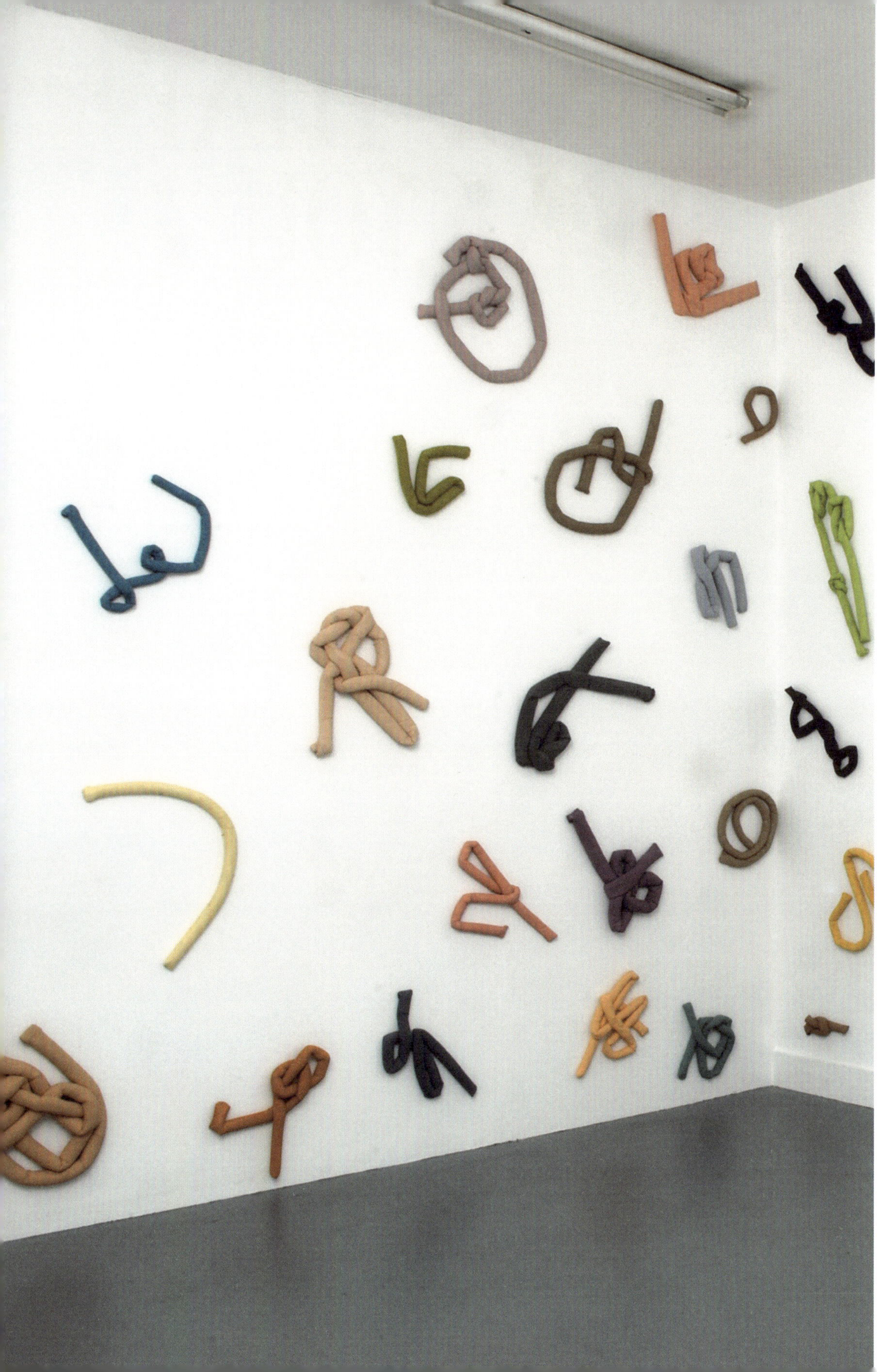

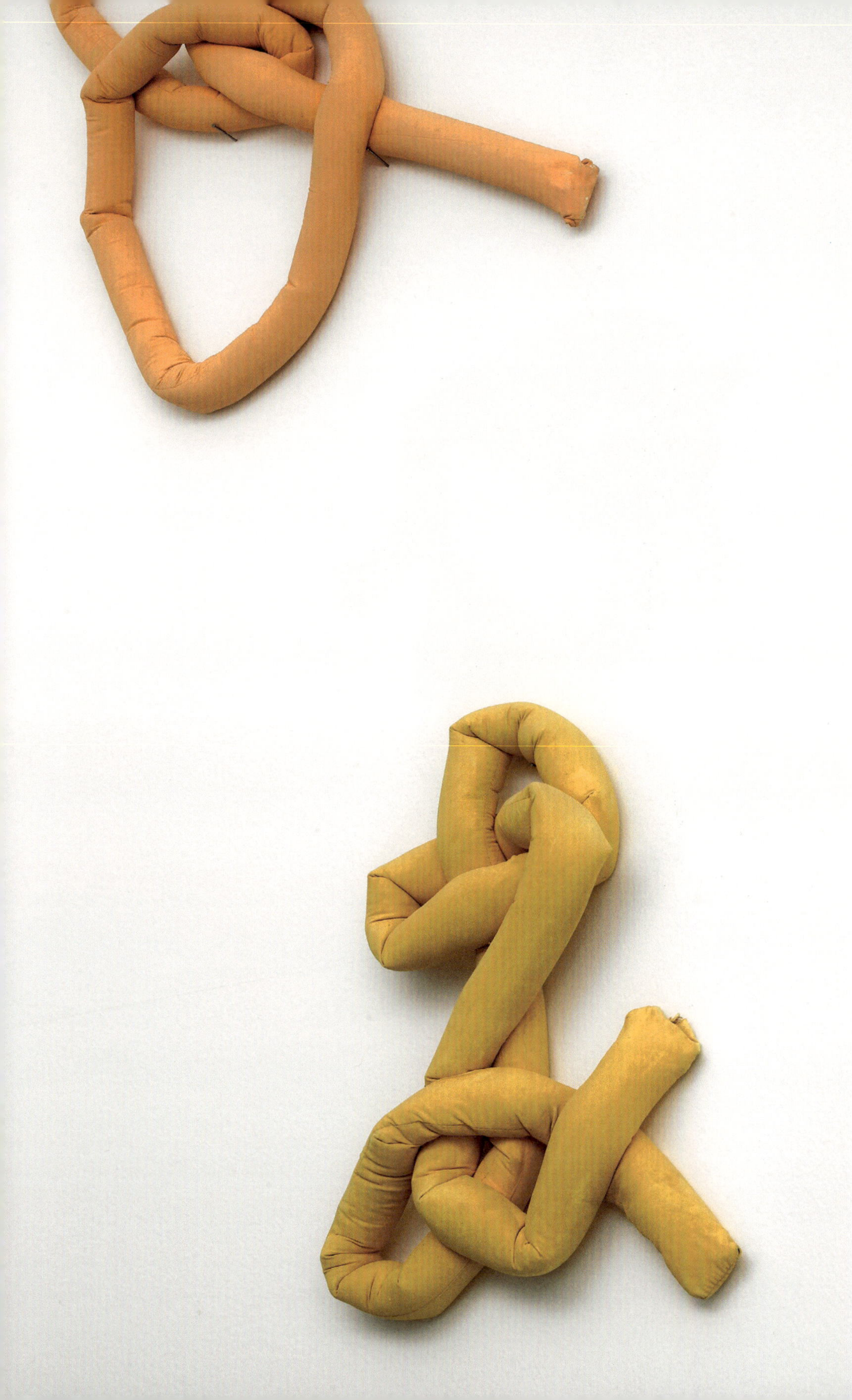

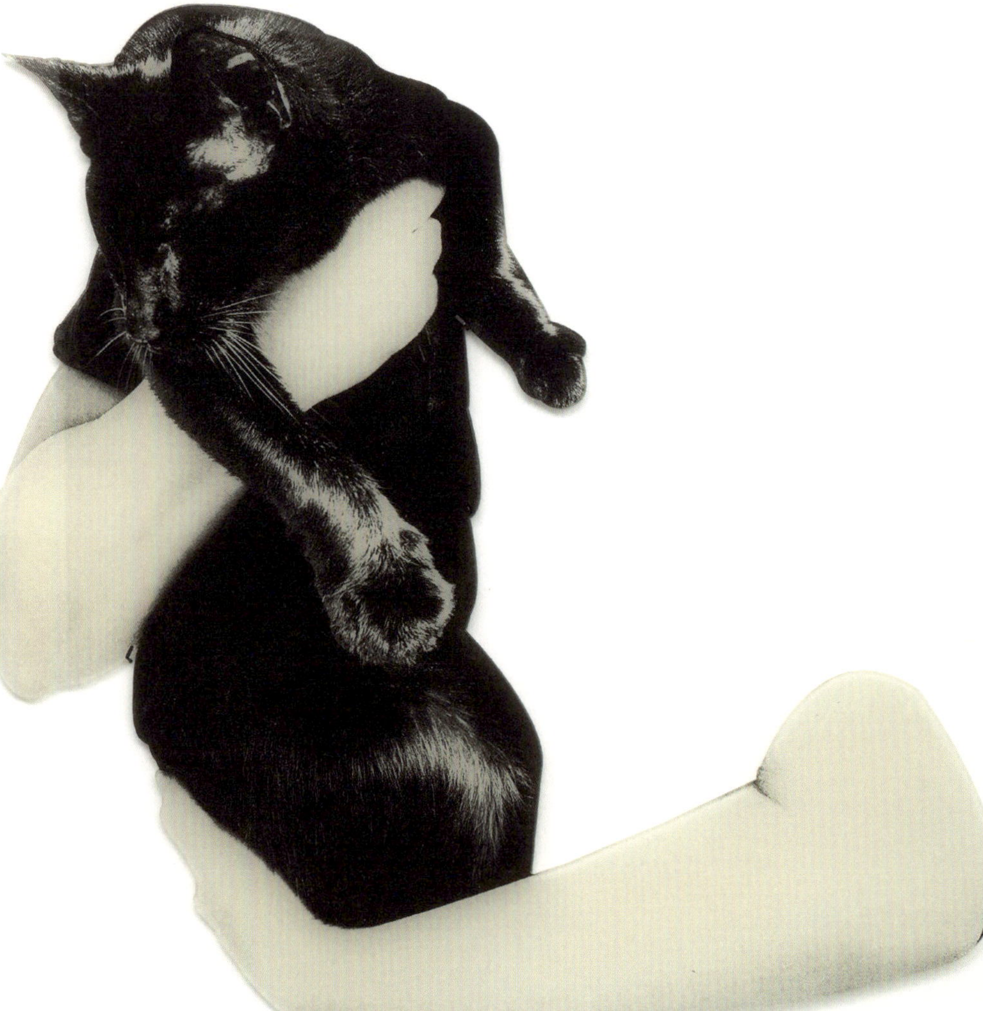

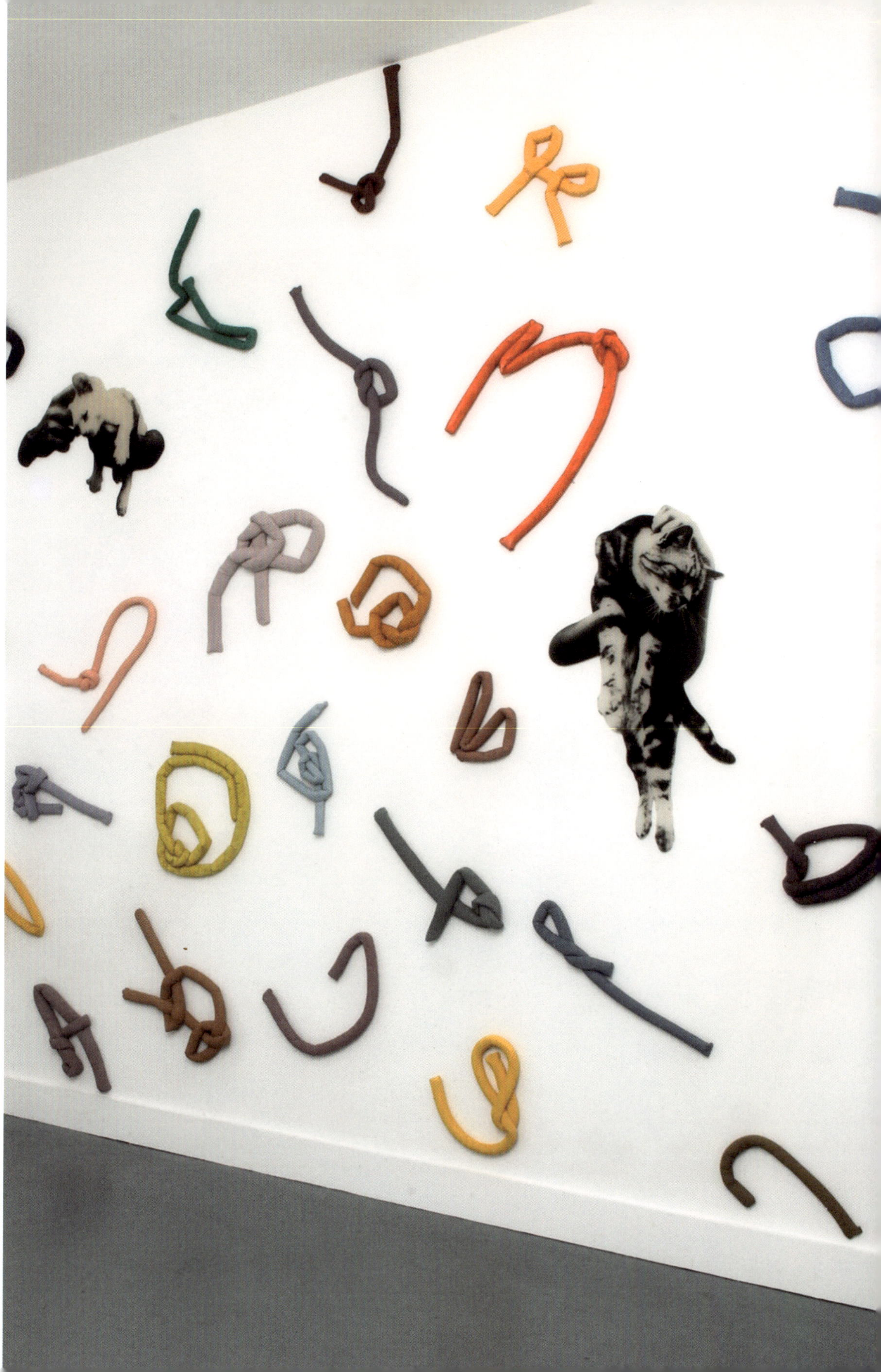

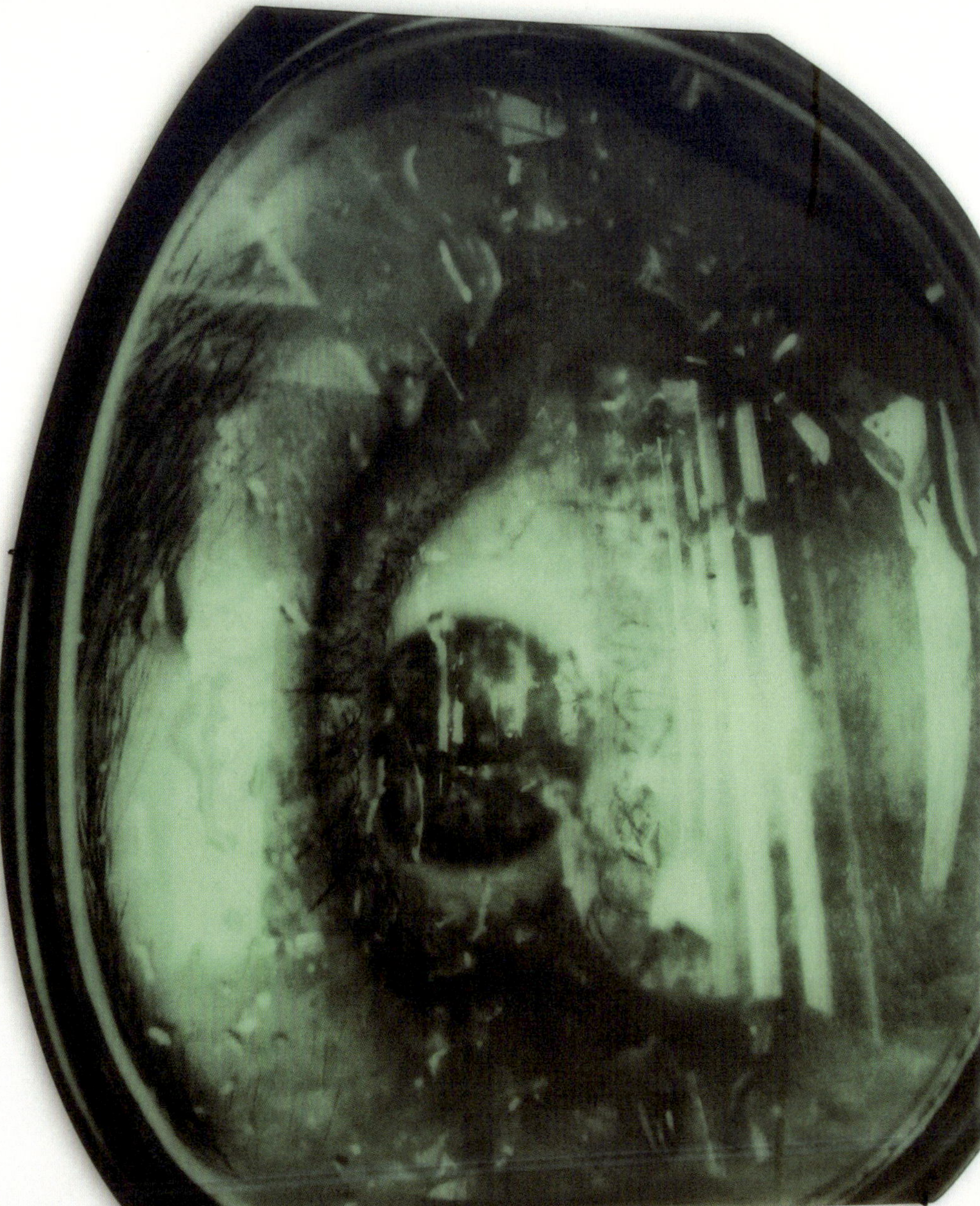

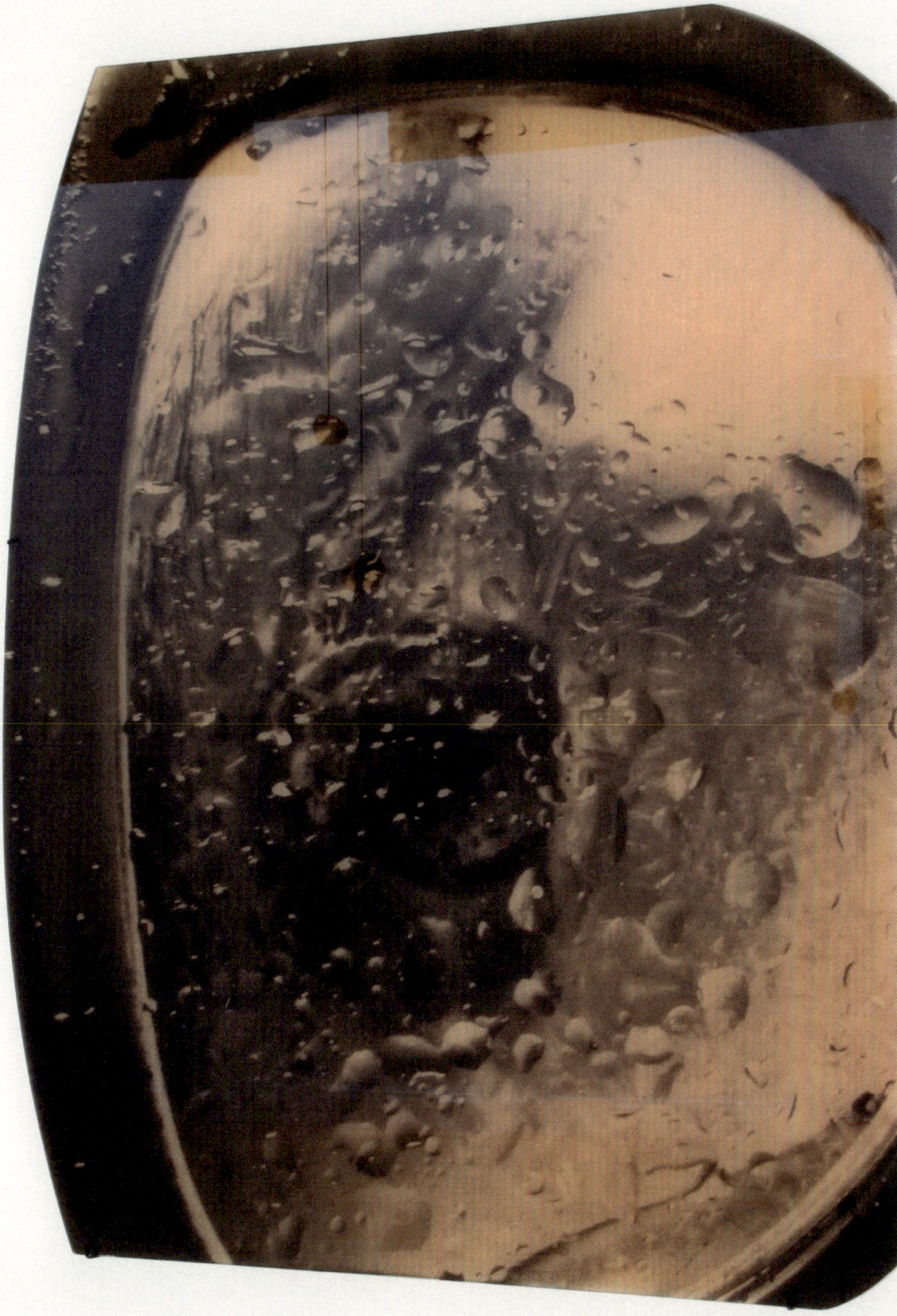

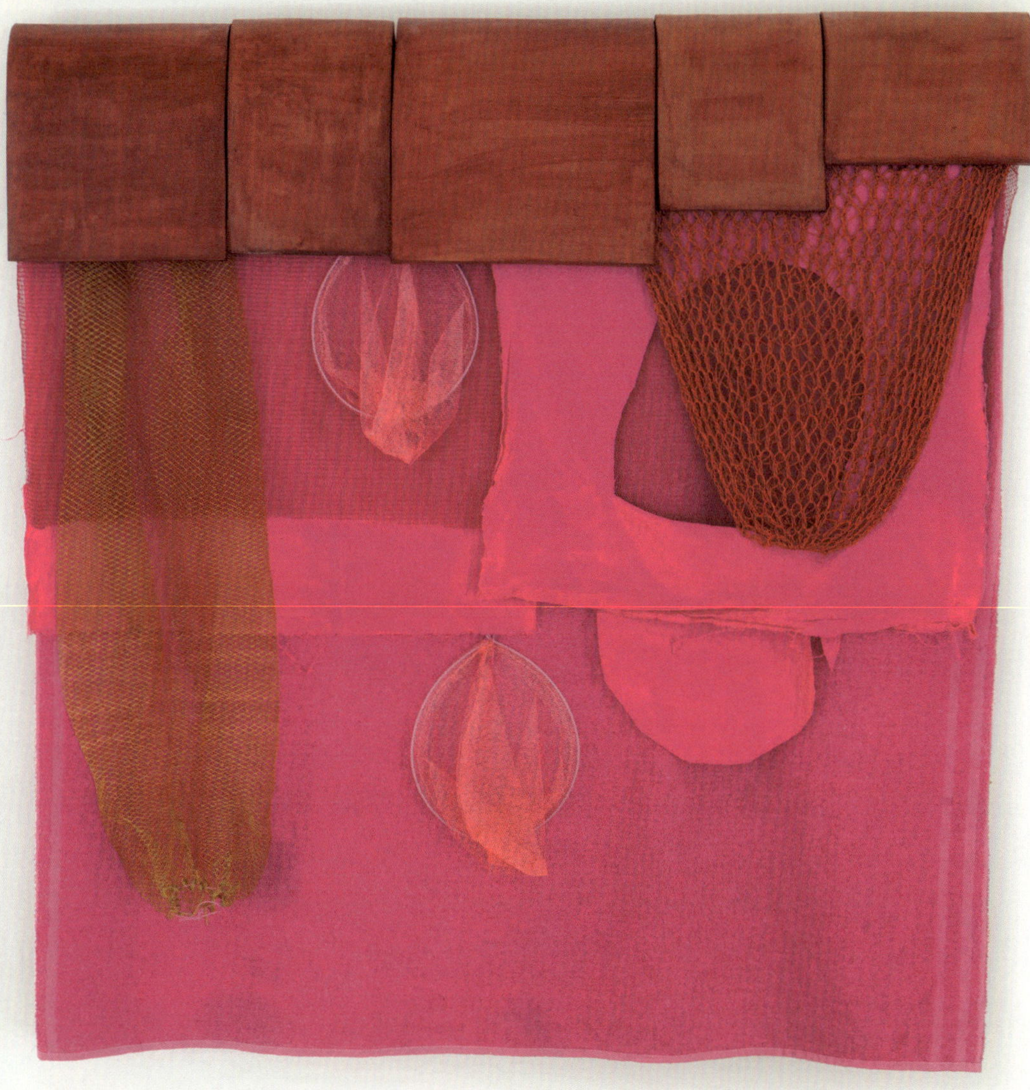

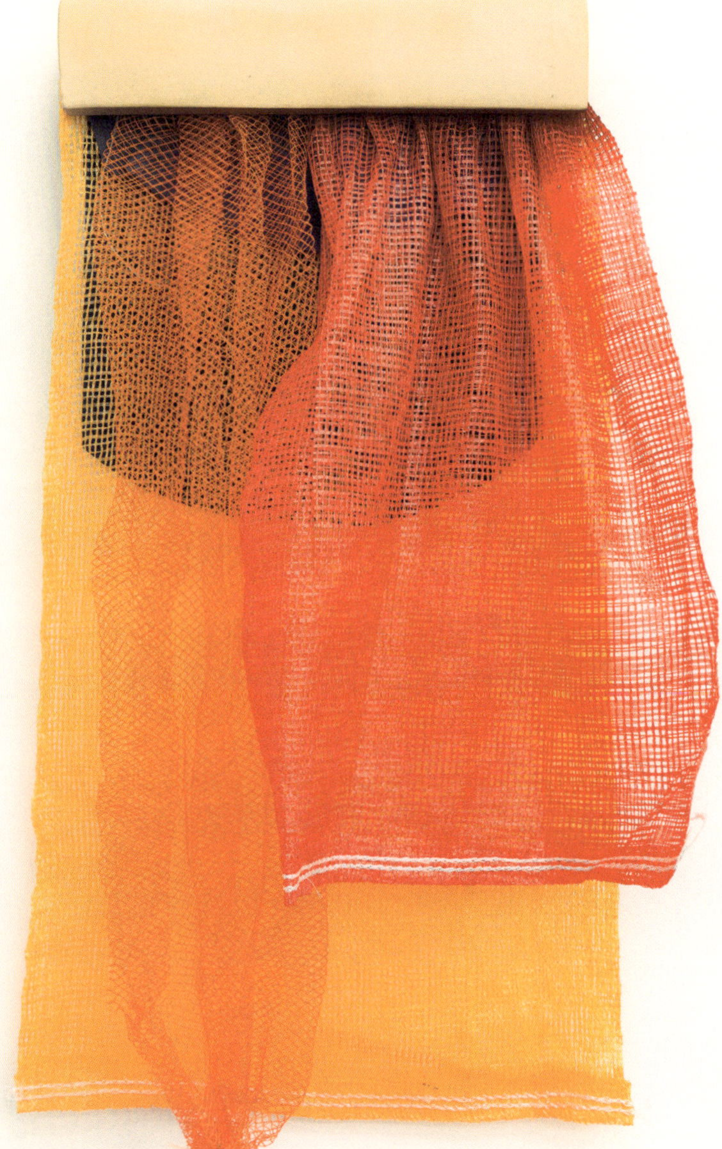

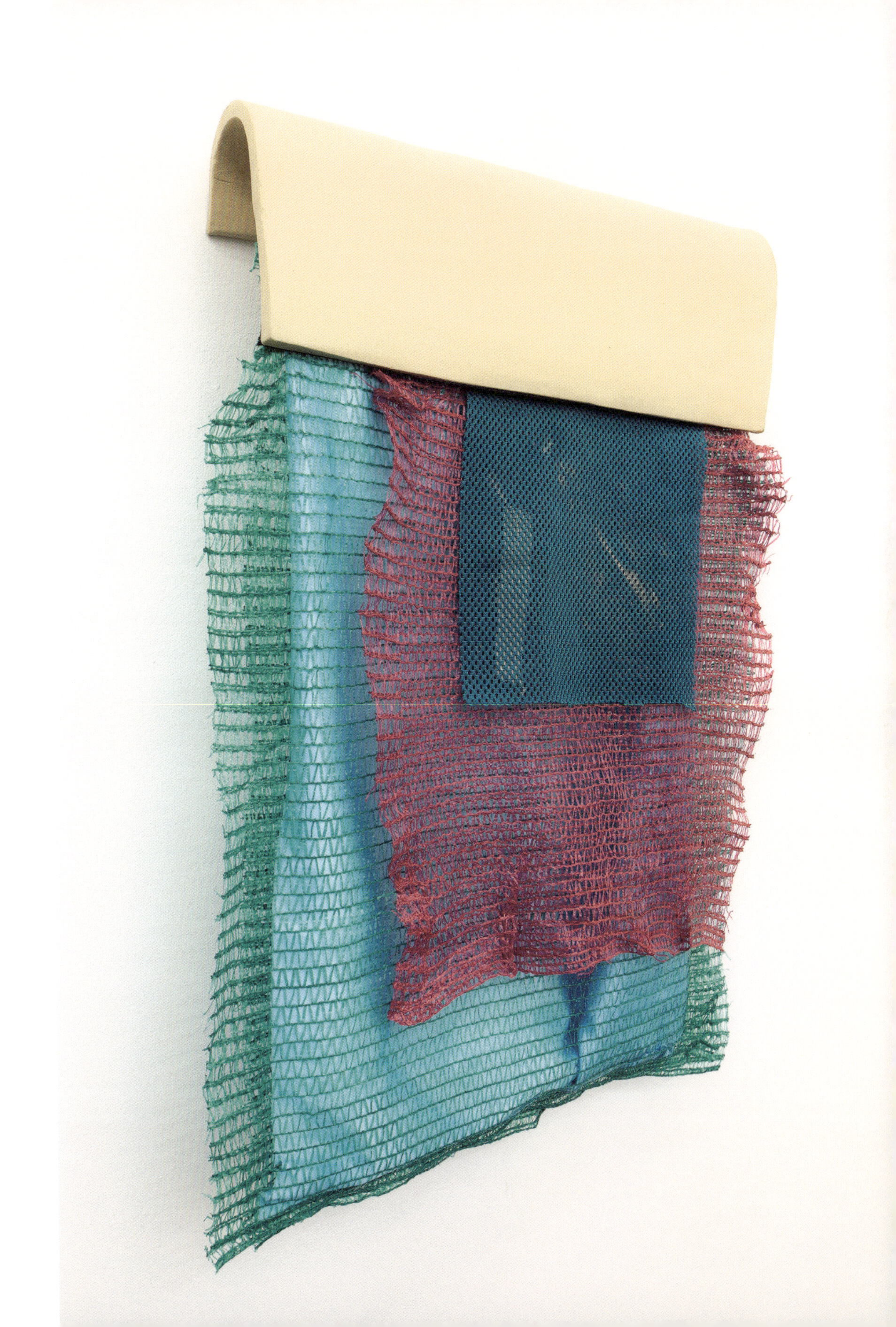

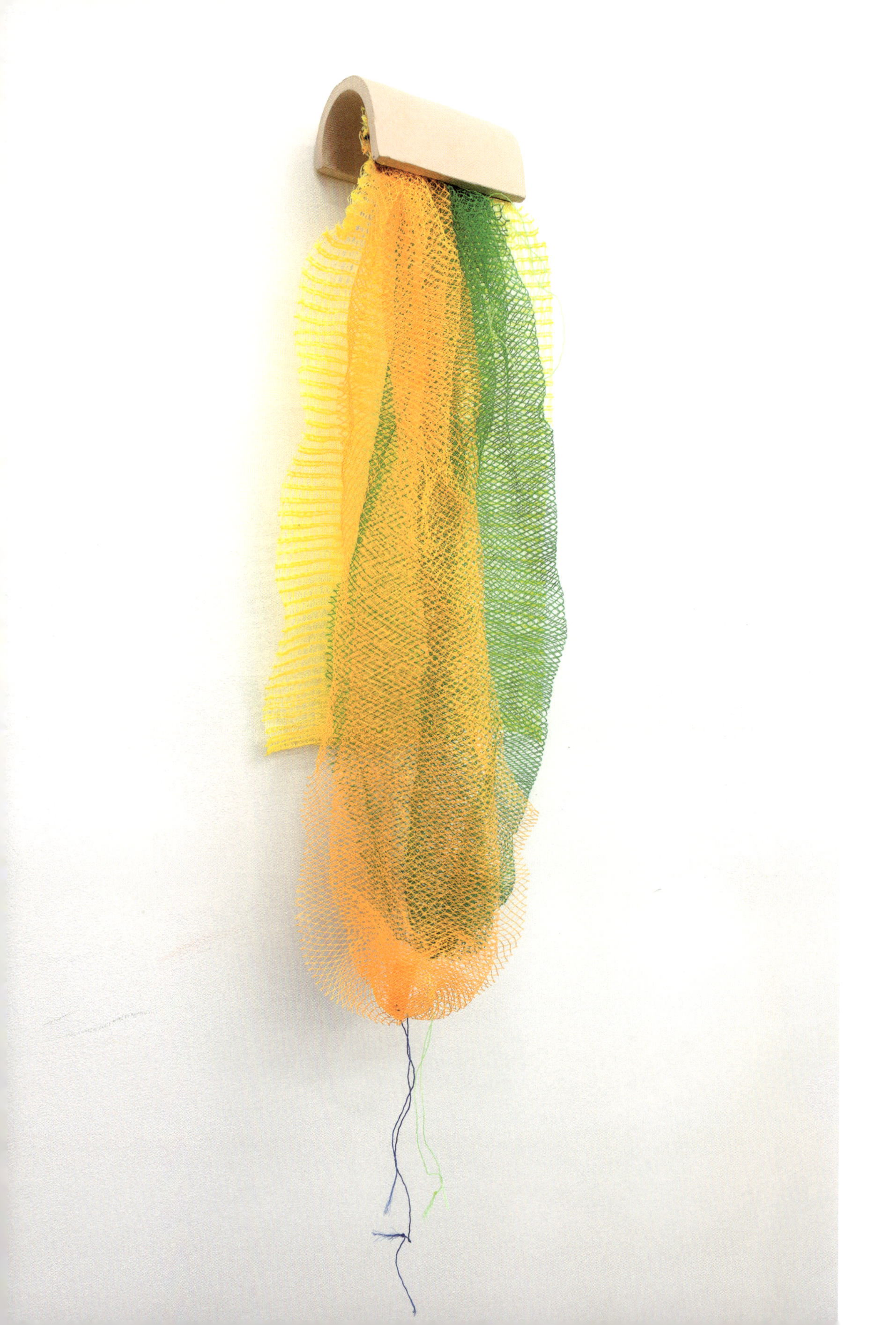

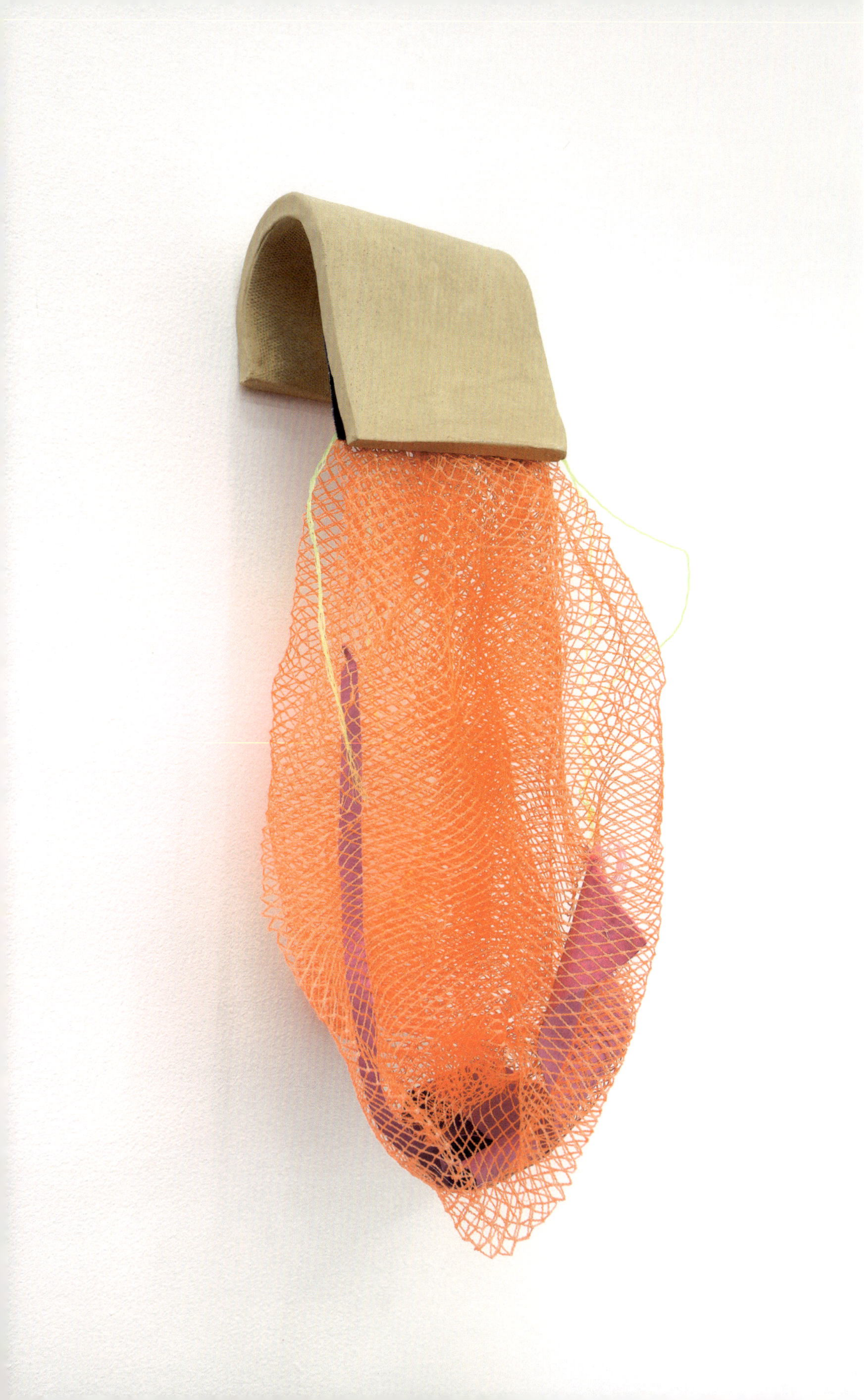

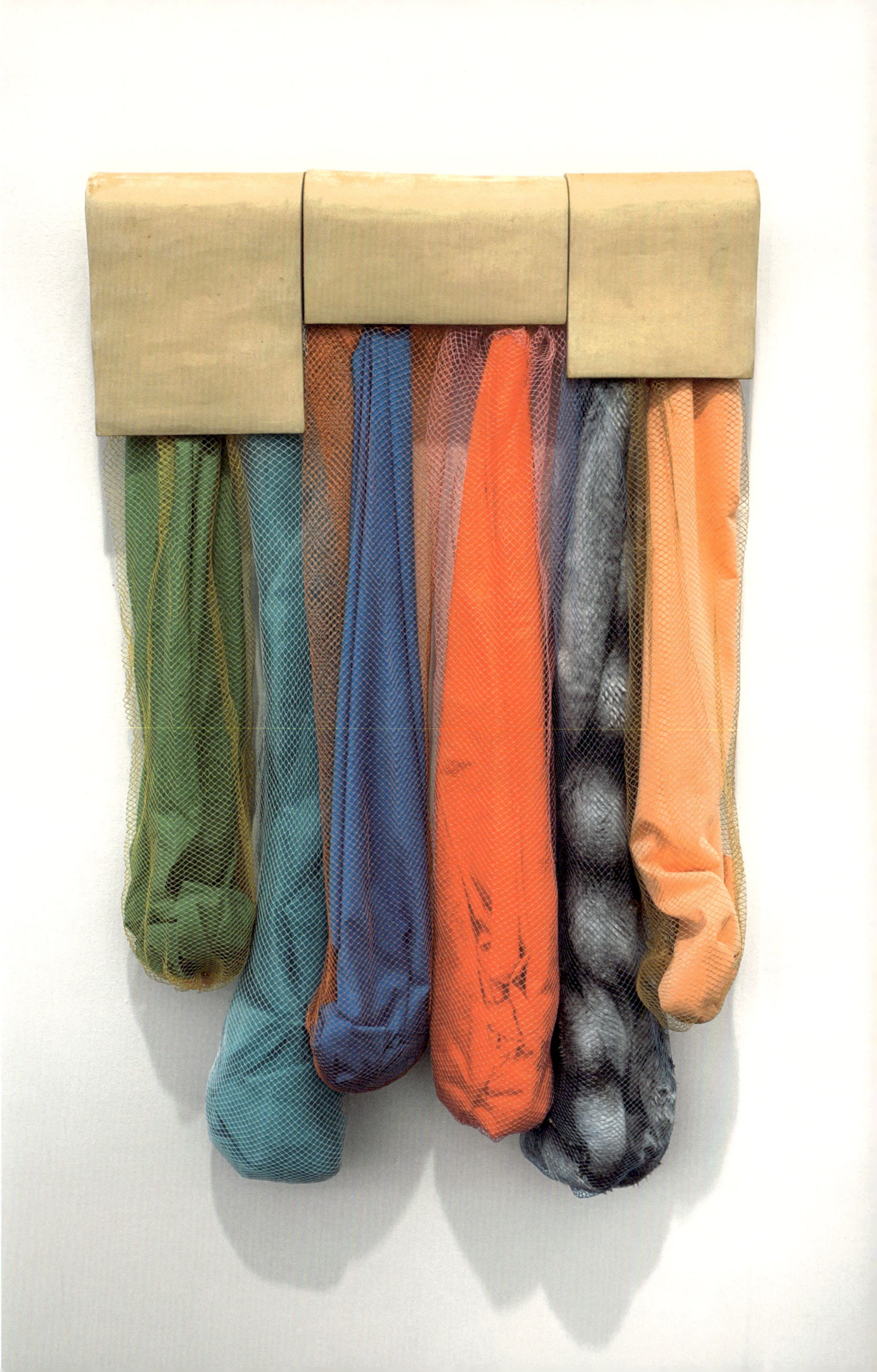

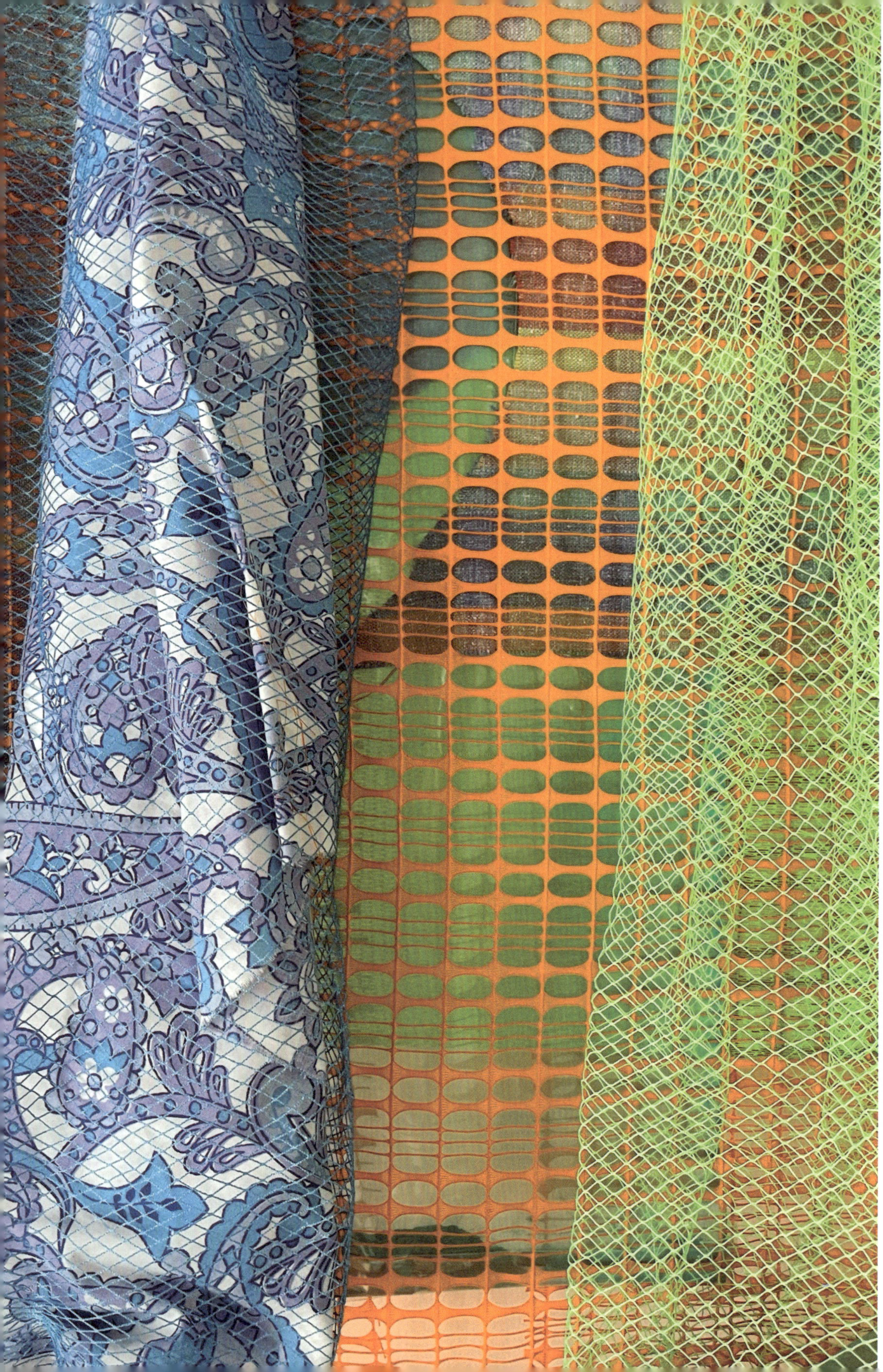

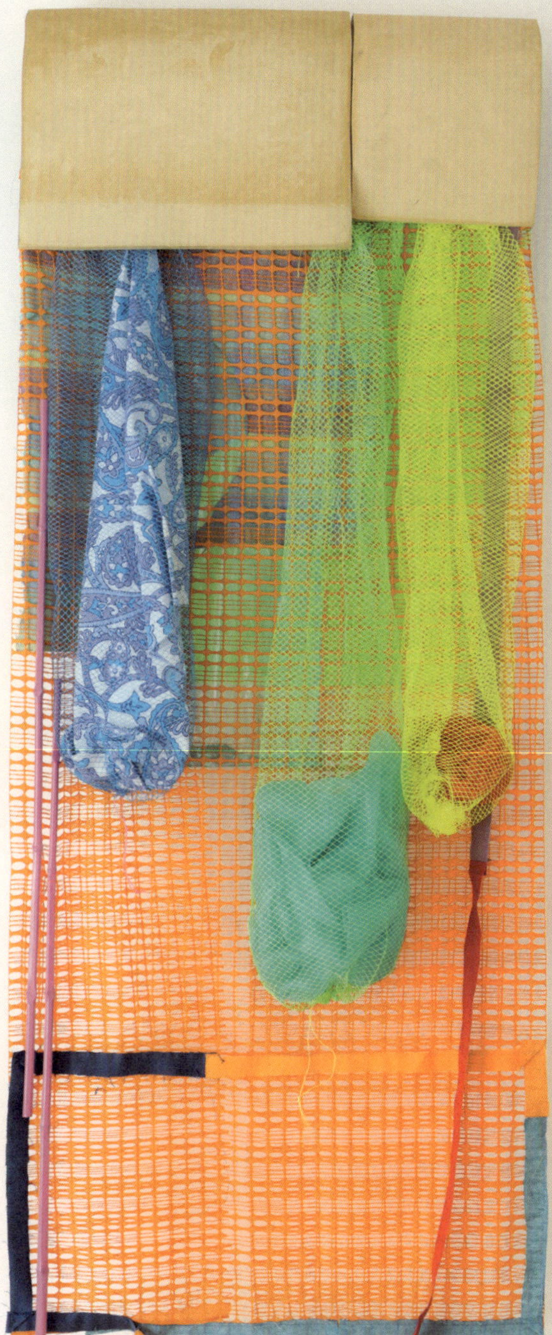

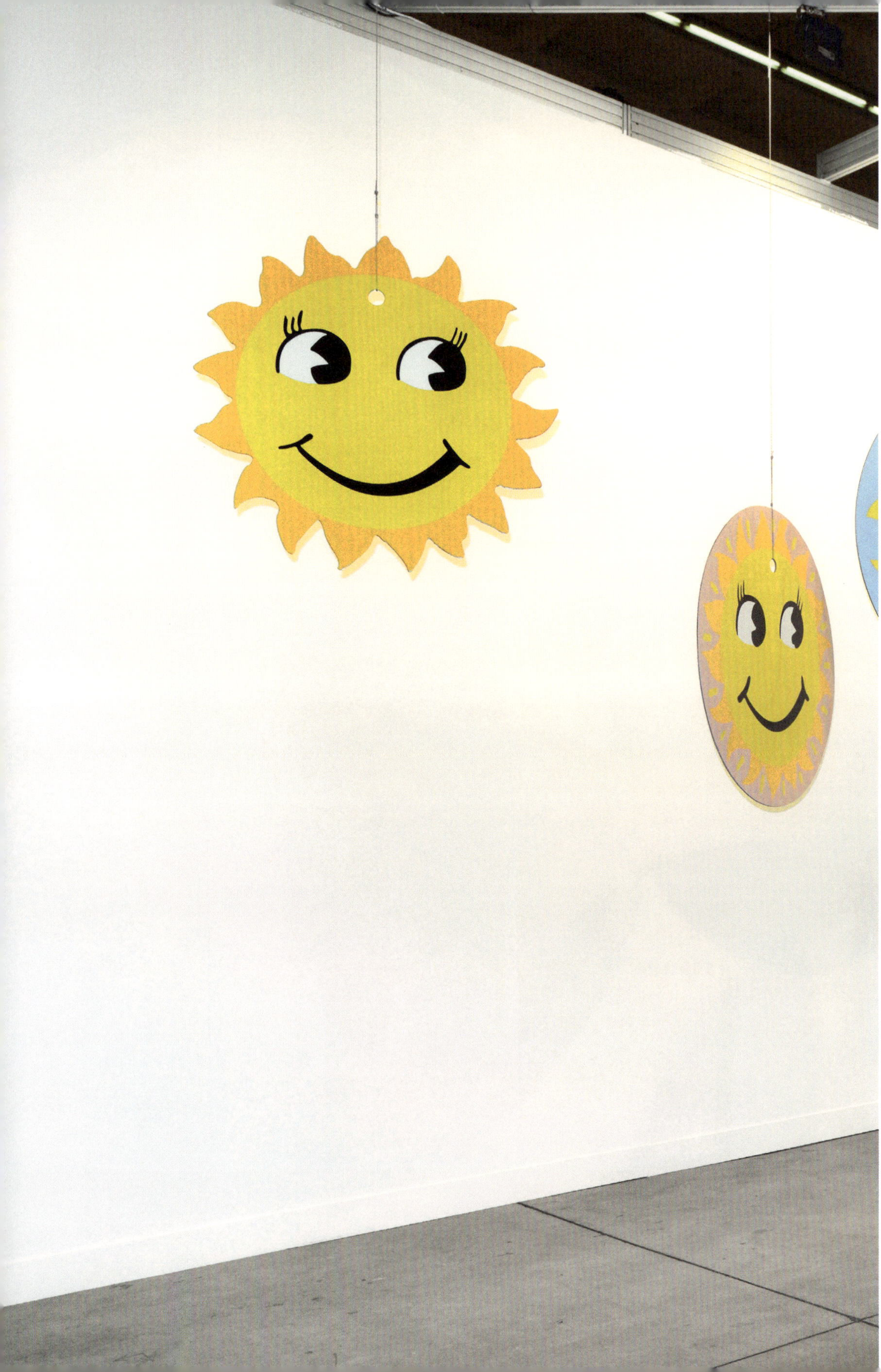

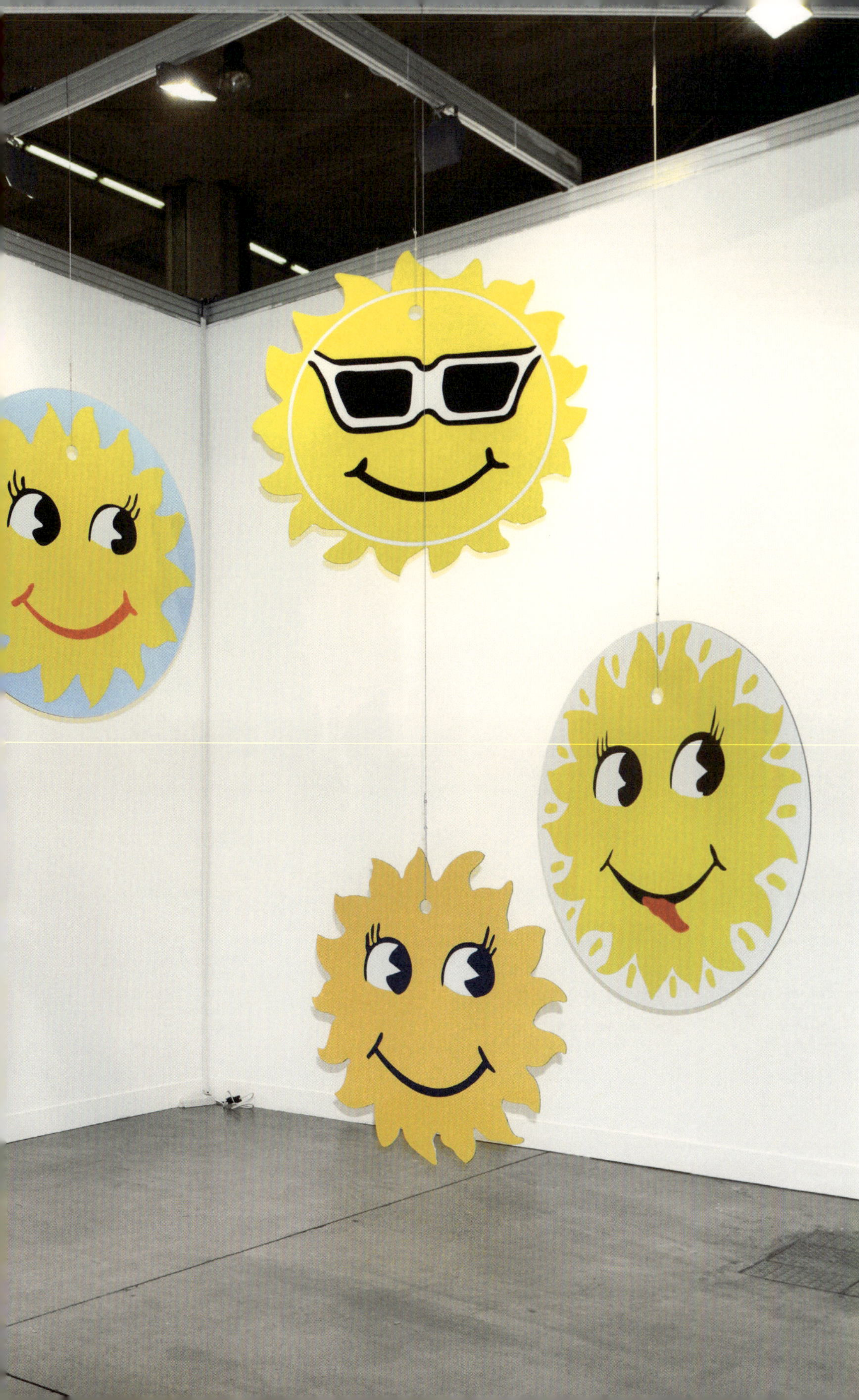

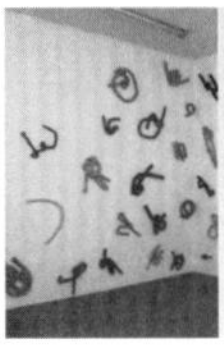
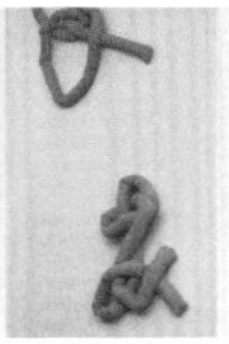

114
Untitled, 2011
fabric, plaster, powder paint, dimensions variable

installation view, Studio Voltaire, London, 2011

115
Untitled (detail), 2011

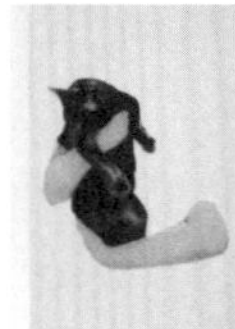
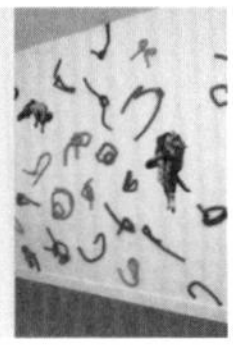

116
Hand Extended (IV), 2011
screen print on Perspex, 65 × 67 cm

117
Untitled, 2011

Hand Extended (V), 2011
screen print on Perspex, 64 × 72 cm

installation view, Studio Voltaire, London, 2011

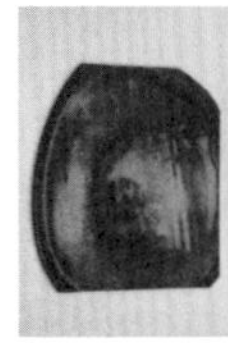
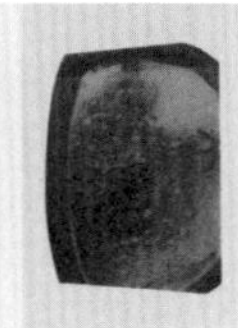

118
Let it grow on, all sides (II), 2011
screen print on Perspex, 75 × 60 cm

119
Let it grow on, all sides (III), 2011
screen print on Perspex, 90 × 70 cm

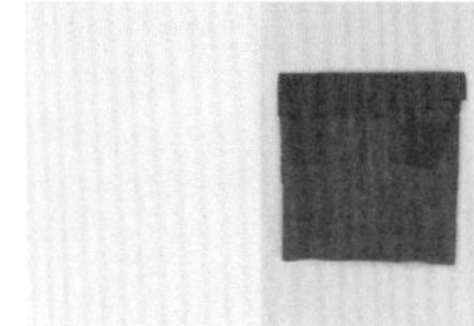

121
Things that soak you (XV), 2021
stoneware, dye, netting, fabric, towel, 124 × 112 × 18.5 cm

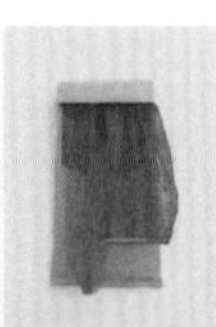
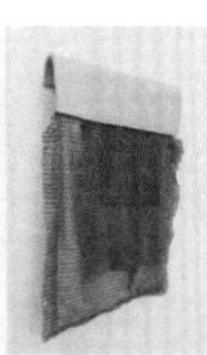

122
Things that soak you (I), 2016
ceramic, net, fabric, 45 × 78 × 10 cm

123
Things that soak you (V), 2016
ceramic, net, fabric, 73.5 × 49 × 9.9 cm

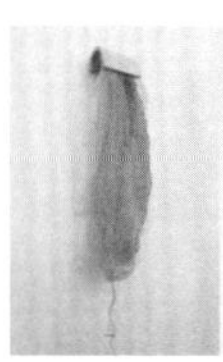
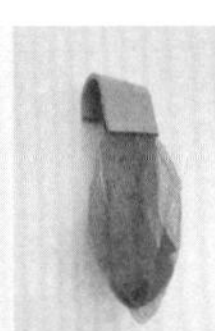

124
Things that soak you (IV), 2016
ceramic, net, fabric, 108 × 31 × 11 cm

125
Things that soak you (VI), 2016
ceramic, net, fabric, 46.5 × 23.5 × 10.5 cm

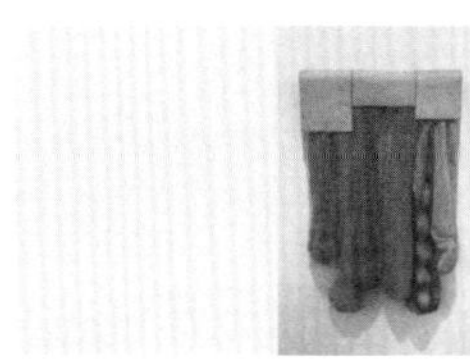

127
Things that soak you (XII), 2019
washing nets, fabric, thread, faux fur, stoneware, 120 × 87 × 40 cm

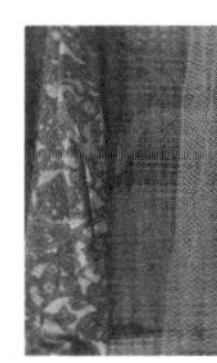
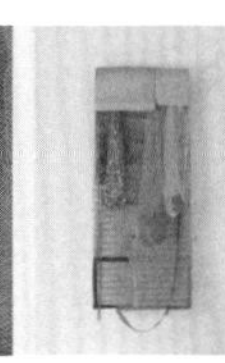

128
Things that soak you (XIV) (detail), 2021

129
Things that soak you (XIV), 2021
stoneware, netting, fabric, plastic sheet, pigment, bamboo cane, 190 × 64 × 17.7 cm

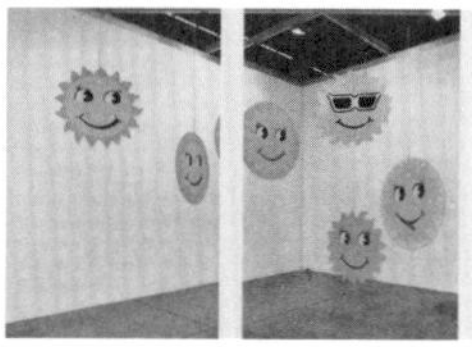

130–131
Be a nose! (I–IV), 2015
vitreous enamel on steel,
dimensions variable

THE OUTSIDE IS INSIDE EVERYTHING WE MAKE

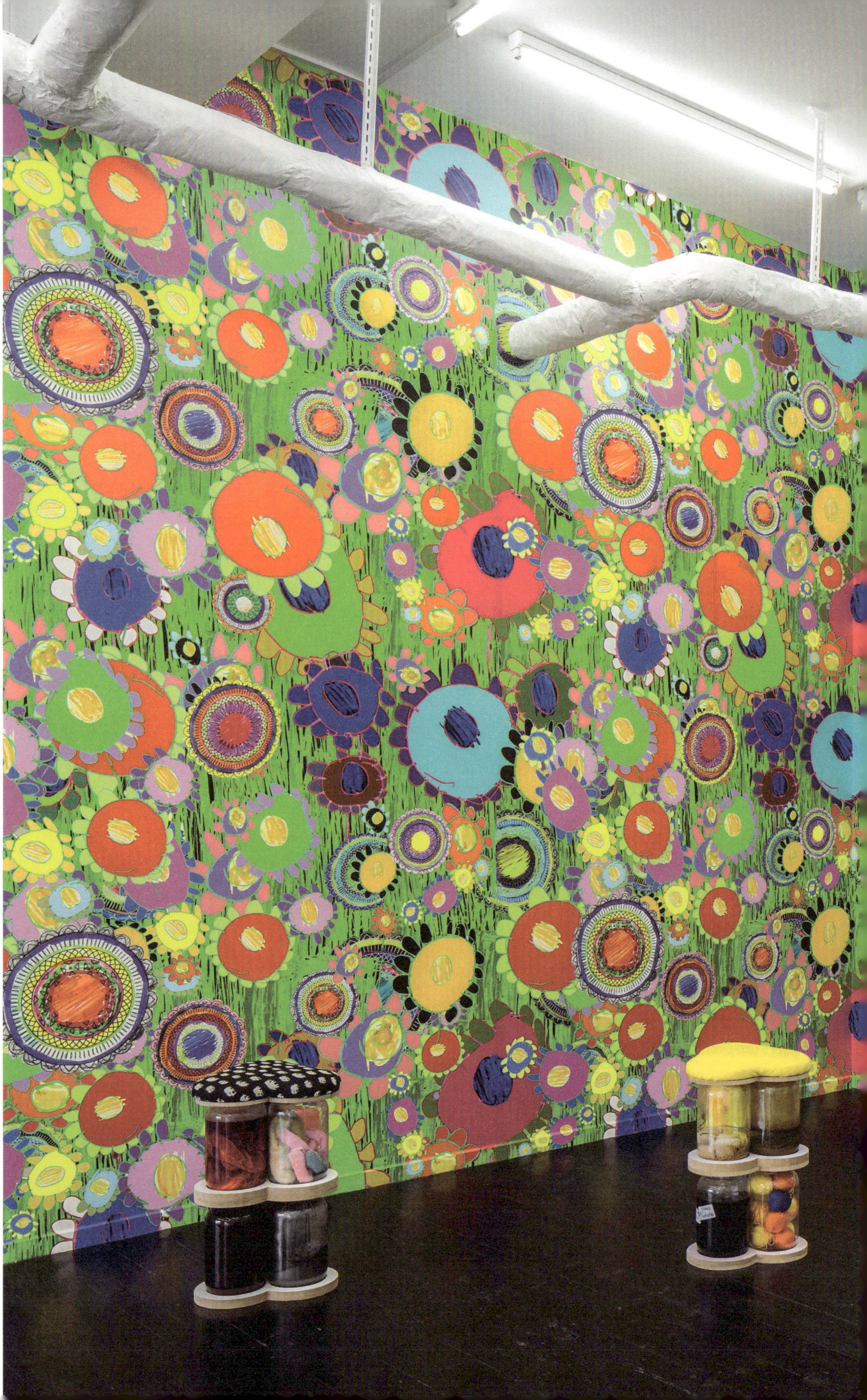

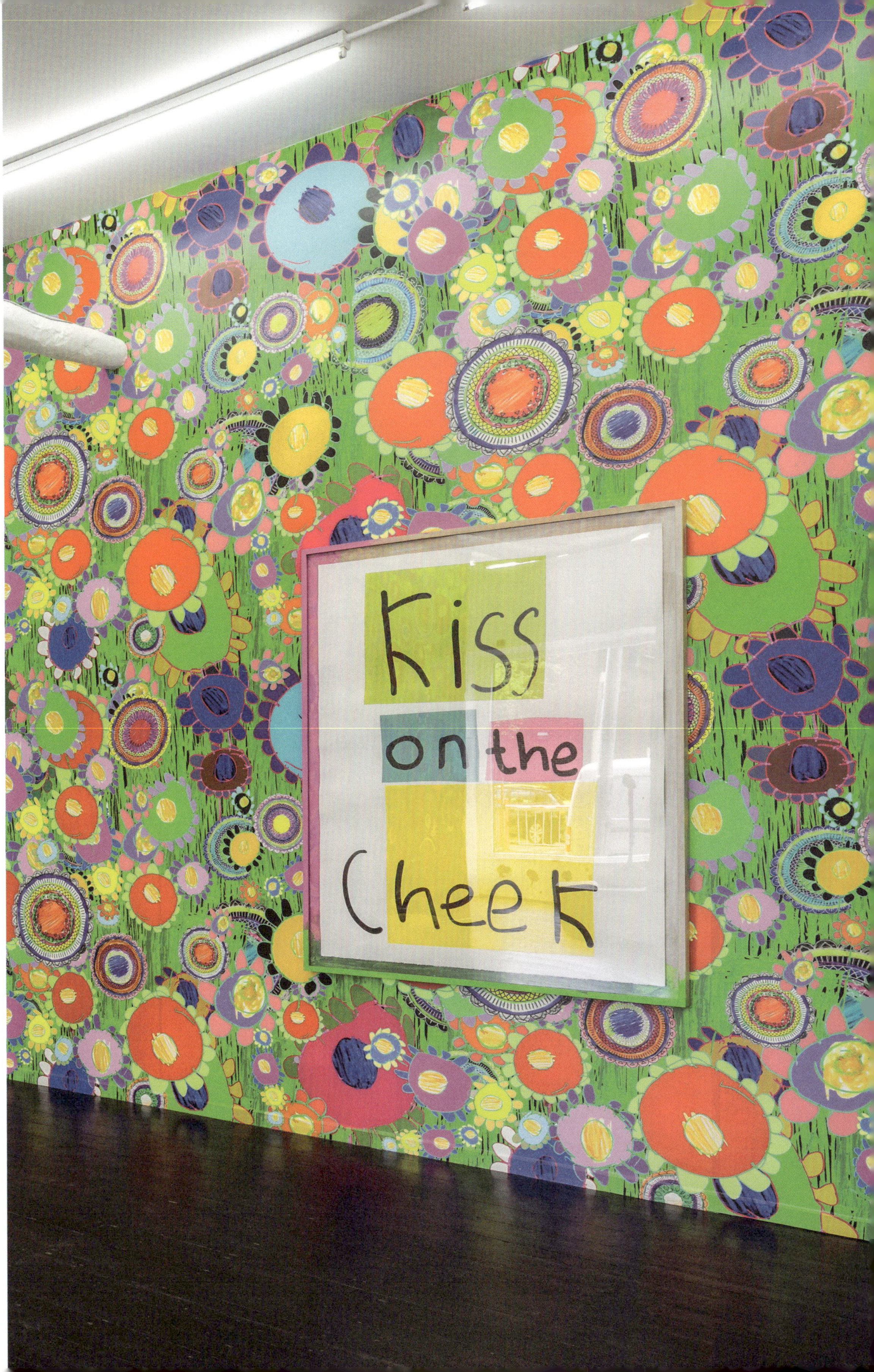
Kiss
on the
Cheek

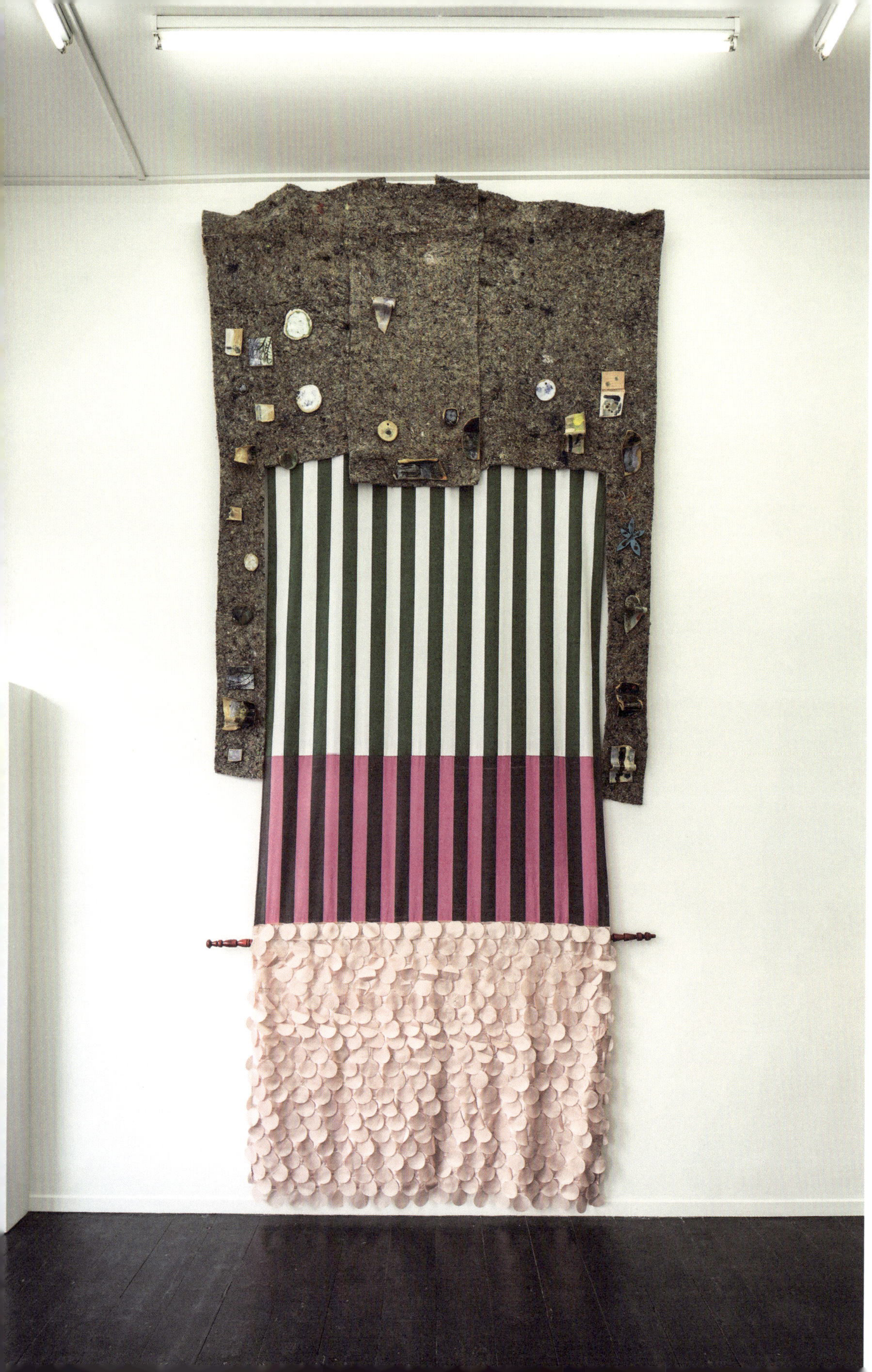

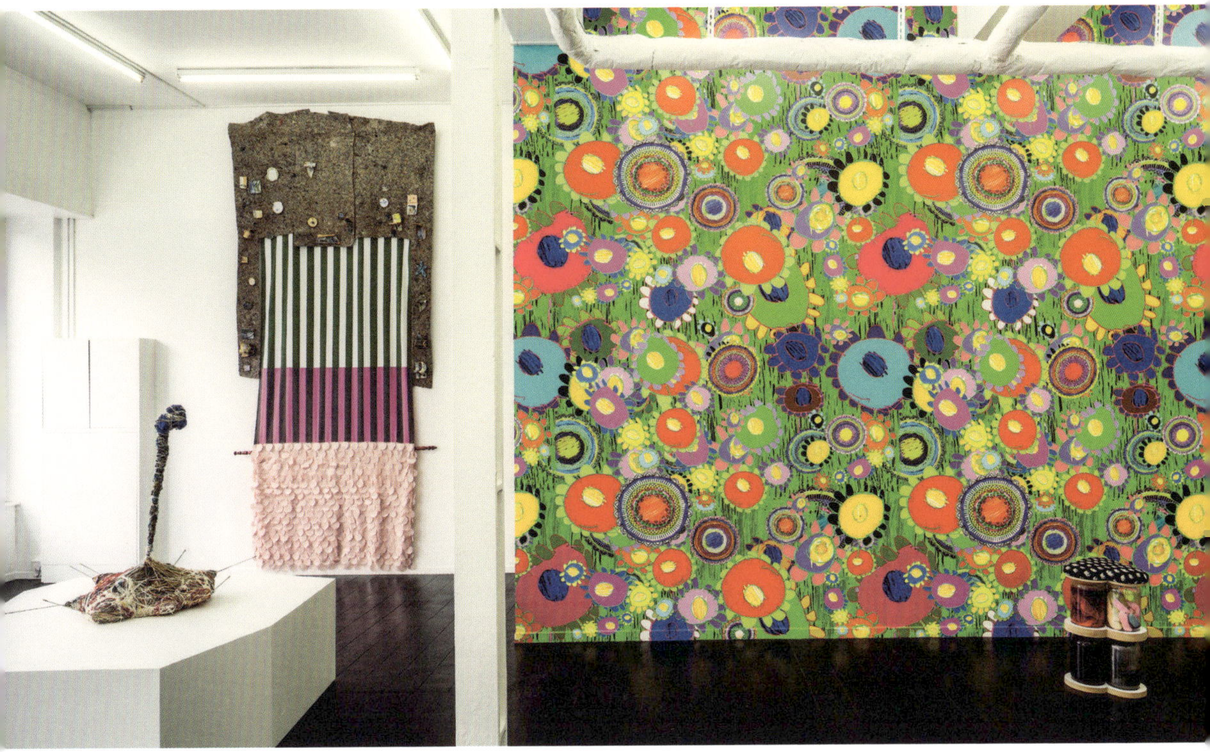

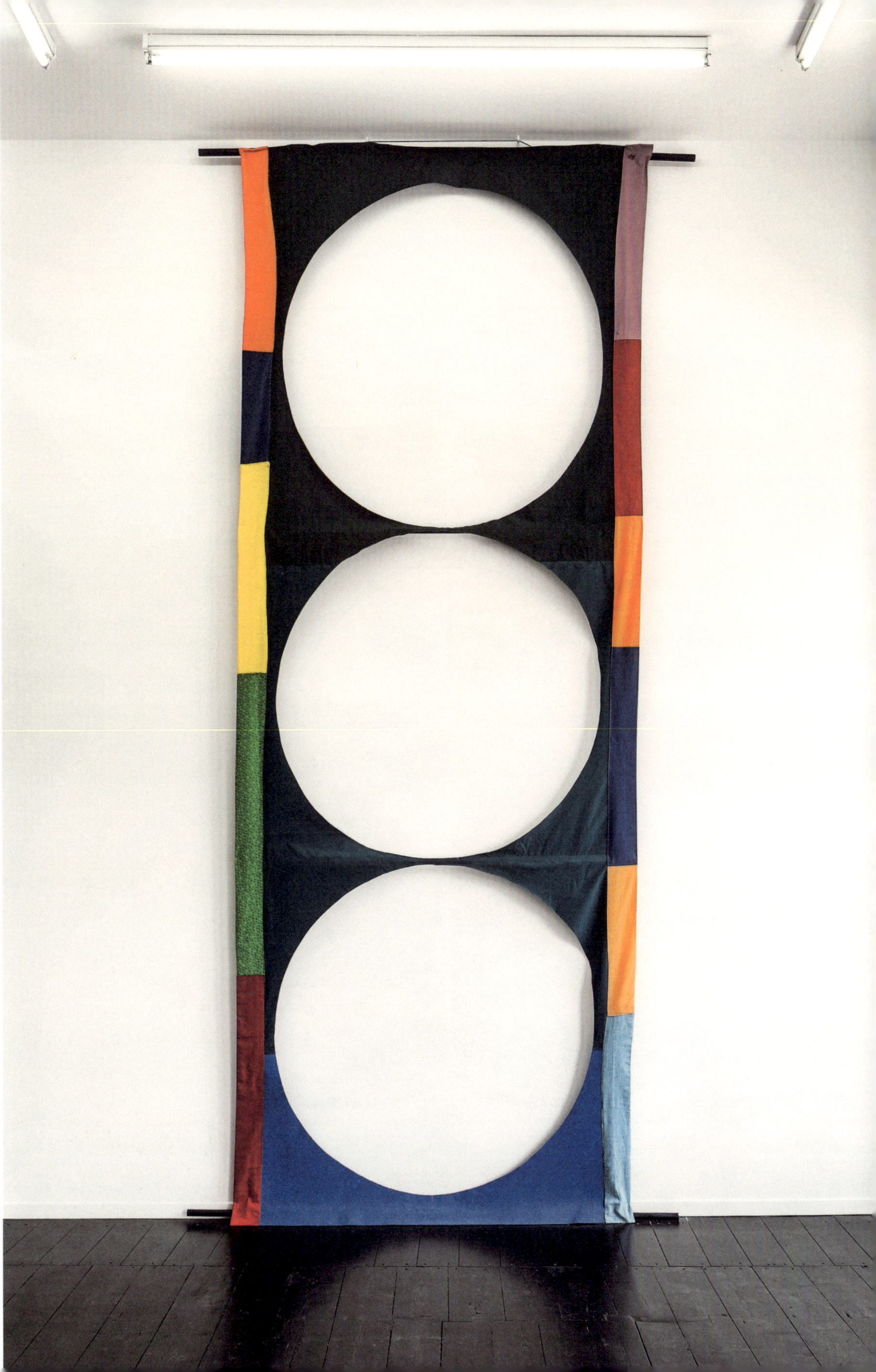

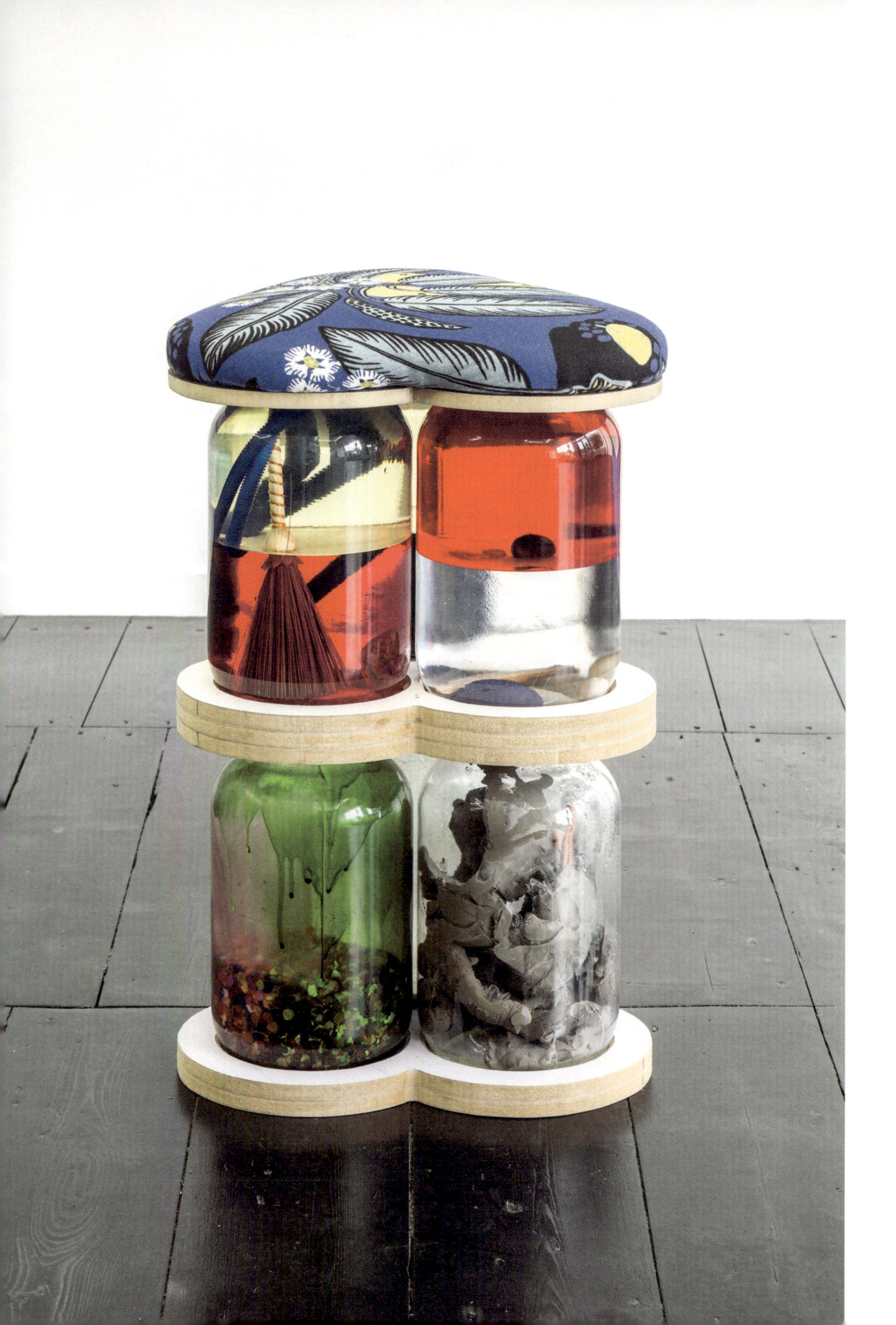

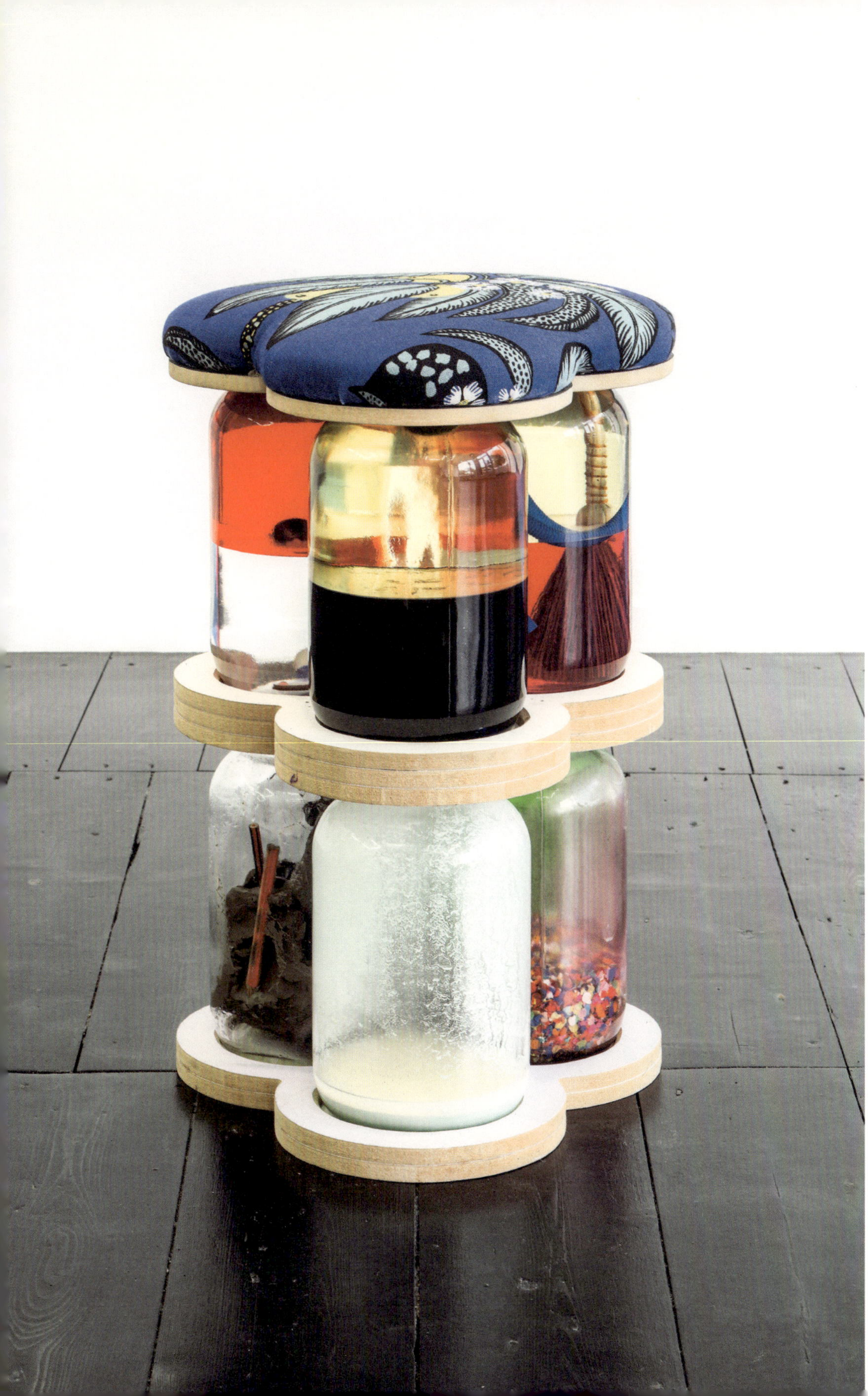

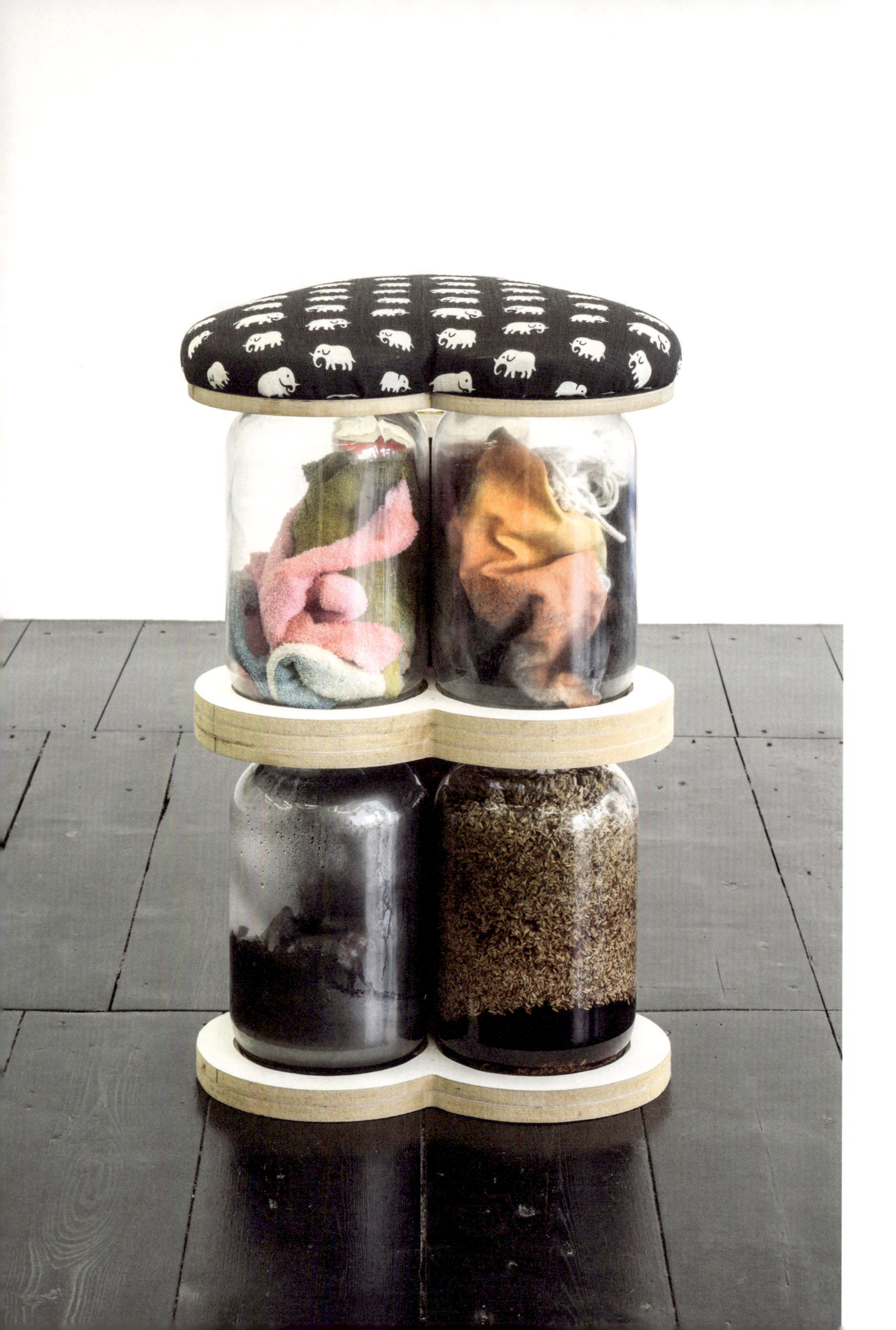

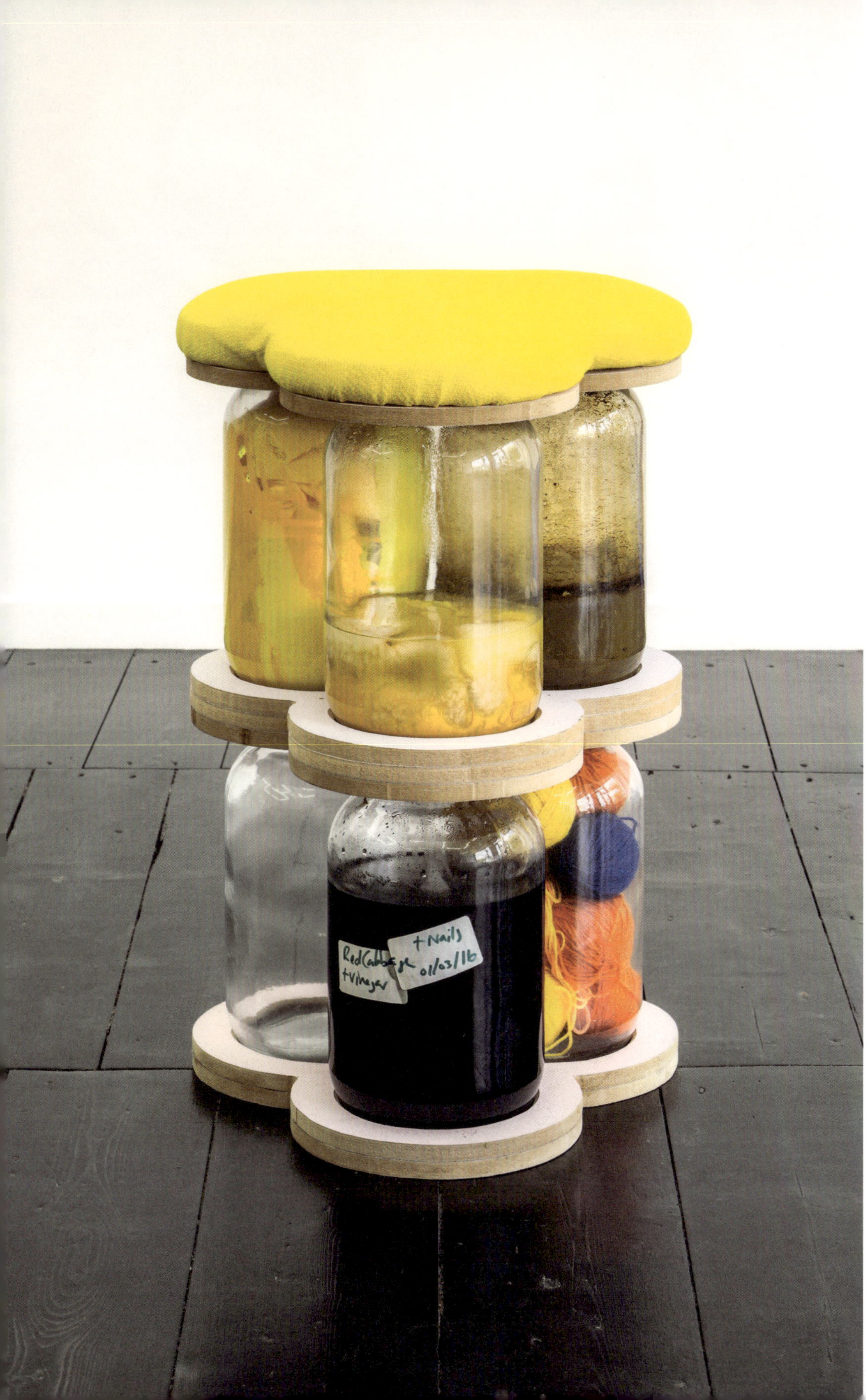
RedCabbage
+Vinegar
+Nails
01/03/16

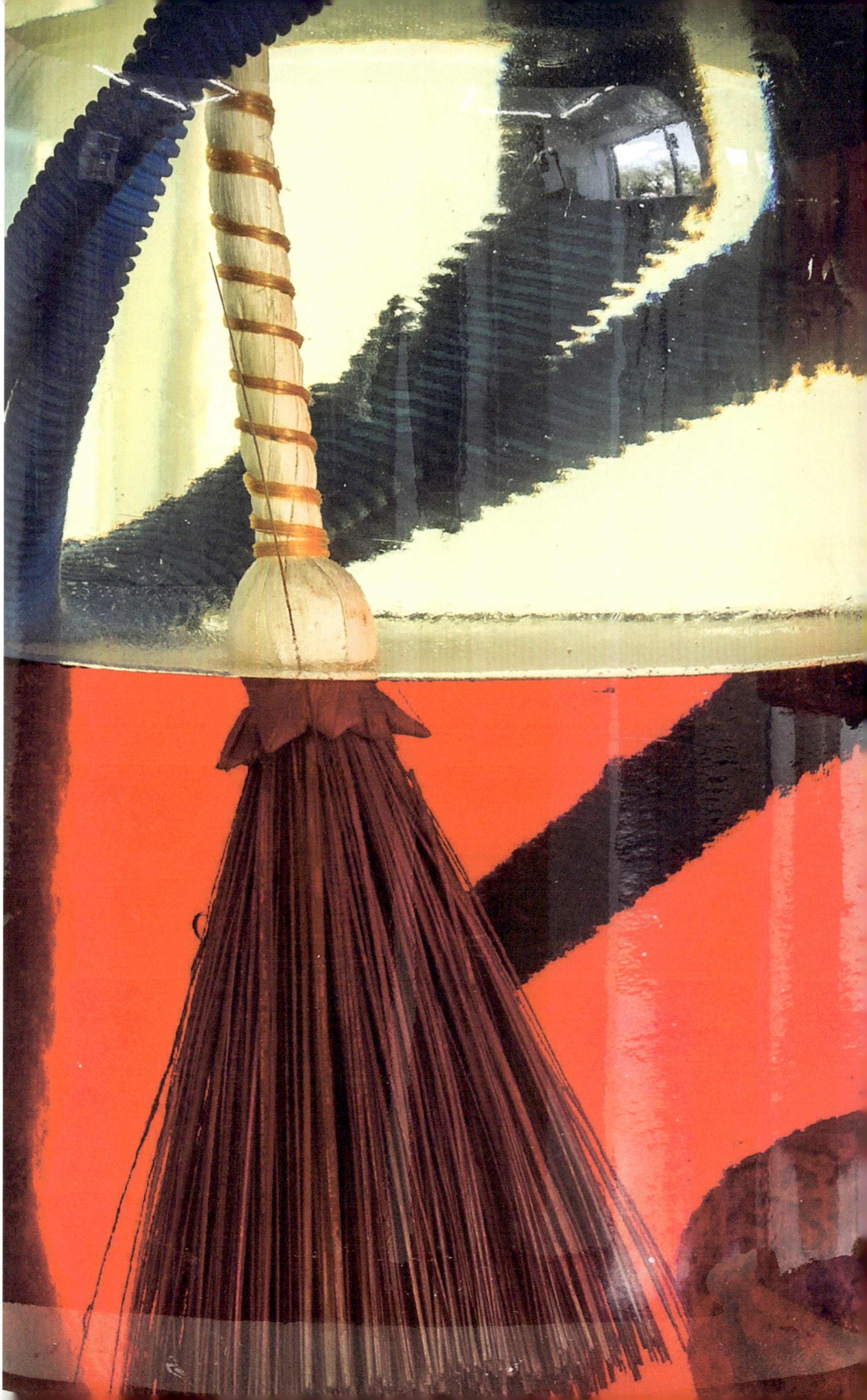

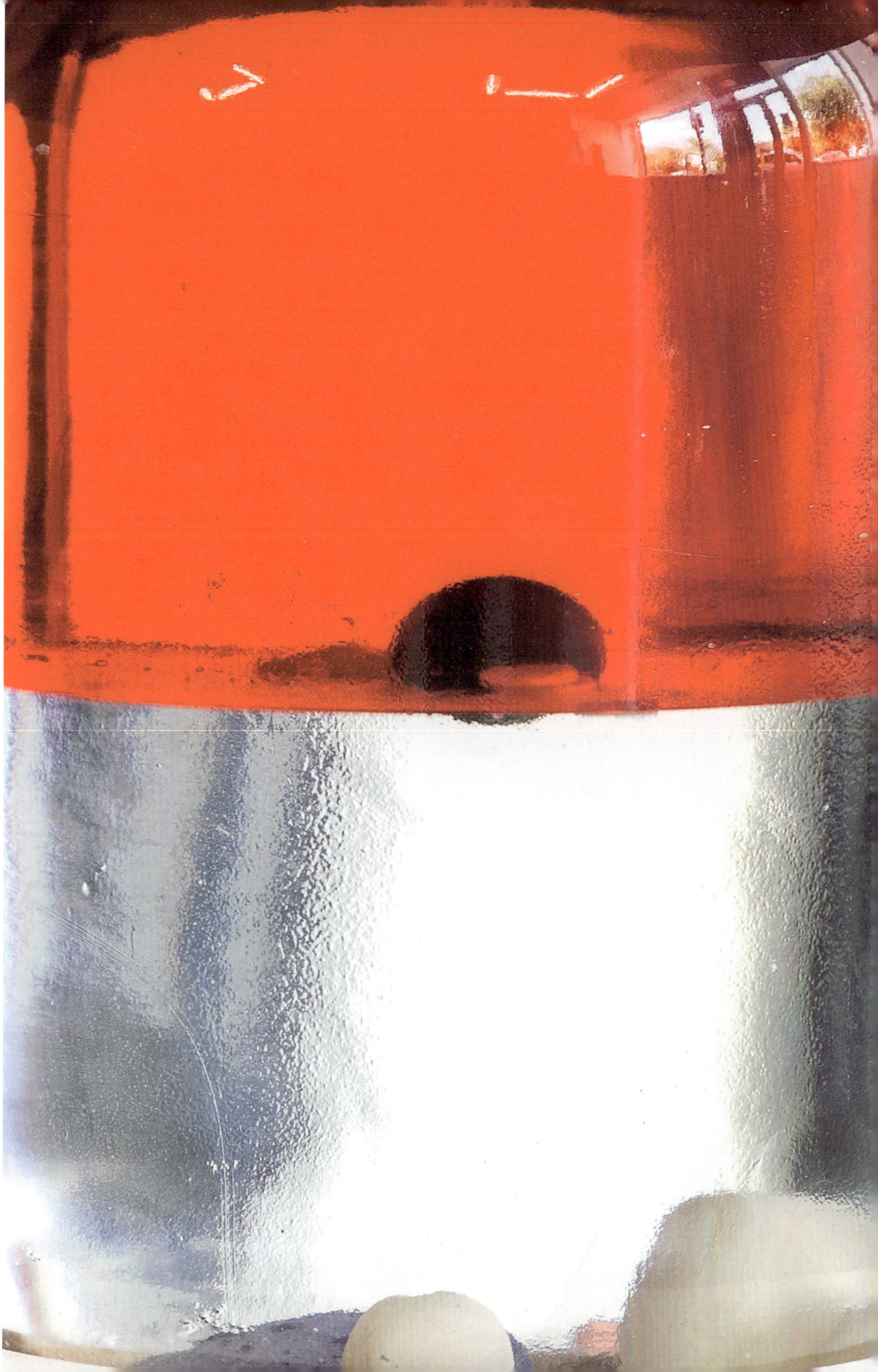

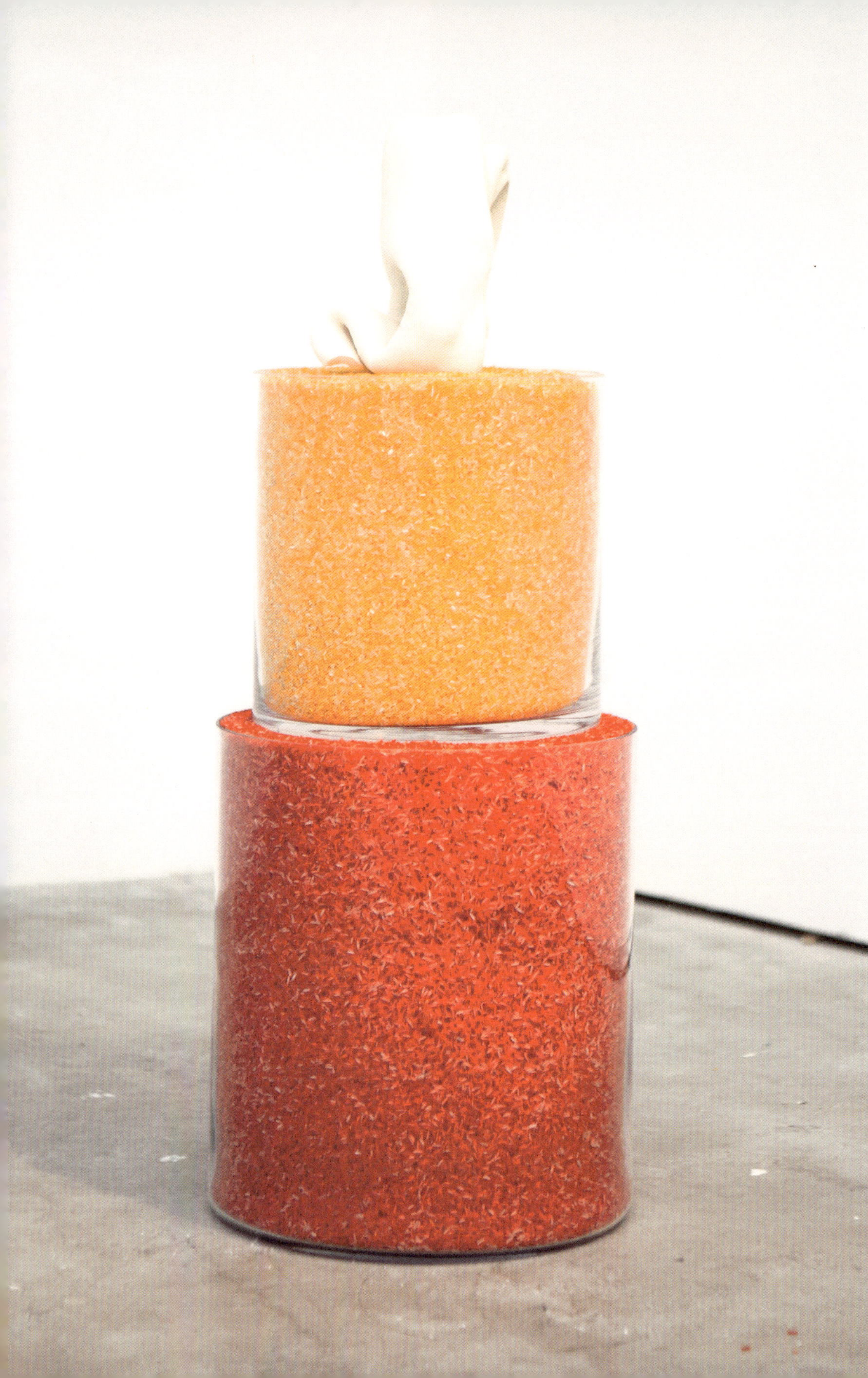

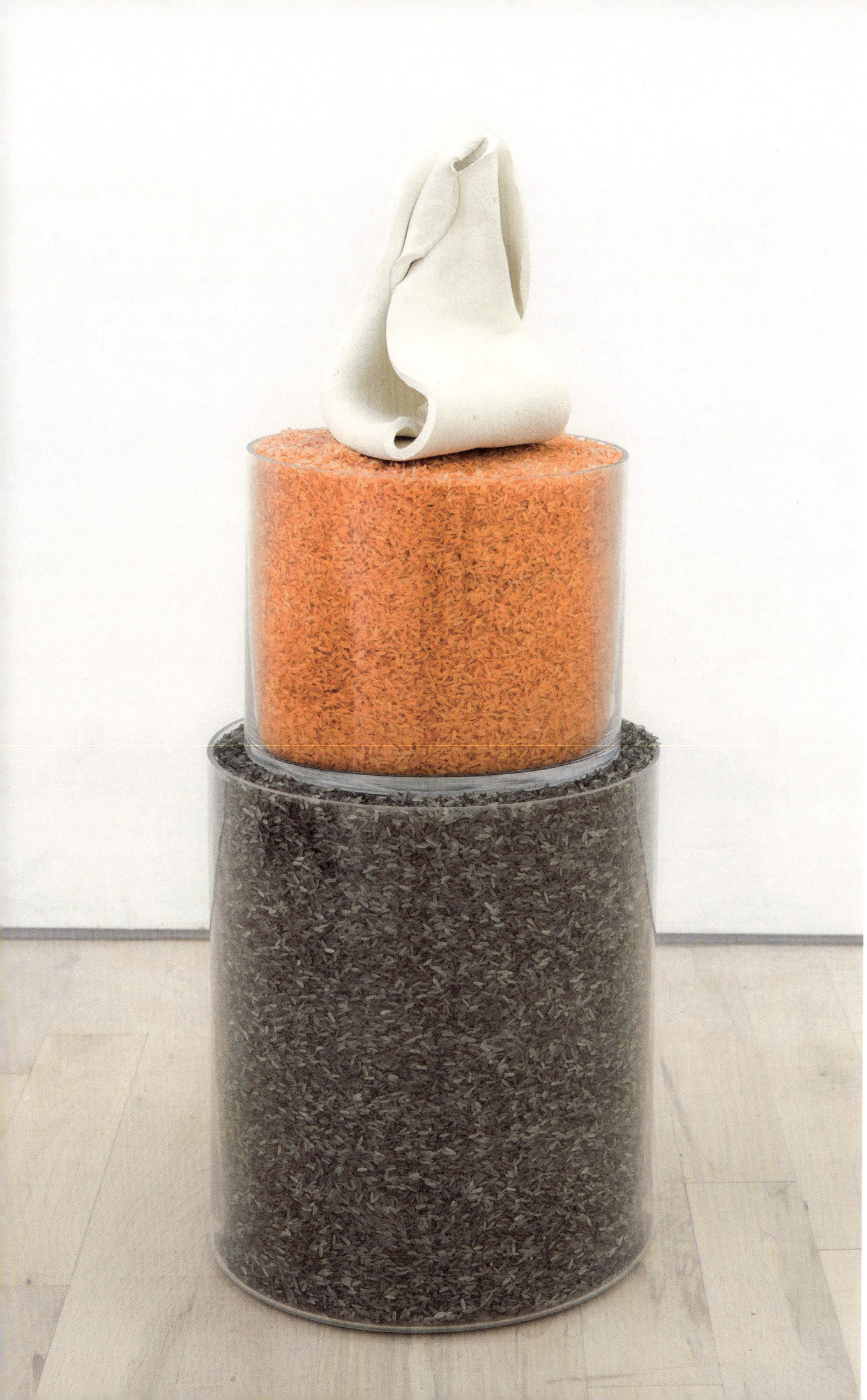

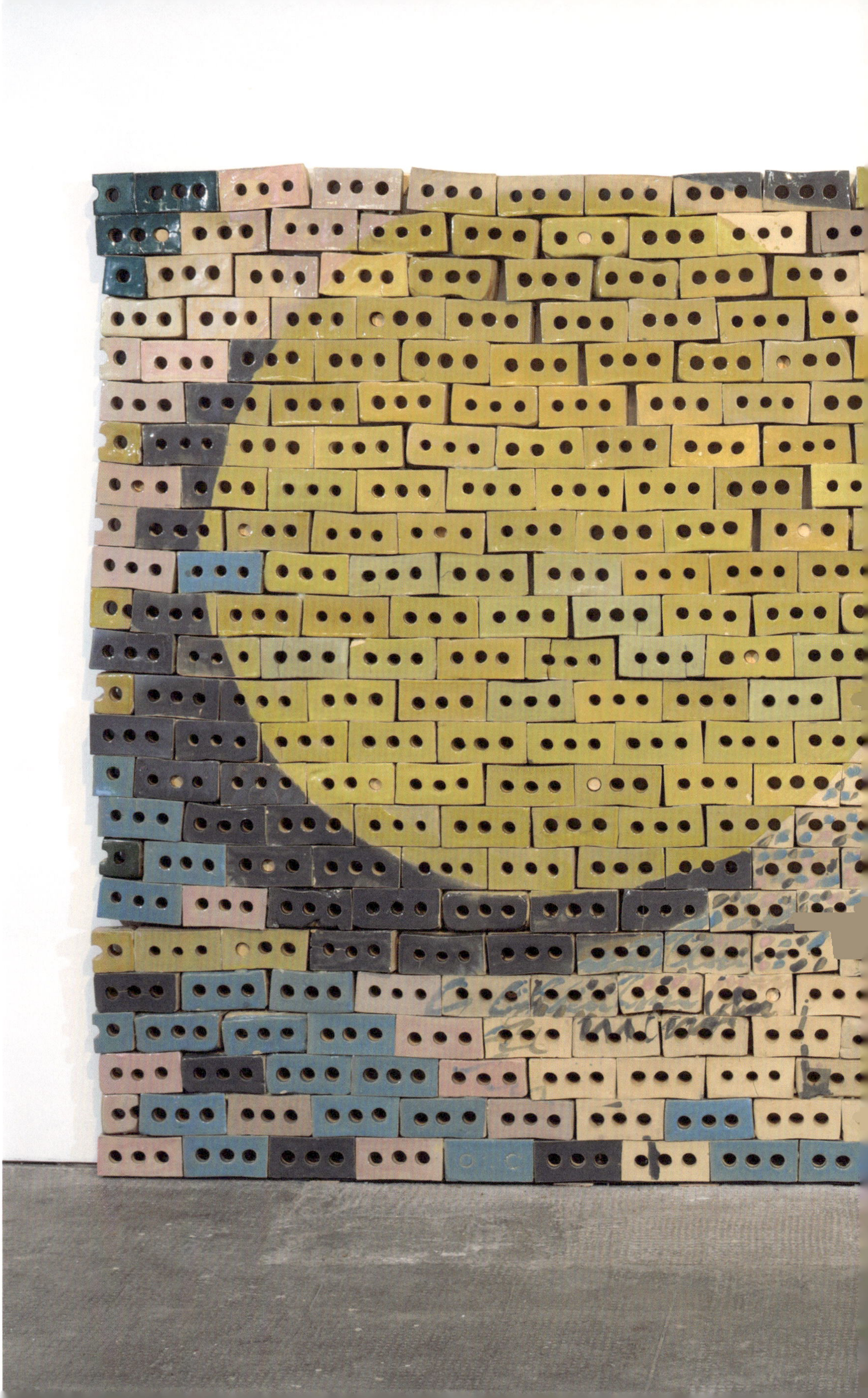

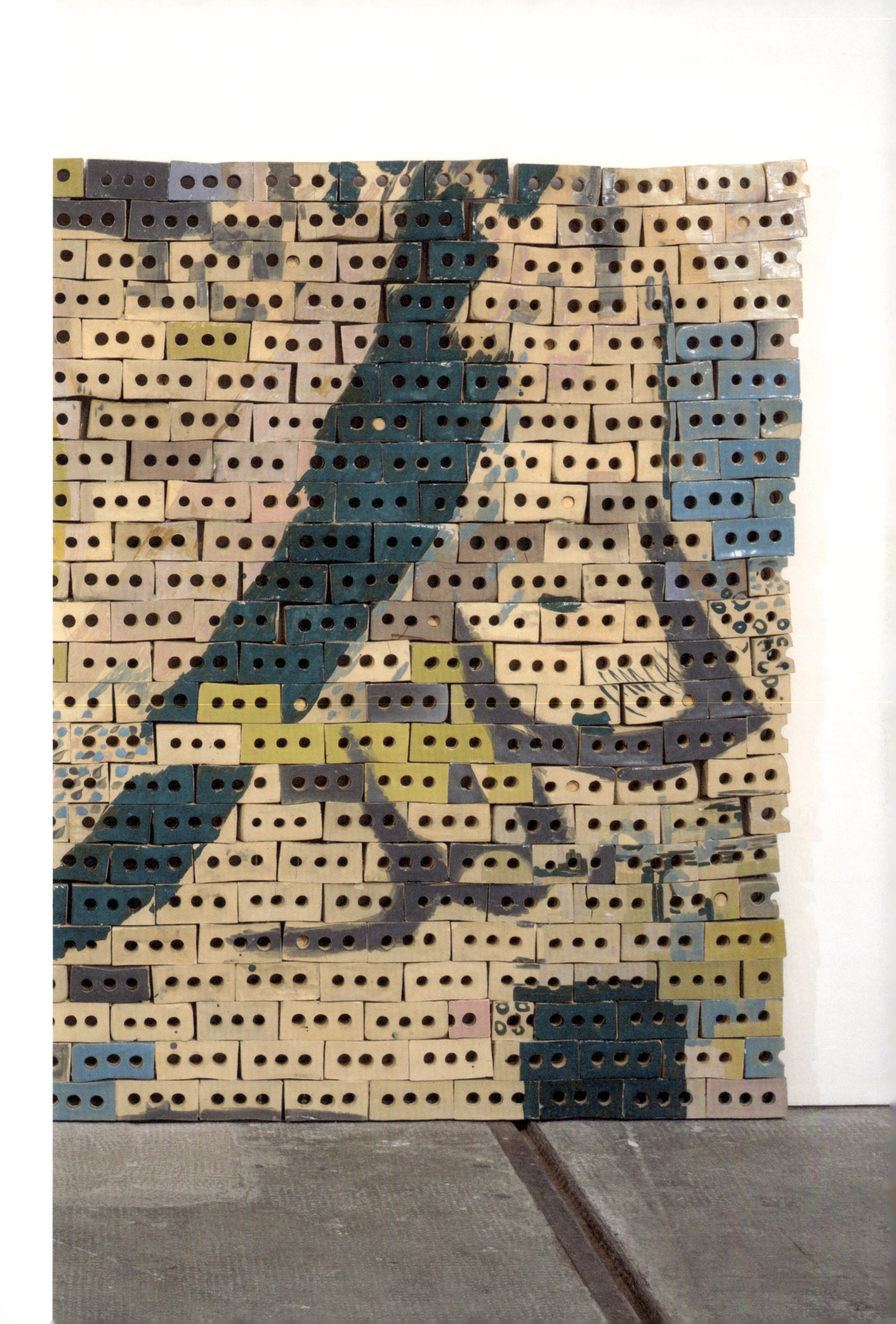

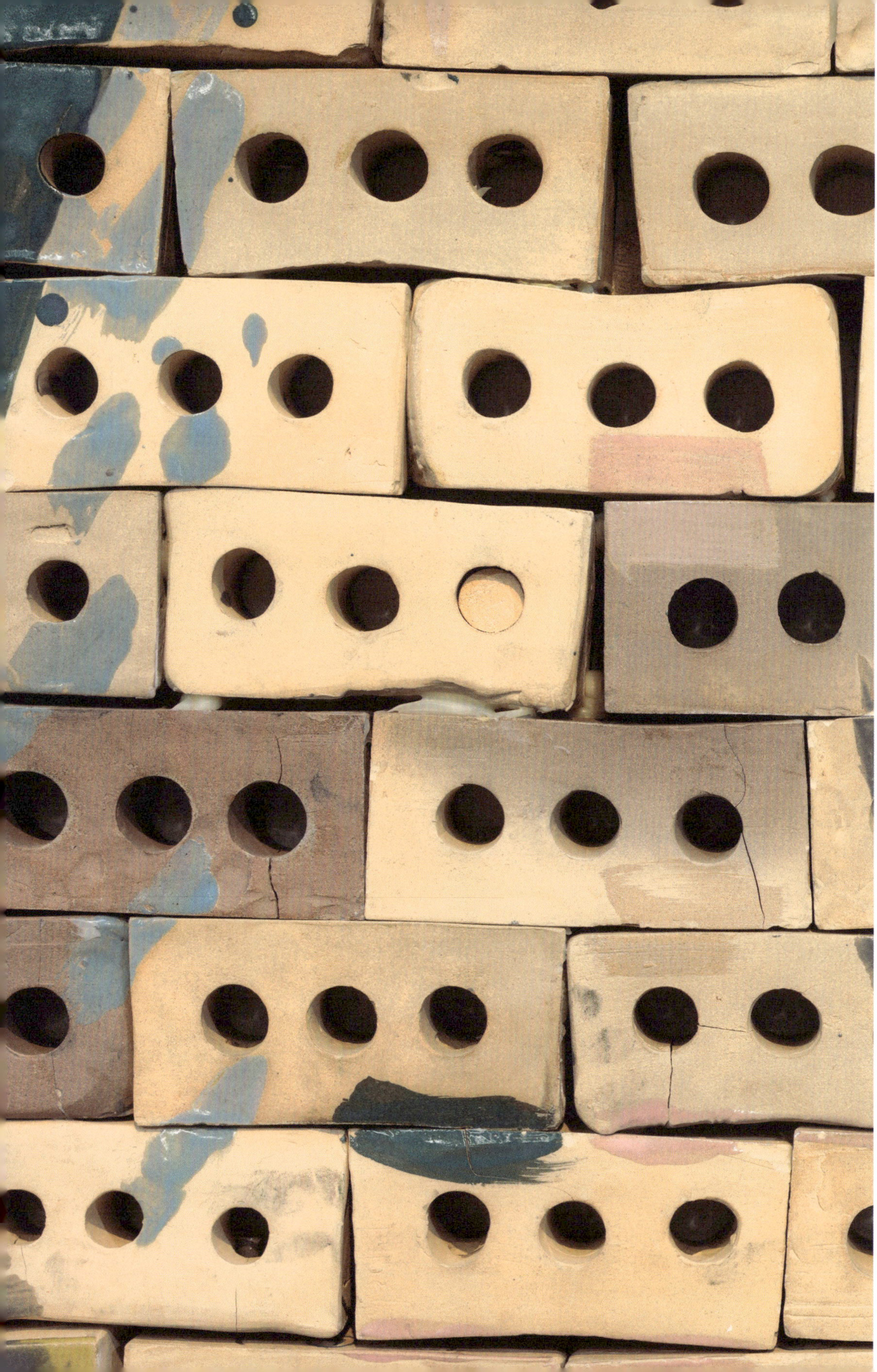

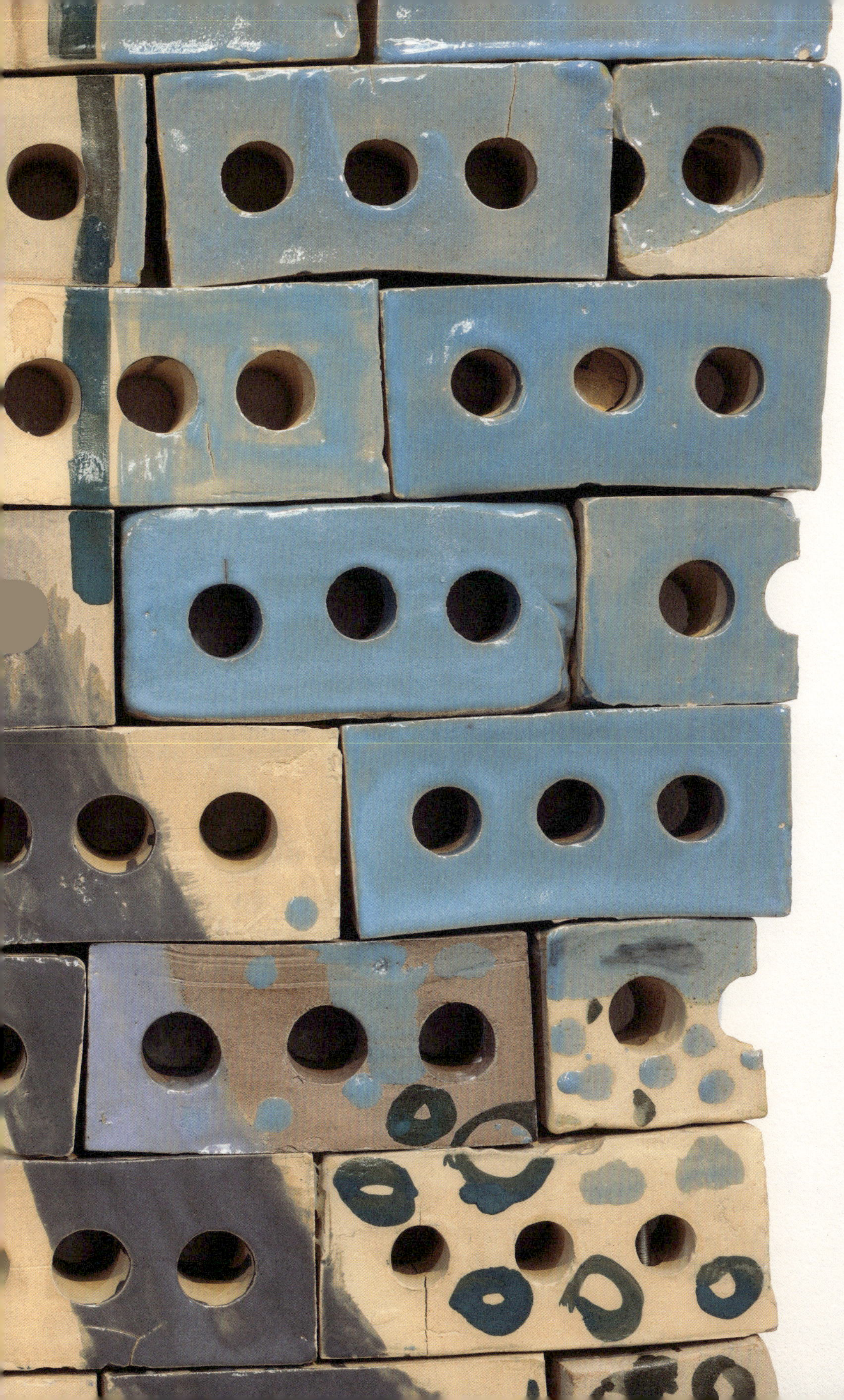

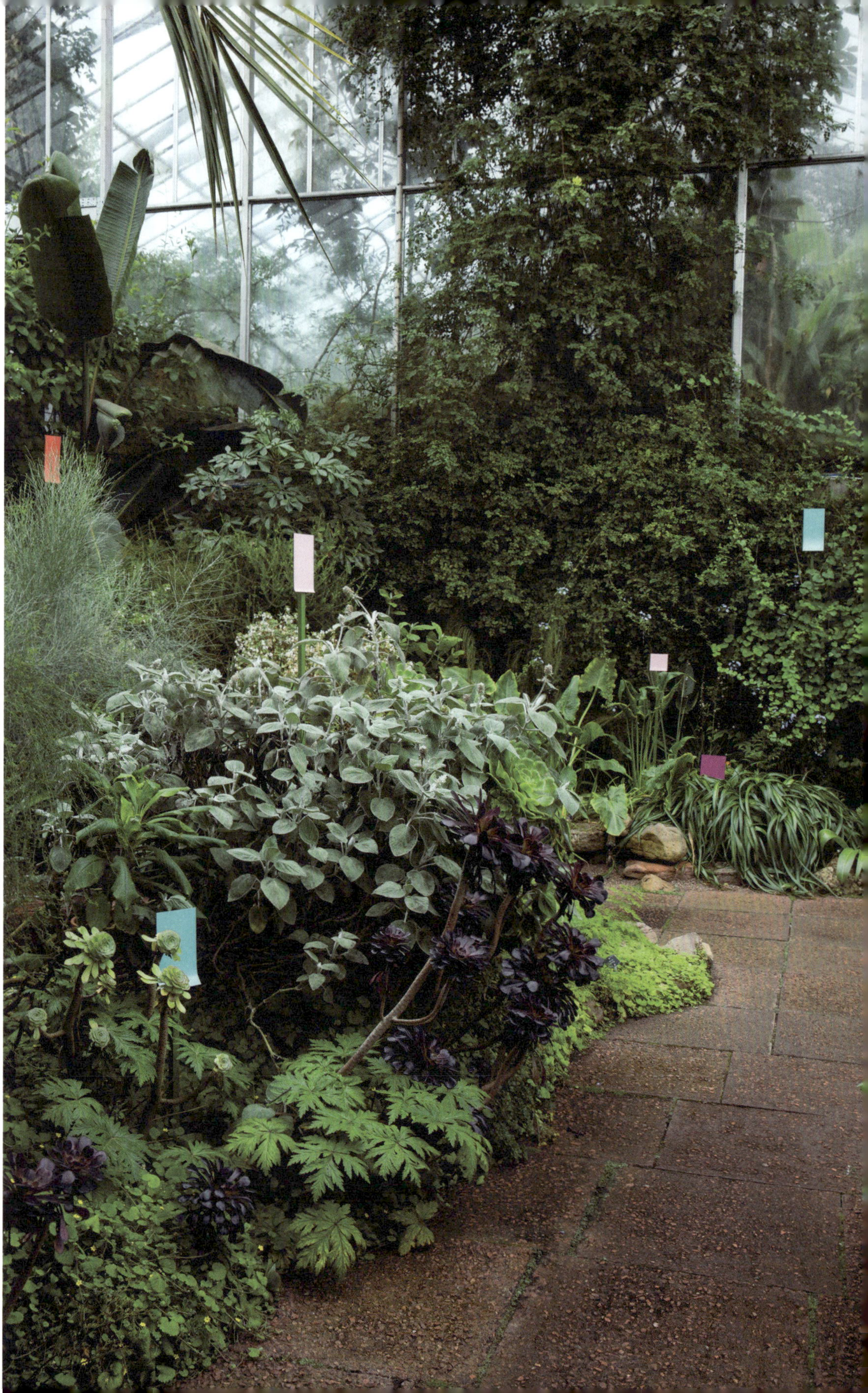

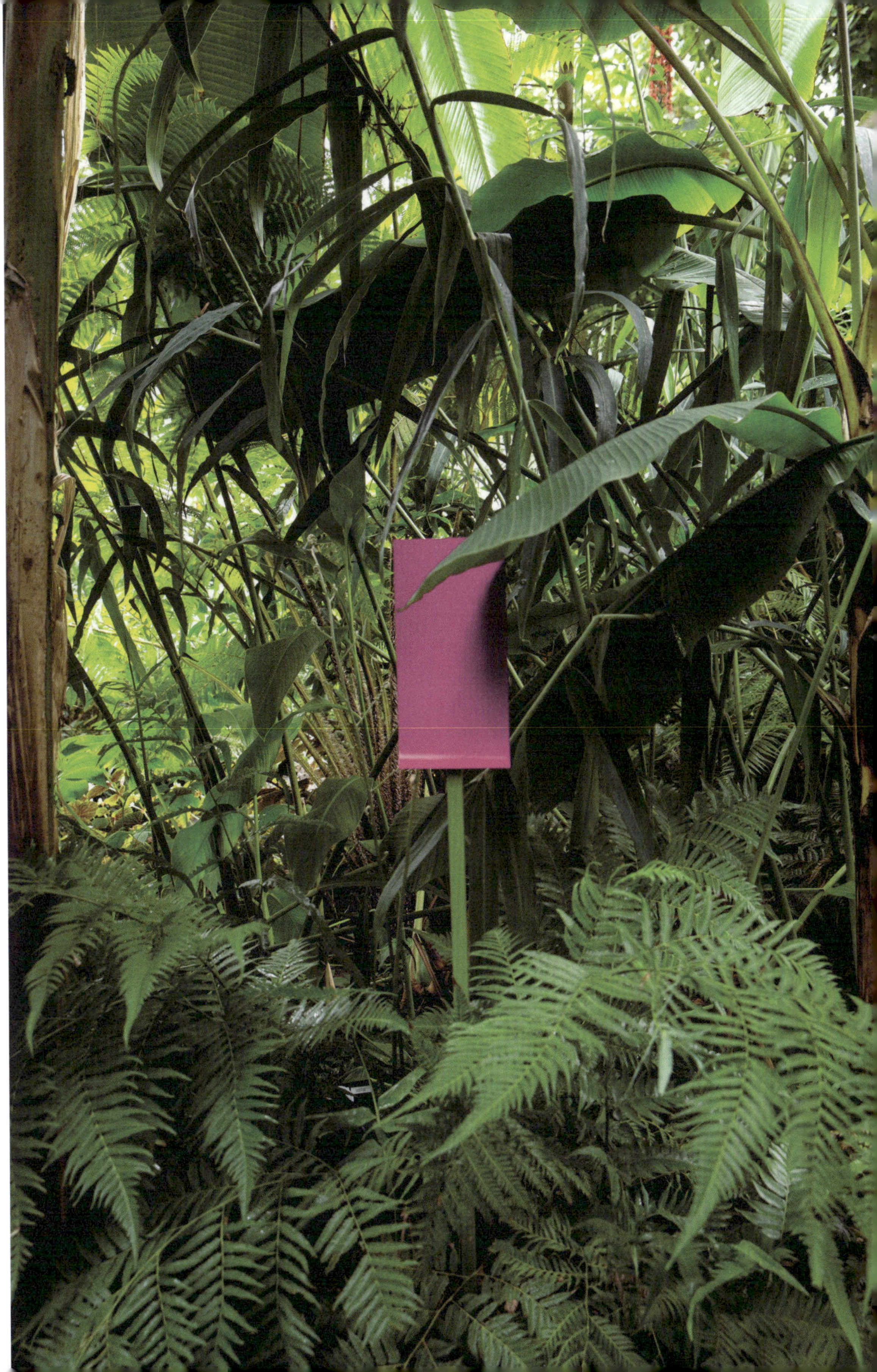

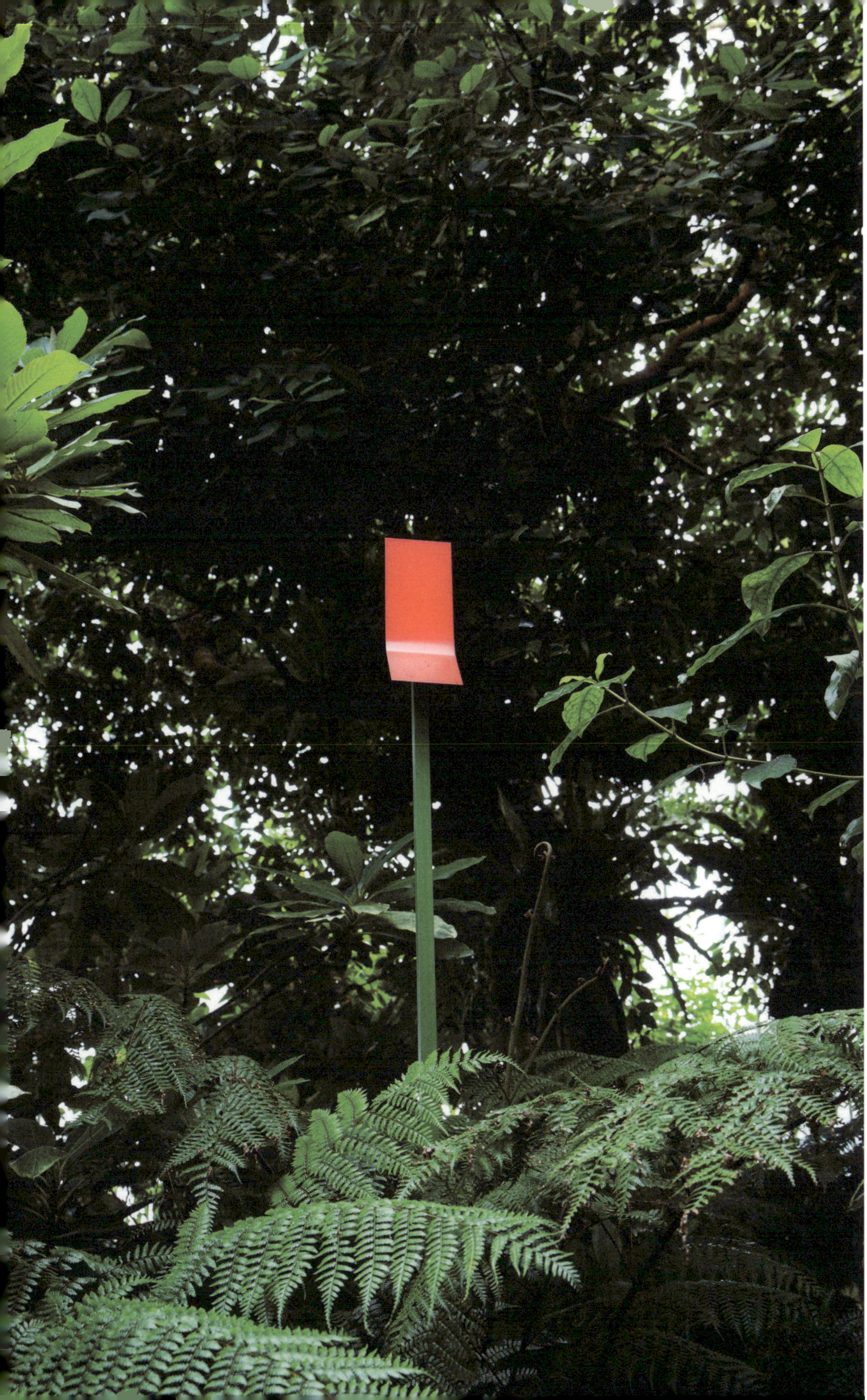

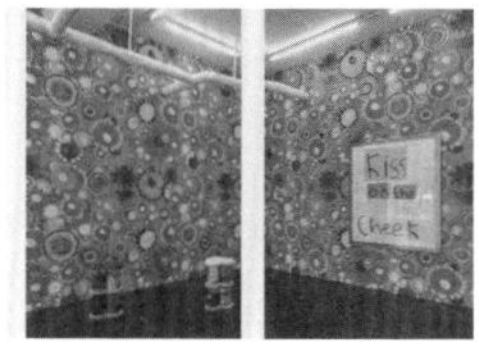

136–137
(wall)
Leanne Ross, *Hot Hot Hot*, 2021
digital wallpaper, dimensions variable

Leanne Ross, *Kiss on the Cheek*, 2021
ink on paper in custom artist frame, 152.4 × 121.9 cm

(floor)
Pickle Stool Prototype (A new thought for an object) II, 2021
mixed media, 59 × 35 × 35 cm

Pickle Stool Prototype (A new thought for an object) III, 2021
mixed media, 59 × 35 × 35 cm

The Outside is Inside Everything We Make, installation view, Kendall Koppe, Glasgow, 2021

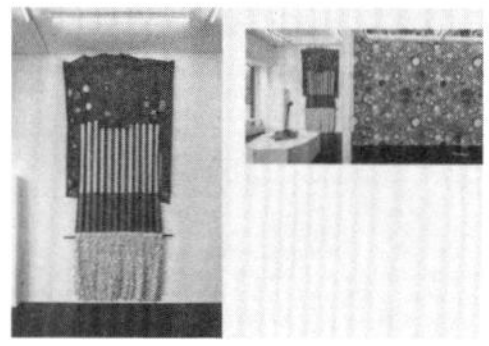

138
Purposeful Abstraction XVIII (scrolling), 2021
fabric, dye, wood, cotton, rope, and glazed stoneware, 395 × 163 cm

139
Judith Scott, *Untitled*, ca. 1990
wool, cotton, string, wood, cardboard, metal, 92.5 × 100 × 100 cm

Purposeful Abstraction XVIII (scrolling), 2021

Leanne Ross, *Hot Hot Hot*, 2021

The Outside is Inside Everything We Make, installation view, Kendall Koppe, Glasgow, 2021

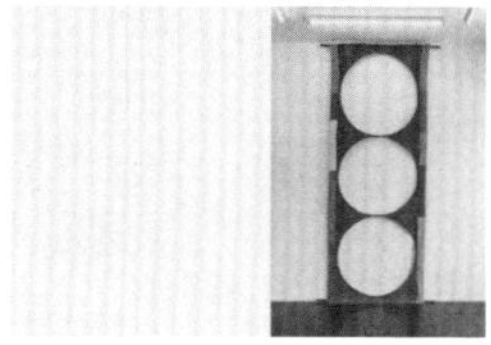

141
Purposeful Abstraction XIX (scrolling), 2021
fabric, dye, wood, cotton, and rope, 400 × 145 cm

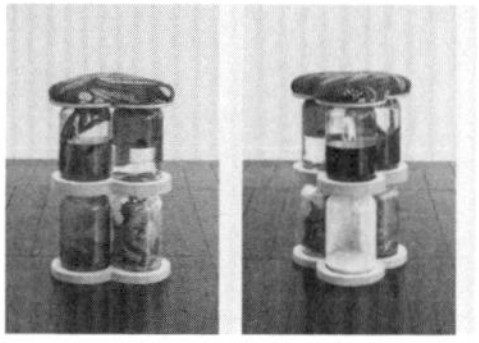

142
Pickle Stool Prototype (A new thought for an object) I, 2021
mixed media, 59 × 35 × 35 cm

143
Pickle Stool Prototype (A new thought for an object) I, 2021

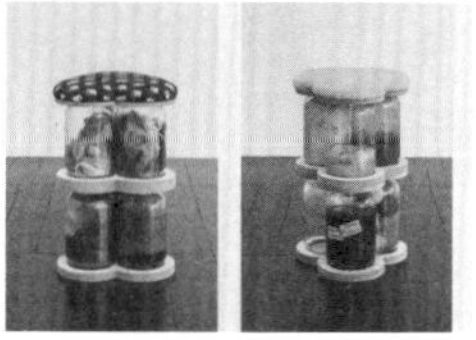

144
Pickle Stool Prototype (A new thought for an object) II, 2021

145
Pickle Stool Prototype (A new thought for an object) III, 2021

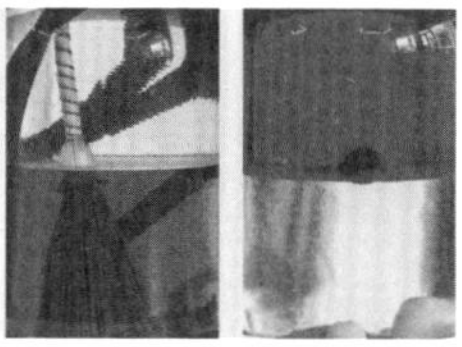

146–147
Pickle Stool Prototype (A new thought for an object) I (detail), 2021

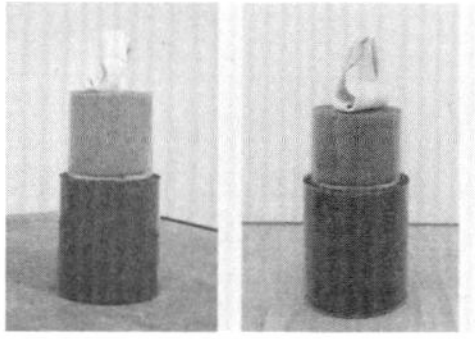

148
Not my elbow (I), 2014
ceramic, glass vases, rice, dye, 81 × 30.5 × 30.5 cm

149
Not my elbow (VIII), 2014
ceramic, glass vases, rice, dye, 81 × 30.5 × 30.5 cm

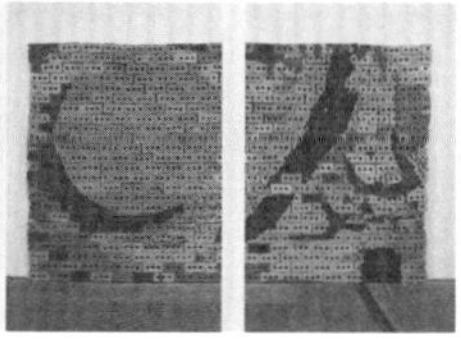

150–151
Laura Aldridge & Alistair Dearie, *Display-scape no. 2: BRICKwork – A misleading, whole new way to do things (or so they say)*, 2015
glazed stoneware, 320 × 214 × 20 cm

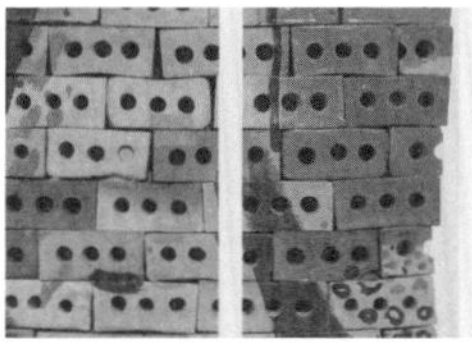

152–153
Laura Aldridge & Alistair Dearie, *Display-scape no. 2: BRICKwork – A misleading, whole new way to do things (or so they say)* (detail), 2015

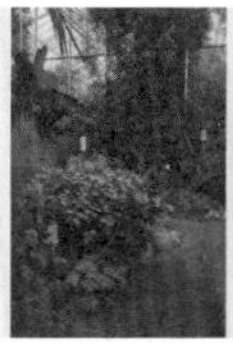

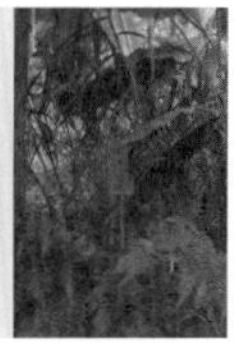

154
Sample and Straps, 2017
painted aluminium, dimensions variable (40 parts)

155
Sample and Straps, 2017

installation views, *Plant Scenery of the World*, Inverleith House, Edinburgh, 2017

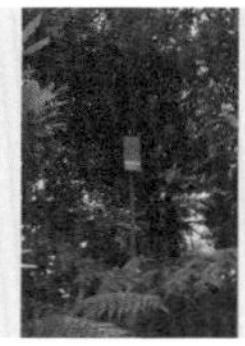

157
Sample and Straps, 2017

installation view, *Plant Scenery of the World*, Inverleith House, Edinburgh, 2017

AND THIS BECOMES MATERIAL

LOUISE SHELLEY

Louise Shelley is a London-based curator interested in collaborative processes of research and production. Her curatorial work has included *Structures That Cooperate* at Cubitt and *Communal Knowledge* at The Showroom, both in London.

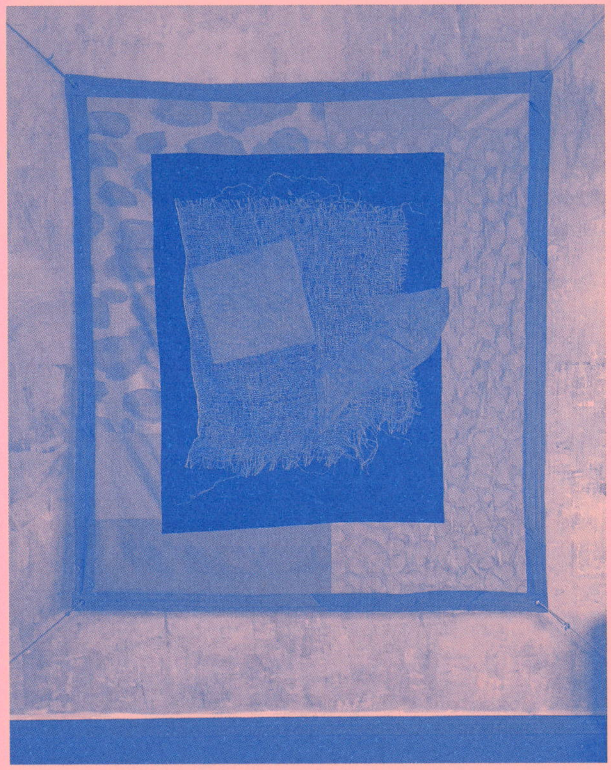

PHYSICAL CULTURE: Raise your vibration and stick this up where it will do some good (IRL), 2020, fabric, scrim, digital print, thread, dye, paint, string, eyelets, washers, 200 × 200 cm

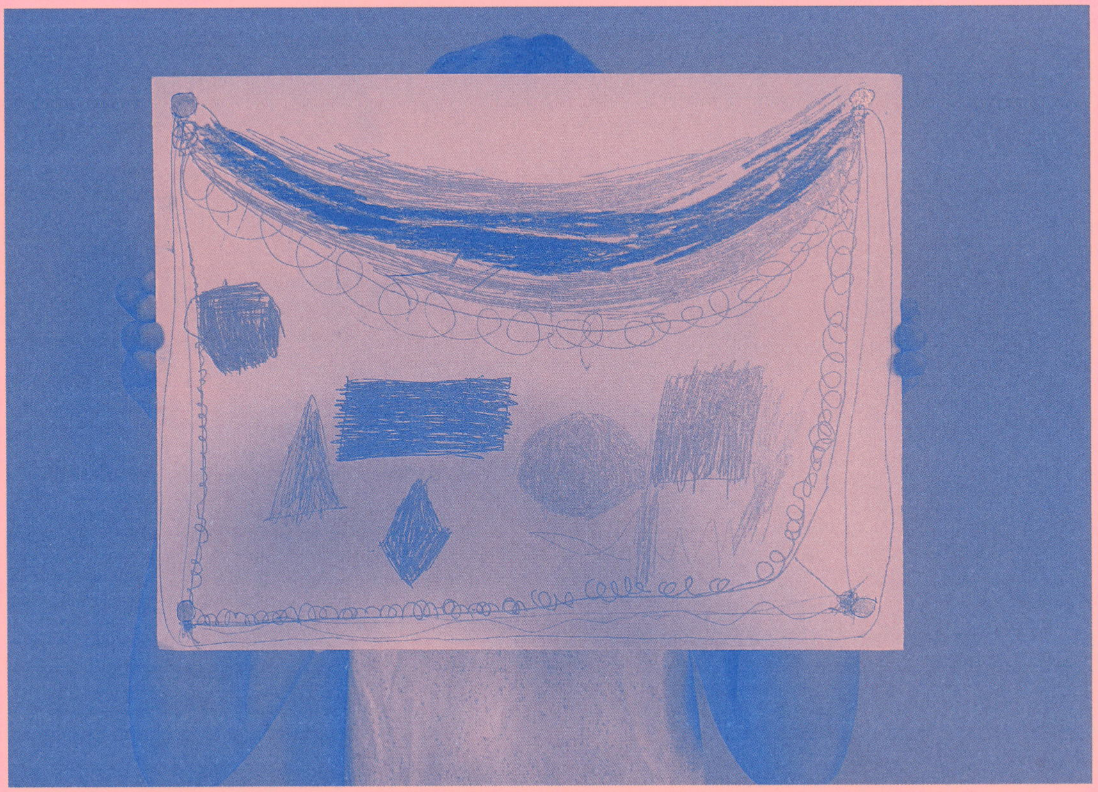

Oliver responds with coloured pencils to *PHYSICAL CULTURE: Raise your vibration and stick this up where it will do some good (AD)*, 2020, audio 5:3 min.

I received an invitation to write, and I want to circle through this work, these thoughts, these materials, these conversations, collaborations, these forms, shapes, and colours. I want to use this text as a way to be more porous with how to read and translate the work.

and I invite you into a process with this work to see with attention to feelings.

The words and lines of these pages are me attempting to think through diagramming and anecdote as an aesthetic language for Laura's work, particularly in trying to think through how the work is processing collaboration, pleasure, and affect. How is it possible to make visible the different resolutions or registers that exist in the work—manifesting contemporary presence, historical practices, multiple spaces and places, and these towards possible futures. How to map the work's movements through both solo and collective conversations and outputs, a visualisation of process almost/maybe performative in emotion?

Firstly, listen,

This is Laura's voice

It's a, it's a big work, it's about, I'd say it's about 200 centimetres across by about 230 down.

And it's a banner of sorts. It's depicting something that is not clear from the outset. And from afar it looks like fabric, but it's quite hard to tell which parts are real and which parts are printed. So which parts are sort of flat representations of colour and texture and which parts are really colour and texture.

It has a blue border of soft-looking fabric. And this is sewn on, but it's sewn on quite loosely, it looks a bit like bias binding, the type you can buy in the sewing shop, or you can buy your own, and it's sort of a way of finishing off a raw edge. But this sort of a much larger kind of bias binding, it feels very homemade, and it's messy, and it's quite unfinished. So it sort of draws attention to the task of finishing something properly, but not really

managing to. In the four corners of the banner, there are these metal eyelets that pierce the fabric, and they're kind of dark grey kind of gunmetal colour. And these eyelets are entry points for some hand-dyed blue rope, and the rope is knotted onto the banner in each corner. And then the work is kind of pulled sort of equal tension from each four of those points to sort of stretch it out onto the wall. So the pulling action of the rope stretches the piece or fixes it onto the wall rather than it simply being a kind of wall hanging that just sort of droops and sags there from two fixed points at the top. The blue edging that's around the banner, it holds inside it a composition which is a composition of colour, texture, and shapes. There's a border of different orange fabric, which creates a kind of background for a more formal black oblong, which sits on top of the combinations of orange fabric. On top of this black oblong sits a combination of this wide mesh scrim, so that's the first fabric that's placed on top of the black. It's the kind of scrim a sculptor might use to reinforce a plaster work. And on top of that scrim is a sort of square of faux fur that's light brown, it's probably the kind of faux fur you'd buy in a haberdashery to make a teddy bear or a lion maybe, it's quite furry. The third element in the composition is a piece of rust-coloured velvet, but not luxe velvet, the sort of cheap stretchy kind that you might use to make a kind of body-con dress or a figure-hugging top. The piece of velvet lies quite messily on top of the scrim in the black fabric, and it sort of spills out into the main composition and onto the background of the orange fabric. The orange background is a, it's a sort of patchwork of different types of fabric with different textures and different thicknesses.

There's a piece of cheesecloth on the right, that has had bright orange acrylic paint sort of daubed onto it, sort of splodges, but you can almost sort of tell that they're brush marks, the thickness of the paint blocks out and fills the loose weave of the fabric and the colour of the paint in contrast to the dull sort of mesh of the cheesecloth, and the flatness of the black oblong makes it look almost luminous, like a light source or like a sort of phosphorescence to it. It's really bright. Opposite the painted fabric, but still part of the background, sits a digital version of this painted cheesecloth. It's been enlarged as well, which heightens the painterly quality of the dabs of paint on the cheesecloth. And sort of through this mediation of being scanned, resized, and then printed, the painting has lost its vitality, sort of flattened itself out, and becomes something else entirely. Any gaps in the background are filled with scraps of orange fabric.

I make notes and I am reading and I am looking
and the work is felt.

There is a process of joining the conversation,
entering into dialogue with the work, and the
work holds intimacy, boldness. We need to insert
new words, to witness, to trace and imagine textures
and process and conversations with others that manifest
into form.

The work, or really I should say *Laura*, invites others in, people she works with, for, whom she cares about and for, their direction is her lead, their skills become shared, her invitation becomes theirs, and this becomes material.

radical openness

collective imagining

collective processes with people, places, and materials

working with others

I have also been in collaboration with Laura. My work as a curator, an organiser, and a cultural worker centres collaborative practice and the politics inherent in this. I am interested to understand how and why Laura works with others. What is at stake, what is shared, what is the service, what is felt, and what is produced?

These moments and processes of creating a work and creating the tools to make the work.

a confidence in making, an energy shared, an abundance, and always learning. A commitment to keeping it open, making it again, making it soft, making it selfishly and generously, learning how to make it, always revising these positions and our relationships to them.

Making for, making with, instructing, leading, following, and returning.

Collective practice, how to negotiate this process, the relations, and a mutual exchange.

big happy workshop
—Leanne Ross

This publication is being produced at a time when the exhibition is a nonachievable moment. A global pandemic has paused the exhibition programmes in institutional spaces, disrupting the art school, the workshop, all events and moments in institutional space. When we last spoke, I was listening to Laura describing a sense of liberation in no longer making for these spaces alone. A renewed commitment to process and keeping it open, to making work without the exhibition being the prioritised outcome. How spaces lead our making and our experience of art—to question where art education happens, where the work is made public, in a moment when it isn't held by a gallery or an institution. What happens without the institution's containment of artworks? What is permitted, in process and in how it is received and by whom? How do we feel differently without the constraint of the gallery's "neutral" or often extractive platforming? How can the sharing of work, process, and collaboration

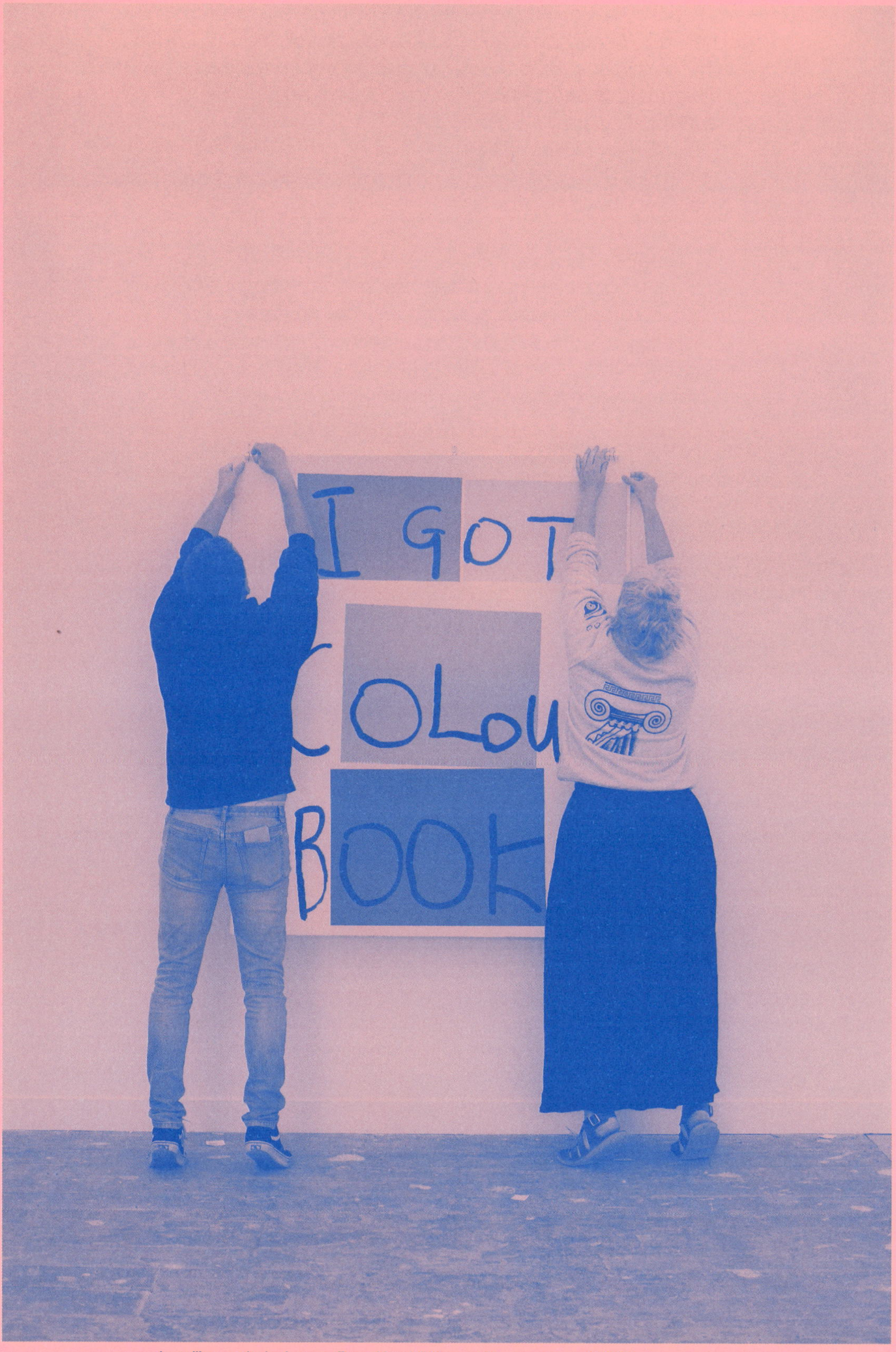

Installing works by Leanne Ross, Kendall Koppe, Glasgow, August 2020

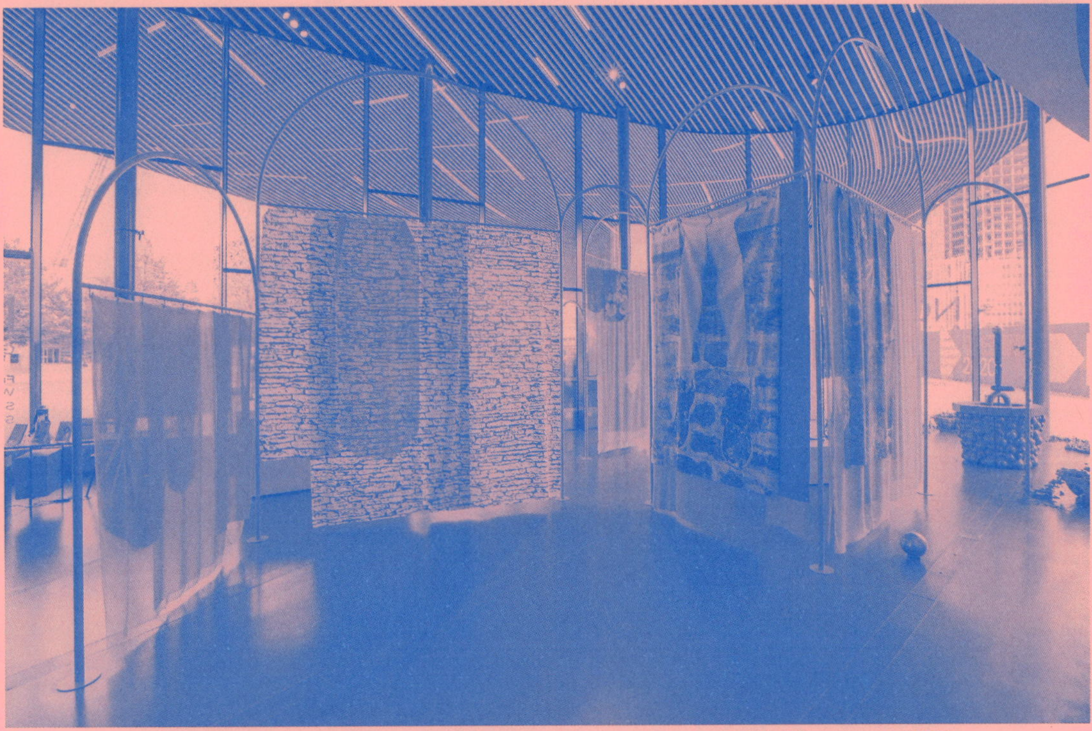

Laura Aldridge & James Rigler, *Indirect Sunlight*, 2018, installation view, NOW Gallery, London, 2018

through a publication be an access point to reconsider a practice? Who and what shapes how we work and produce, which is ultimately a question of power and how bodies, languages, and spaces navigate, exaggerate, and hold onto this power? There is a commitment in Laura's practice that is prioritising the formation of relationships and process, to attend to and support the needs of these relationships, how to access what we really need through acts of making and remaking it again.

Access and encounter for whom?

Leaving questions open,
How can the making of art imagine new forms of living and working in common?
Can we foreground our understanding of artworks as a social and embodied experience?
How to propose an idea, a set of questions, and take people with you on a process that feels connected and meaningful?
How is an artwork collectively shaped in relation to the initial idea?
I am feeling happy looking,
filling my eyes and vision with colour
Visually tactile, visually feeling.

pleasure created the object.

Now this is my voice:

There is a folder shared with me on Google Drive, "images for Louise's essay." I move my cursor to this folder, and I open this folder with a click. Inside there are many other folders. I click on one called "sensory workshops." In that folder there are many images, and there's a short movie file, it's documentation of a moment. It's documentation of a sensory workshop.

I press "play" on the movie. I'm taken into a dark room that seems to have multiple projections onto a wall. These projections also seem to fall onto a hanging fabric or curtains that are gently folded or draping down in the room—that gentle, sort of curved curtain closed shape. The projection is of spectral colours that look like moving liquids, falling snow or glitter. There are maybe three layers of projections that shine light onto, and through, and behind, and on top of these fabrics in the space. In between the hanging draped fabric is a person, and they are sitting in the work, projections cover their body and light up their face. And they are still and they are staring and they are watching, and it looks warm and calm. There is sound, cinematic, it's atmospheric, it's like a build-up of a string orchestra maybe, and it adds to the feeling and the movement. It's not theatrical, it's more dreamlike, or like being in outer space. It's sort of hypnotic, and also overwhelming or all-encompassing. It's sort of slow, sort of magical. Maybe relaxing? This person looks quite relaxed. I wonder how long this experience will be. The colours... the room is dark, but the projected colours are a sort of pastel pink, sort of a yellow, orange, white, there's a blue, a sort of inky blue moving across the larger part of the projection, like when you drop ink into water and it sort of dilutes and spreads like clouds moving across the sky. Also, the glitter is like stars, like being in a planetarium. And the video stops while the experience continues.

I am conscious I say *sort of* all the time, but I am trying to be precise and clear in my description.

Please
bring strange things.
Please come bringing new things.
Let very old things come into your hands.
Let what you do not know come into your eyes.
Let desert sand harden your feet.
Let the arch of your feet be the mountains.
Let the paths of your fingertips be your maps
and the ways you go be the lines on your palms.
Let there be deep snow in your inbreathing
and your outbreath be the shining of ice.
May your mouth contain the shapes of strange words.
May you smell food cooking you have not eaten.
May the spring of a foreign river be your navel.
May your soul be at home where there are no houses.
Walk carefully, well loved one,
walk mindfully, well loved one,
walk fearlessly, well loved one.
Return with us, return to us,
be always coming home.

—Ursula K. Le Guin

Objects as conduits, sculptures to orient ourselves around and materials to feel in relation to

how does our work change when we create
from a place of joy, support, learning? How does the work change
when
we make it with others, for others?

by turning to the question of how we can theorise positive affect and the politics of feeling good [...]
I do not assume there is something called affect that stands apart or has autonomy, as if it corresponds to an object in the world, or even that there is something called affect that can be shared as an object of study. Instead, I would begin with the messiness of the experimental, the unfolding of bodies into worlds, and the drama of contingency, how we are touched by what we are near.

—Sara Ahmed[1]

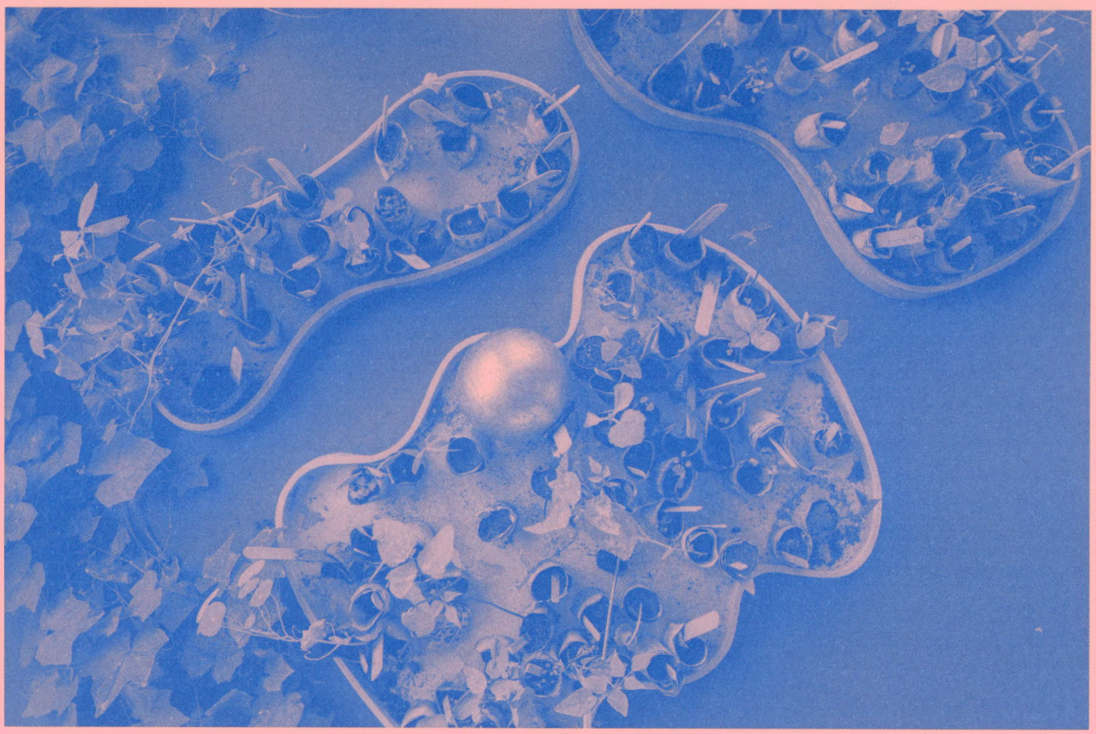

Laura Aldridge & James Rigler, *Indirect Sunlight*, 2018, installation view, NOW Gallery, London, 2018

they, the work, we, stretch, dance, adorn ourselves and the space around us

read it aloud, sound it out, slowly, up close, with your body, with others.

I am legs against a brick wall, I am a nasturtium growing in a gallery, I hang, I am weight, I need support and to grow

I love the titles, the material lists, language gives form to touching, feeling. They move and expand, they breathe life and emotion over, into, out of the work

Things that soak you
Washing nets, fabric, dye, stuffing, rice, hair, net, net
woven sacks, thread, mop head, stoneware
Things That Soak You XI, Washing nets, fabric, thread,
faux fur, stoneware
I am a Dependent Object,
Indirect Sunlight
Some Language, screenprint on paper (cat paws)
What noise is garden?
Signals and get wet
Round the outside (looking as a means of attachment)
fabric, wood, and string

Things that soak you (VII) ceramic, net, fabric

Display Scape #5: Drop. Cloth (Remove shoes and
collapse your metonymic impulse, replace it with a refreshed
sense of how we relate to the things around us)
plants, nails, fabric, copper, steel, hairpins, and Meabh's keys.
Dimensions variable
indirect sunlight
The workshop has survived because we love each other

x

1
Sara Ahmed, "Happy Objects," in *The Affect Theory Reader*, Melissa Gregg and Gregory J. Seigworth, eds. (Durham, NC: Duke University Press, 2010), http://hemi.nyu.edu/courses/sp2016-performance-and-activism/wp-content/uploads/sites/8/2016/02/02242016-Ahmed.pdf

BIOGRAPHY

Born 1978 in Frimley / lives and works in Glasgow

2005
Academic Exchange, California Institute for the Arts, Los Angeles

2004–06
MFA, Glasgow School of Art

1998–2001
BA (Hons) Fine Art (Painting), Wimbledon School of Art, London

SOLO EXHIBITIONS

2021
sumVIGOUR, CAMPLE LINE, Dumfries and Galloway

2020
#fromKStoYou, Kunsthall Stavanger

2019
NO MATH METHOD, Curfew Gallery, Edinburgh

2018
What Noise is Garden?, Peles Empire, Berlin

2017
GO WOMAN GO!, Headquarters of Federal Ministry of Women Affairs & Social Development, HOUSE 33, Abuja

2016
Inside all my activities, Koppe Astner, Glasgow

2015
One to another, one-to-one, Passerelle, Brest

California WOW!, Tramway, Glasgow

THINGS HELD INSIDE//THE NEW SEA, Kendall Koppe, Glasgow

Underside, backside, inside, even, CCA Centre for Contemporary Arts, Glasgow

2011
Cairn Gallery, Pittenweem

Studio Voltaire, London

2010
Low Hanging Fruit, Project Room, Glasgow

Cats are not important, Transmission, Glasgow

2007
The Workshop Has Survived Because We Love Each Other, Glasgow Sculpture Studios

COLLABORATIONS

2018
Indirect Sunlight, with James Rigler, Now Gallery, London

2014
OPENARIES, with Anna Mayer, Glasgow International

2013
Taking back our bodies (refund please), with Joe Scotland, Infernoesque, Berlin

GROUP EXHIBITIONS

2021
The Outside is Inside Everything We Make, Kendall Koppe, Glasgow

2019
I am a Dependent Object, Brno Biennale of Contemporary Art

2018
The Life and Opinions of the Tomcat Murr together with a fragmentary Biography of Kapellmeister Johannes Kreisler on Random Sheets of Waste Paper, Rob Tufnell, Cologne

Perceptions, British Council Touring exhibition: Cetinje, Montenegrin Art Gallery; Serbia, Novi Sad, Gallery of Matica Srpska; Pristina, National Gallery;

Banja Luka, Museum of Contemporary Art of Republic of Srpska; Skopje, Museum of Contemporary Art

Sculpture Showroom, Glasgow International Festival of Visual Art

2017
Plant Scenery of the World, Inverleith House, Edinburgh

Things That Soak You, Kate MacGarry, London

31 Women, Bresse Little, London

The Artists House, Eastside Projects, Birmingham

2016
In Sense of Place, Highlanes Gallery, Drogheda

Jack and Diane, Kate Werble Gallery, New York

2015
Ceramics and Graphite, Chert, Berlin

DIDING – An Interior That Remains an Exterior?, Künstlerhaus, Graz

2014
Earth Minutes, Andrew Kreps Gallery, New York

On the devolution of culture, Rob Tufnell, London

Rubbernecking in the Stacks, Greene Exhibitions, Los Angeles

Wearing Potentiality, Paradise Row, London

Illusions, Hospitalfield House, Arbroath

2013
Out of doors, Supplement, London

The Cat Show, White Columns, New York

The Collection Exhibition, The Collection Museum, Lincoln

Laura Aldridge, Sara Barker & Sue Tompkins, Shane Campbell, Chicago

Every Day, GOMA, Glasgow

2012
Tiling, Seventeen Gallery, London

Easy Living, Less is More Project Space, Paris

Pavilion, David Dale Gallery, Glasgow

Folklore Contemporain, SWG3, Glasgow

Studio 58: Women Artists in Glasgow Since WWII, MacIntosh Museum, Glasgow School of Art

2011
Industrial Aesthetics: Environmental Influences on Recent Art from Scotland, Hunter College/Times Square Gallery, New York

2010
Reflections on Black: Artists Cinema, CCA Centre for Contemporary Arts, Glasgow

2009
Maison Domino, Generator Projects, Dundee

SELECTED BIBLIOGRAPHY

2021
Sarah Unwin Jones, "Kiln Time," *The Herald*, June 26

Chloë Ashby, "Is Scotland Now the Artistic Heart of Britain?," *Elephant* (July 8)

2017
Emily Steer, "31 Women," *Elephant* (June)

Anna McNay, "31 Women," *Studio International* (June)

Roberta Smith, "Out-of-town Galleries Arrive, Bearing Art," *The New York Times*, July

Susan Mansfield, "Plant Scenery of the World," *The List* (August)

Catriona Gallagher, "Plant Scenery of the World," *Map Magazine* (August)

Giles Sutherland, Exhibition review, *The Times*

2016
Judd-Leonard Okafor, *The Daily Trust*, December 4

Agwu Enekwachi, "Laura Aldridge," *This Day Live*, December 11

GO WOMAN GO!, with essays by Linsey Young, Charlotte Linton, and Michelle Wipplinger (London: The British Council)

Claire Shea, "Throwing Shapes," *Elephant*, no. 26

2015
Exhibition Preview 24 January 2015, *The Herald*

George Vasey, *Art Monthly*, no. 385

Matthew McLean, "In Focus," *Frieze*, no. 170

Moira Jeffrey, "Laura Aldridge," *The Scotsman*, February 14

Laura Campbell, "Laura Aldridge: California WOW!," *This is Tomorrow* (February)

2014
Alhena Katsof, "Laura Aldridge & Lee Maida," *BOMB Magazine* (August 8)

2013
Kate Morrell, Laura Aldridge, Louise Shelley, *Laying down and kissing the love in the mist: Part three* (Glasgow: Laura Aldridge)

2012
Talitha Koetze, "Things Held Inside // The New Sea," *The List* (October)

Joey Villemont, Camille Le Houezec, "Laura Aldridge & Travess Smalley: Folklore Contemporain," *This Is Tomorrow* (November)

Underside, backside, inside, even, with an essay by Anna Mayer (Glasgow: Laura Aldridge)

2010
A book by Laura Aldridge with an essay by Leslie Dick (Glasgow: Transmission)

Talitha Kotzé, "Cats are not Important," *The List* (March 19)

Sarah Lowndes, "Laura Aldridge," *Frieze*, no. 131

Mason Leaver-Yapp, "Laura Aldridge," *Map Magazine*, no. 22

2009
Fiona Jardine, "Maison Domino," *Map Magazine*, no. 19

James Garner, "Maison Domino," *The Metro*, August

2008
Polly Staple, "Emerging Artists," *Frieze*, no. 112

2007
Francis McKee, "Laura Aldridge," *Map Magazine*, no. 11

Fiona Jardine, "The workshop has survived because we love each other," *pamphlet* (July)

Leon McDermott, "Laura Aldridge," *The Metro*, July

LAURA ALDRIDGE
THINGS THAT SOAK YOU

Publishing Editor
Ilaria Bombelli (Mousse)

Editorial coordination
Vittoria Mieli (Mousse)

Texts
Tina Fiske, Joe Scotland, Louise Shelley, Linsey Young

Copy editing and proofreading
Erica Olsen
Vittoria Mieli (Mousse)

Graphic design
Massimiliano Pace (Mousse)

Published and distributed by
Mousse Publishing
Contrappunto s.r.l.
Corso di Porta Romana 63
20122, Milan–Italy

Available through
Mousse Publishing, Milan
moussepublishing.com
DAP | Distributed Art Publishers, New York
artbook.com
Vice Versa Distribution, Berlin
viceversaartbooks.com
Les presses du réel, Dijon
lespressesdureel.com
Antenne Books, London
antennebooks.com

With the support of
Creative Scotland
Kendall Koppe, Glasgow
Patricia Wolf

First edition
2021

Printed in Italy by
Faenza Group S.p.A.

ISBN 978-88-6749-500-9

EUR 27 / USD 30

Photo Credits
© Roberto Luigi Ama
© Ostyn Ami
© Mike Bolam
© Tom Carter
© Ruth Clark
© Katy Davies
© Michaela Dvorakova
© Trevor Good
© Keith Hunter
© Patrick Jameson
© Erik Sæter Jørgensen
© Andy Keate
© Kendall Koppe
© Aurélien Mole
© Tom Noland
© Caro Weiss

(p. 10 left–bottom, p. 60)
© Estate of Ree Morton. Courtesy: Alexander and Bonin, New York
(p. 10 right)
© Su Richardson (for the *Fenix* Travelling Installation in collaboration with Kate Walker, Monica Ross, Suzy Varty). Courtesy: Richard Saltoun Gallery, London. Photo: Joerg Lohse
(p. 139)
© Judith Scott. Courtesy: The Museum and The Gallery of Everything, London

Laura Aldridge would like to thank:
Brenda & Christopher Aldridge, Debi Banerjee, Isobel Barr, Matilda Barr, Craig Brownlie, Amanda Catto, Jon Court, Emma Dove, Nick Evans, Tina Fiske, Hadrian Garrard, Lauren Gault, Kendall Koppe, Stephen Palmer, James Rigler, Leanne Ross, Joe Scotland, Louise Shelley, Alison Stirling, Celia Pym, Patricia Wolf, Nicola Wright, Linsey Young.